The Nikolais/Louis Dance Technique

* PLEASE CHECK FOR DVD AT
BACK OF BOOK *

The Nikolais/Louis Dance Technique

A Philosophy and Method of Modern Dance

including *The Unique Gesture*

Alwin Nikolais & Murray Louis

Routledge

New York • London

Published in 2005 by
Routledge
Taylor & Francis Group
270 Madison Avenue
New York, NY 10016
www.routledge-ny.com

Printed in the United States of America on acid-free paper.

10 9 8 7 6 5 4 3 2 1

Library of Congress Cataloging-in-Publication Data
    Nikolais, Alwin.
     The Nikolais/Louis dance technique : a philosophy and method of modern dance / by
    Alwin Nikolais and Murray Louis.
        p. cm.
      ISBN 0-415-97019-9 (hb : alk. paper) — ISBN 0-415-97020-2 (pb : alk. paper)
     1. Modern dance. 2. Modern dance—Philosophy. I. Louis, Murray. II. Title.
     GV1783.N54 2004
     792.8'01—dc22   2004021542

CONTENTS

PREFACE

The Nikolais/Louis technique is a composite technique. It deals with the total person—physical, mental, and spiritual—for who is to say which part learns easiest or is of greatest importance. Over the past fifty years, the principles and vocabulary of this technique have become a part of standard dance teaching methods everywhere. As a result many readers will find that they already have a familiarity with the Nikolais/Louis technique. Others may be encountering it for the first time. Readers, dancers, and teachers alike should feel free to use this book however it might apply to their own unique situation.

The teaching of dance is not an exact science. However, where specifics of movement are concerned, the technique is exacting. Many factors are involved in teaching the simplest movement phrase. These include the manner and character of the teaching voice, the clarity of the ideas, the use of devices to stimulate motivation, the necessity of insightful criticism, and the maintenance of spontaneity and energy during repetitious corrections. In addition, the teacher must account for such things as the physical size and temperament of different students. All of these factors are at play in the classroom, often simultaneously.

Verbally describing an improvisation or dance is a difficult, often hopeless task. When, after Nik's death, I was faced with the prospect of writing a book to provide a guide to the Nikolais/Louis technique, the task seemed insurmountable. I had Nik's own philosophy of dance, *The Unique Gesture*, in manuscript form, but a complete approach demanded a step-by-step manual as well. I wanted to be true to Nik's vision and also to highlight the collaborative nature of both our dance technique and our pedagogy. To accomplish this, I kept Nik's words intact but interspersed my own insights when I felt inspired or called to do so. I organized the chapters thematically, but allowed the play of

dialogue to suggest itself by retaining the unique voices of two speakers. So as not to jar the reader, the two speakers are indicated simply in the design of the book. Nik's writing has all been retained as he wrote it and is signaled by a bold font throughout. My own musings are in a regular typeface. Through this arrangement, I hope our individual voices ring clearly, as well as our shared approach to dance.

One method Nik and I employed in the classroom to overcome the difficulty inherent in speaking about dance was to use the various written notes that students had made for themselves. These usually consisted of comments and criticisms made in class by us as teachers after they were funneled through a student's mind and put in their private notebooks. This was how the students remembered and recreated the dance studies for themselves. Since these notes and "crits" worked for them, I used the same device here in the hope they would evoke in the reader a similar tangible understanding.

Each class had its own balance of elements. The physical exactness demanded by stretches, alignment, and plies was fueled by a more vague, though no less urgent, wellspring of motivation and imagination. All of this the teacher had to provide. Excepting the photographs used to illustrate the stretches, the accompanying visual materials in this book—the DVD and photographs—do not specifically depict the creative premises. Limiting creativity by illustration with a specific photographed movement would defeat the richness suggested by the technique. Let the DVD and photographs, like the stories and the crits, suggest a mood of creative exploration. Let your imagination roam freely.

The studio spaces we used at Henry Street were unusual in that mirrors were seldom permitted, and if they were, they were off to the side. They

Murray with Cybil at West
Broadway studio.
Photo by Nan Melville.

were never in the front of the room, lest the dancers become absorbed with what they looked like. The mirrors were used for rehearsal purposes so that dancers could check their ensemble accuracy. Again the focus was to remain on the dance itself.

The classes were filled with many stories and references to professional experiences. What also made the studio an especially productive environment was the presence of the studio cats, who lent a calming and constant reminder that there were other life forms who shared space with us, and had other opinions about life.

Overall, the approach of this book does not follow a rigid line, but instead reaches out to encompass a wide and inclusive path. It can be considered a reference book to be consulted for specific information even as it can also be used more broadly, as a place to dip randomly when looking for inspiration. It is, of course, a manual and is not intended to be read all at once.

There is no precise beginning or end with this technique. The training is meant to serve a lifetime. It is continuous and ongoing. The technique intends to broaden the definition and the vocabulary of the dancer's art. How one executes a movement technically is as important as the movement itself. This book's main purpose is to create the ability to experience to the fullest the marvel of the moving body, and to give a voice and vocabulary to this endeavor. It seeks to speak to the dancer in total: as teacher, student, choreographer, and performer.

A final caveat: I must apologize in advance for using the male gender as my pronoun of choice. I am fully aware that the majority of dance students are female but the limitations of grammatical syntax make it difficult to address both sexes at the same time and retain the clarity of one's thoughts. Above all, I wanted clarity. But rest assured, it is all you dancers, dancers of every sex, every stripe, and every size, who were on my mind as I wrote.

Murray Louis
New York
January 2005

BIOGRAPHY OF ALWIN NIKOLAIS

Alwin Nikolais (Nik) was born at midnight on November 25, 1910, in Southington, Connecticut. Geographically this would make him a Connecticut Yankee, but his German mother and Russian father both lent him their national attributes, and he in turn became both methodical and flamboyant.

Nikolais's first artistic exposure was to the piano. His mother, who had no artistic inclinations of her own, dutifully felt that all her children should play the piano, and so once a week the music "professor" arrived and the children had their turn "at the piano." This led to his later becoming a skilled organist, and eventually brought him work as an accompanist in silent film houses. His job there was to match music with action, which developed his skill in improvisation. He also became involved with the small theatrical group in his town, where he was more valued as a scenic designer than for his acting abilities.

In 1934, by pure happenstance, Nikolais attended a concert by Mary Wigman, the great German modern dancer. He was profoundly impressed, and with this searing experience, his destiny was forged. At that time, *dance* was hardly a word in common usage in rural America, least of all as an art form. However, Wigman's presence, choreography, and, most of all, percussion accompaniment stimulated and challenged his imagina-

tion. Happily, the encounter came at a time when his creative instincts were already awakening.

He visited nearby Hartford frequently and there met Truda Kaschmann, a Wigman disciple. Truda, on hearing of his interest in percussion, said, "Very well, but you must also study dance to learn this musical accompaniment," and thus his first dance training began. Shortly afterward he made his debut with two other young men in a pageant portraying industry arising from the Connecticut River (amid a large chorus of pulsating young ladies, in swaths of blue voile, representing the river).

On one of these visits he met the director of the Hartford Parks Department, who asked him if he knew anyone who could direct their newly created marionette theater. Nik promptly recommended himself and got the job. With these new prospects, he left Southington and moved to Hartford. Nikolais had now expanded his theatrical experiences to include music, drama, dance, and puppetry. This early training prepared him for his later multimedia excursions.

In 1937, he attended his first summer session at Bennington College, where he was directly exposed to the great innovators of modern dance: Martha Graham, Doris Humphrey, Charles Weidman, Hanya Holm, Louis Horst, and John Martin. Thanks to

Alwin Nikolais.
Photo by Dan Ziskie.

these overwhelming stimuli, Nikolais's focus on dance was securely affirmed. In 1939, with Truda Kaschmann and composer Ernst Krenek, he was commissioned to create a new modern ballet. *Eight Column Line* was well received and further encouraged his career. He began a school and formed a dance company in Hartford.

The World War II years, 1942 to 1945, found him in the U.S. Army as Sergeant Nikolais. Upon his discharge, he relocated to New York City, where he concentrated his study with Hanya Holm, Wigman's former associate. In 1948, he assumed the directorship of the Henry Street Playhouse, located on New York's Lower East Side. The Playhouse was a beautifully designed theater, but it was in an almost derelict condition when he arrived. With the help of the young people he attracted, he rejuvenated and restored the building and brought it back to the international importance it had originally experienced.

Here, for the next twenty years, Nik and his dedicated young company revitalized the theater and established a major school of dance for both children and professionals. Although he became known as the "Father of Mixed Media," his primary focus was dance. And in dance he was a purist. The training at the school focused on dance, not on the dance theater that he chose for his own creative direction.

During this time his theories of motional qualification evolved, including his belief in giving movement its own sentient intelligence and its own interior identification, and, through the practice of improvisation, equipping the dancer with the skills to perform. He created a vocabulary pertinent to his theories. Judgments and application during the technical training included such concepts as *decentralization, totality, immediacy, presence in stasis, intuitive judgments, sensings,* and *grain*—concepts to which he brought new meaning.

His first works at the Playhouse were programs for children, and his genius for developing the theatrical in dance began to take form. Later, his use of color, costumes, and light became some of his major contributions to dance. He made dance a visual as well as a kinetic art.

In 1956, Nikolais created *Kaleidoscope,* which was based on his principles of dance in terms of space, time, shape, and motion. Its success thrust him into prominence in the dance world, an ascendancy from which he never faltered. *Prism* (1956),

which dealt with aspects of lighting and light, followed. Other major works he created at the playhouse were *Allegory* (1959), *Totem* (1960), *Imago* (1963), *Sanctum* (1964), *Galaxy* (1965), *Somniloquy* (1967), and *Echo* (1969). During this period, his experiments in lighting for dance advanced steadily. He created new devices to light and isolate the dancing figure. He restructured projectors to transform the stage with light and color. He created a range of dazzling slides to stimulate the eye and enhance movement, and painted the stage with atmosphere and mystery.

In 1964 and again in 1967, he received Guggenheim fellowships. These enabled him to purchase the electronic and synthesizer equipment he needed to create the sound scores he provided for all his productions. In the spring of 1993, a compact disc of his scores was released by Composers Recording Inc. in New York City.

In 1970, when the Settlement House administration changed, Nikolais left the Playhouse. By then his work had become known and was in demand throughout the world. His productions of *Imago* and *Tent* in Paris in 1968 won him the Grand Prix, and he became an international star. He regularly toured Europe, Asia, South America, and Africa, in addition to the United States, and his became one of the foremost American companies touring internationally. He received the French Legion of Honor and the keys to almost fifty cities throughout the world.

During the seventies he created television programs for British, American, German, Italian, Swedish, Danish, French, and Yugoslavian stations. He also continued to create for his company: *Scenario* (1971), *Foreplay* (1972), *Crossfade* (1974), *Tribe* (1975), *Guignol* (1977), *Arporisms* (1977), and *Gallery* (1978). In 1980, the Paris Opera commissioned him to create *Schema,* a full evening length work for their company. This was followed by more creations: *Pond* (1982), *Mechanical Organ* (1982), *Persons and Structures* (1984), *Crucible* (1985), *Blank on Blank* (1987), *Intrados* (1989), and *Aurora* (1992). Nikolais received five honorary doctorates from American universities, the Scripps Award, the Capezio Award, the Kennedy Honors, and the Presidential Medal of Art, among others.

Alwin Nikolais was not only a philosopher/ pedagogist but a multifaceted artist as well. He was a colorful world traveler with a lusty sense of humor. He was a connoisseur of good wine and good food, and was himself a superb chef. He held opinions about many things. He was a designer of costumes, stage slides, scenery, and lighting, and was a composer and teacher. As an observer of social and political change, he made it his business to be active in the politics of dance in America.

He dined with presidents and workmen. He could play Beethoven sonatas and compose electronic music. He watched the sun rise over the Taj Mahal and went disco dancing in Los Angeles.

He was generous and frugal and knew elation and despair. He was naïve and sophisticated, serious and playful. He lived through the Great Depression, World War II, and the awesome explorations of outer space. He lived both ends of everything, including the twentieth century. But most important, he lived fully.

For fifty years, Alwin Nikolais's genius helped shape modern dance in America, giving it an articulate pedagogical basis for training and for creating a multimedia theater of abstraction on stage.

BIOGRAPHY OF MURRAY LOUIS

Murray Louis was born in New York City on November 4, 1926. Upon his mother's early death during the Depression years, he was placed in an orphanage together with his older brother and younger sister while his two older sisters maintained some semblance of a home in the city. At the orphanage, which was built like a turreted palace, he spent some of the happiest years of his life.

Thanks to an older brother who looked after him, and an older sister, Frances, who became a loving surrogate mother, the orphanage years proved to be more of an adventure than a traumatic experience. The orphanage had a large and well-stocked library, which he immediately appropriated. He organized it and over the years read about half the books that it contained. He read everything: the encyclopedia, science books,

classics, mystery stories. Words drew him in like a magnet. Social life at the orphanage included "talent" nights, where he invariably won the prize with his abandoned free-style improvised dancing. On Sundays his sisters took him to museums and events. One memorable visit was to the Macy's farm display on the fifth floor of the department store, where he encountered his first cow. It was love at first sight. The visit also provided his first experience with gardens and flowers, which later became a passion.

The "movies" became a major influence during this period. It was here he became addicted to the style and wit of Fred Astaire's dancing, which he emulated at the talent shows. His older sister Frances had become secretary to the director of the W.P.A. Writer's Project, and he was able to see

Murray Louis.
Photo by Nan Melville.

performances of the W.P.A. theater and dance programs. These were his first introduction to modern dance. At sixteen he sat in the music pit and turned pages for a Helen Tamiris concert. He saw several other modern dance concerts, but none made the impression upon him that Astaire's skill and style did. During the orphanage years, the library fed his mind and Astaire's dancing fed his body.

At age eighteen he was promptly drafted into the navy and nineteen months later, when WWII ended, he found himself in San Francisco, free at last to determine his own life. Would he pursue archaeology or exploration? His brother assured him that there was nothing new to discover, but perhaps there were some ancient kings still buried. Should he become a writer or composer? Music turned out to be a very short-lived ambition. He was thoroughly familiar with much of Beethoven, Mozart, and Tchaikovsky, but solfège put an end to that ambition. The list of options grew: gardener or scientist? Everything interested him. With no one to coerce him into a career decision, he finally decided to undertake a profession he would enjoy, one that came easily to him: dance. Dancing was natural for him; it came easily and he had a passion for it. "Why not enjoy work?" he thought. It was a decision he never regretted.

For his remaining time in San Francisco, he enrolled at San Francisco State College, majoring in dance; he worked with Anne Halprin for a summer session. In 1949, Louis set out to return to New York City and Broadway. En route, he enrolled in Holm's Colorado Springs summer session. There he fatefully met Alwin Nikolais. Hanya Holm had been delayed that summer, and so Louis had two concentrated weeks with Nikolais. That was enough time for him to discover Nikolais's genius. The meeting had a profound impression on each man. Here was a young man bursting with energy and a mature mind able to direct that energy.

Nikolais had just been made director of the Playhouse of the Henry Street Settlement, on the Lower East Side of New York. He invited Louis to join him in this new enterprise. Louis looked at this blonde, blue-eyed, New England country boy and thought, "Someone has got to look after him. He can't go back to the Lower East Side alone," and he agreed to go.

For the first five years (1949–1954), the work at the Playhouse was arduous and often grueling.

But the vision that lay ahead was so bright and promising that the labor to physically restore the building and develop a school, which peaked at five hundred students both young and professional, was its own reward. Louis contributed to the evolution of Nikolais's philosophy and methods while reshaping his own body and finding his own creative direction. He made his debut in 1953 together with Gladys Bailin. In 1957 with a small group he presented *Journal*, a thirty-minute work, which gave evidence of his performing and creative range. Thus the Murray Louis Dance Co. was born.

Throughout the sixties he presented a new major creation every year, including: *Entre-Acte* (1959), *An Odyssey* (1960), *Calligraph for Martyrs* (1961), *Facets* (1962), *Interims* (1963), *Landscapes* (1964), *Junk Dances* (1964), *Chimera* (1966), *Go 6* (1967), and *Proximities* (1969). His range was considerable, from comic to abstract, dramatic to lyric; his formidable technique and wit served him in all his endeavors.

Up to this point he had been the leading dancer with the Nikolais Company, but with the success and growing prominence of his own company both he and Nikolais decided that he should concentrate on his own work. During the seventies, the school, which had by now relocated from the Henry Street Playhouse to mid-Manhattan, had become a major national and international center. A good deal of the teaching became his responsibility as "Nik" was carried off on international tours. His skill as a teacher of creative dance was honed to a fine point.

During the next years, his own touring took him to five continents, and he played every state in the union. In the early seventies he released a five-part video series, *Dance as an Art Form*, which became a standard for dance departments across the country. He was asked by the U.S. government to undertake a pilot program in dance with young people. The result was so successful that the Artist-in-Schools program was born. He continued producing works, such as *Personnae* (1970), *Continuum* (1971), *Hoopla* (1972), *Scheherazade* (1973), *Index* (1974), *Geometrics* (1975), *Porcelain Dialogues* (1976), *Four Brubeck Pieces* (1984), *The Station* (1986), *Sinners All* (1996), and *Tips* (1997). In total, he has composed 130 works. In 1989 a video, titled *Murray Louis in Concert*, was released.

Louis has received two Guggenheim grants, as well as grants from the Ford, Rockefeller, and

Mellon Foundations. He has been a grantee of the National Endowment for the Arts since 1969. In 1984 he joined forces with Dave Brubeck and together they toured the United States and abroad for four seasons. With Rudolf Nureyev he shared seasons in London, Paris, Madrid, and New York City. He wrote monthly essays for *Dance Magazine*, which led to the publication of *Inside Dance* by St. Martin's Press, later followed by *On Dance*.

The two dance companies were joined when Nikolais's health began to falter; in 1993, a forty-four-year relationship ended with Nikolais's death. Carrying on the work of the company, in 1996 Louis became a lecturer for a Phi Beta Kappa "distinguished lecture" tour of twelve universities and colleges, and he returned to the stage with the acclaimed *Sinners All* and completed a five-part video series titled *The World of Alwin Nikolais*.

In 1999, on the fiftieth anniversary of the inception of their lifelong collaboration, the extensive Nikolais/Louis Archives found a home at Ohio University. Work on the archives will continue for several years and eventually be made available worldwide. The vast collection of films, videos, photos, music, designs, flyers, posters, and manuscripts are also being prepared to eventually go on the Web.

Murray Louis received an honorary Doctorate of Performing Arts from Ohio University in Athens, Ohio, in 1999, and an honorary Doctorate of Fine Arts from Rutgers University in New Brunswick, New Jersey, in 2000. November 2001 marked the premiere of his most recent work, *Isle*, with the Jose Limon Dance Co.

As Hanya Holm said of him on the presentation of a *Dance Magazine* Award, "Murray Louis is a dancer, choreographer, teacher, writer. All his parts are the sum of an enormous energy which he spends generously in the service of the dance."

The Henry Street Playhouse.
Photo by David Berlin.

INTRODUCTION

The Nikolais/Louis technique is based on the philosophy that the undertaking of dance training is not a simple or singular event, but a lifelong investment in personal enrichment. It was originally presented as a daily, three-year course at the Henry Street Playhouse in New York City. We always presented the principles of the technique in various combinations and challenges, and adjusted them according to the changing times and social scene. Alwin Nikolais designed the course to begin with a two-hour technique class, followed by one hour of improvisation and, after a half-hour break, a period of composition, percussion, or pedagogy. The criterion for success was the fulfillment of the premise presented in class that day. All classes demanded full participation from the students and a lively, encouraging presentation from the teacher. The overall aim was to impart the skills of performer, choreographer, and teacher to the student, since, practically speaking, the dancer would need all three skills to earn a professional income. More than this, mastering or at least being familiar with all the facets of dance gave the student a richer understanding of the profession.

The Playhouse's success was unique in many respects. The school was housed in a beautiful but rundown theater; as its director it had Nikolais, a man whose genius was primed to flourish in such an environment. It drew on a rich source of possible students in the form of hundreds of children who lived within walking distance and therefore did not need parents to accompany them. It also had a national and international professionally oriented adult enrollment. All of these factors allowed Nikolais, along with his dance company, to build a large school for professionals and children within a short period of time. At the Playhouse, they performed concerts, presented children's productions by both the dance company and the children, restored the theater, and—after seven years of hard and visionary work—built a school and dance company that commanded respect.

The pedagogy taught for twenty years at the Henry Street Playhouse and then for the following twenty-five years at various New York City studios created individual dancers and choreographers, not copies of a rigid, singular approach. The Nikolais/Louis technique was taught worldwide, and it still is.

Today its pedagogy and principles are represented in many American university dance programs. Many of France's contemporary dancers were nurtured in the three-year program at the school Nikolais created at Angers in 1978 at the request of the French government.

Although it is called the Nikolais/Louis technique, it should be thought of as a *basic* technique, one that is applicable to any dance form. The technique is not limited to technical proficiency alone, but includes improvisational, creative, choreographic, and performing skills. It is an inclusive approach to movement and dance.

The Nikolais/Louis technique is based on many decades of trial and error. Its lineage can be seen covering over 100 years, stretching from Rudolph Von Laban to Mary Wigman, from Hanya Holm to Alwin Nikolais to Murray Louis and beyond. These artists have contributed to the technique as educators, performers, and creators. Each one taught and created differently, but they shared a rich understanding of—and dedication to—dance as an art. They stimulated each other and built on each other's ideas, yet remained individual and unique artists.

The technique covers four areas with which dancers should be familiar because they relate to all facets of the profession: technical training, improvisation, choreography, and performance. A dancer's career will include performing, choreographing, or teaching—or most likely some combination of the three.

Performance is the skill of presenting choreography to its best advantage to an audience. In the Nikolais/Louis technique, by exploring and examining the internal as well as the external nature of dance, the dancer learns how to approach and analyze movement and choreography rigorously. An astute awareness of movement qualities gives a performance intelligence and richness: just as an actor dissects and analyzes a role, the dancer enhances the choreography through clarity of spatial, temporal, and sculptural understanding. Adding nuance and depth to a gesture is the performer's responsibility. Armed with an enriched understanding of movement gained from this technique, the dancer is prepared to meet the demands of the discipline. The technique was created and refined to reveal the fullness and clarity of form, not to interpret it, as interpretation rests primarily in the domain of the audience.

In the same way that it is important for a musician to understand the nomenclature of his musical instrument, it is also important that a dancer is familiar with the instrument he will employ to make his art: the body. The body is an incredible structure that houses a world of complex beauty. Tangible components like bones, muscles, cells, and nerves mingle with the intangible mysteries of intuition, imagination, talent, and emotion. There is no single definition for the human body, just as there is none for a dance work. The body is designed in different shapes and sizes and is charged with an unimaginable range of emotions that guarantees that no two people are alike. It is with this complicated equipment that the dancer begins his training. So, too, it is the students' variety and uniqueness that most challenges the teacher's imagination.

Although this may sound daunting for both the dancer and the teacher, it is not as difficult as it appears. It is manageable if both teacher and student speak the same language—the language of dance—and not the personal language of ego and personality.

This book, which deals with principles of basic dance, is in a way applicable to any training or creative class because it is about teachers and students and how they communicate with each other. Because dance is primarily a nonverbal art, it is important that the teacher and student develop a rapport—an open, clear avenue of contact. This book aims to clear such a path and to lend perspective to what can otherwise be a confusing and often misunderstood learning process.

Teaching, the process of imparting information from one person to another, challenges both the teacher and student. It involves the intellect and the imagination, although in dance training the physical is usually emphasized over the mental. Dance requires real dexterity in many spheres: attuning the sentient capabilities, paying attention to the feedback of the muscles, and engaging the imagination's large and varied spectrum. At the same time, dancers need to grasp what is being asked of them and teachers need to be sure that dancers understand what teachers are saying. Effective communication is as necessary in dance education as in any other successful relationship.

The Nikolais/Louis technique is a technical and creative method geared toward creating this shared communication. With a focus on presenting the fullness of the dancer's art, the technique does not define movement patterns, but presents material in a conceptual frame. In this sense, the technique employs the nonverbal language of abstraction to help encompass the enormous range of human communication. The Nikolais/Louis technique creates a vocabulary that enables communication between student and teacher that is both precise and flexible.

The mutual understanding of criticism is essential in learning and teaching, and the instructor's verbal skills, his use of the literal and the figurative, must be sharp if he is to minimize the vagueness and ambiguity that often clouds criticism. Words mean different things to different people, and it is difficult to retract an inappropriate word completely. An unclear or confused criticism can stick like glue, defeating the value of a class. For the teacher, it is as important to be able to see and help the student who has not been successful as it is to recognize and encourage the one who has achieved success. For this reason, the book includes a collection of criticisms gathered from our years spent in the classroom. By reading them, one can get a sense of the varied verbal range one should try to employ to fire the imaginations and muscles of many different students as they each engage with the same premise.

SECTION I: DEFINITIONS

BASIC DANCE[*]

Man was not the first creature to dance. Long before he appeared upon the evolutionary scene, some animate thing sensed its life and moved solely as an expression of ecstasy. Through its own movement it was transported into an awareness of life beyond its more ordinary functions. This I call dancing.

Man, too, at some early point in his evolution lifted himself in acknowledgement of his endowment with life and motion and of being at one with the mechanism of nature.

It is likely that he did this simply and directly for that purpose. He had no intent of advertising his skill, cunning, or physical endowments for the purpose of either sex or war. Neither did he do this to pursue or exploit his artistic inclinations. Nor did he do it as a catharsis; nor as a means of expressing himself. It was not a way of stretching or warming his muscles. Nor was it a humble acquiescence either to man or to a god.

Dance was a simple psycho-biological statement of his living, moving presence in which he realized a force common to all universal functions coursing through his body. Thus he acknowledged his kinship to all living matter. Within this elemental act there was magic. There was a mystical sense of belonging to nature—a sense beyond his conscious intellectual reasoning.

It is little wonder that, of all the arts, dance became the most vital act in primitive worship. Through dance, man could become the sun, the moon, the earth, fire, and all of the unpredictable occurrences that surrounded him. Through such identification, he sensed a union with nature, which otherwise perplexed him.

In this primary state of dance, for both the early creatures and for man, there was no art. These were actions happening directly in time and space. If beauty occurred (as it must have), it was innocent of artfulness. There was no abstraction or idealization for the conscious purpose of beauty; there was no translation or reproduction into an artifact or action that could contain this wonderment; consequently there was no art. Yet this basic dance contained an elemental power that could be harnessed into an art_one that could serve as a synapse or catalyst from which art could emanate.

Dance in this primal sense is separable from art. However, the art of dancing must retain its contact with the unique motional acts, which trace a lineage back to the primordial dancing creature.

At the opposite pole from these virtually static exhibitions, we find dances of violent physical maneuverings hardly distinguishable from football skirmishes. In the course of history and even in the forms existing today, we find an amazing range of motions designated as dance, from ancient ethnic ceremonies to the gyrations of present-day social dance. One might surmise that the maximum invention of human motion has been reached. Yet it's certain that the future will continue to add new dimensions to the art.

It is in the area of "art dance" that new invention most frequently occurs, and it is here that there is a tendency to lose sight of the basis upon which the art is built. There is usually vehement negative outcry whenever a new form arises. The statement "It is not dance" can be found in profusion in critical writing whenever any new development emerges.

Every period of art creates its own jargon and analytical summations. These tend to establish tenaciously guarded rules, forms, methods, subjects, and so on, which inevitably must be broken or disregarded by the next revolutionary creator. He does this to shatter the peripheral encumbrances so that he may find again the germinal matter that drives his art. Out of this, then, he creates new structures congenial to his time and temper. In effect, he rediscovers and reasserts the naked power of his experiences, out of which he then forms his art—for in its primary form it is not yet art but rather a means through and with which art may occur. So too, in dance: its basic stuff is not art, but without this primary ingredient the resulting art cannot warrant the title of dance. The basis of dance embodies highly volatile factors. If one loses keen, sentient contact

---

[*]Throughout this book, the font type indicates the author. The bold font indicates a section written by Nikolais, while a section in the lighter font was written by Louis.

with them, definition, although easily comprehensible, becomes shallow.

In its purest essence, dance is the motion of a neurologically and kinetically endowed body in which the purpose, meaning, or value of that motion is inherent in the motion itself. In ordinary circumstance movement is a means toward another end, and thus does not call attention to itself but rather to a point of interest or achievement beyond it. The unique character of dance is that motion itself is the end; reason is within it rather than beyond it. Dance accomplishes itself.

The word "motion" as used here means something quite distinct from movement. It is used in the sense that movement implies the displacement of matter from one location to another; whereas motion ascribes a particular nature to the action itself. This is a qualitative distinction. We may say, for example, "The object moved through space in spiral motion." It is meant, then, in this definition, that dance refers primarily to motion as the inner detail of movement—implying qualitative content and definable itinerary.

It is the containment of the function or purpose within the action itself that distinguishes dance from other actions. An arm may be moved for the simple purpose of setting it elsewhere. However, when the motion itself supercedes as the purpose over and above the changing location, then dance takes place. If the arm describes a circle solely for the purpose of describing a circle, it does not qualify as dance in the pure sense. However, if the act places value on the inner sentient content of the kinetics involved during that circular execution, then dance takes place. Motion is a consciously engaged action.

In sports, action directs itself toward attainment of a goal or an achievement to which motion is subservient. No matter how carefully practiced and skilled the action may be, it is nevertheless relegated to the function of carrying out a purpose beyond itself.

Basic dance requires a different attitude toward the action, a frame of mind of the performer, a state of being in which relatively all other factors involved become subservient to the motion. It does not matter from the point of view of definition whether the result is monotonous or poetical. Dance is a category of action that basically is unconcerned with degree of interest or artfulness. Like food it can be good or bad, but it is food nevertheless!

When a child skips down the street, it is perhaps a release of excess energies, but it is not necessarily dance. When a child skips in a dance studio, purposefully and consciously executing the motion for its own sake, then the skip becomes dance.

In the art of mime, motions and gestures may be highly ordered and sensitive. Yet mime is distinguished from dance in that it focuses on motion for the purpose of descriptive, literal expression rather than on the values of motion itself. If it goes beyond this purpose, it may become dance. And, in the same way, the dancer who resorts to literal gesture borrows from the art of mime.

From two extreme points of view, then, if a person raises an arm, no matter how slowly, with consciousness of the kinetics as the end value, then the act can be defined as dance. Also, if one moves with great speed and with consciousness of that speed as the reason and focus itself, then that too, artistic or otherwise, becomes dance. Basic dance begins with an awareness of motion.

In its strictest analysis, basic dance in its most complete and purest sense is rarely seen, for in exemplary instances it would embody the intrinsic coincidences of primary laws of motion as a direct language. It would involve the activation of matter in time and space, engaging gravity, centrifugal and centripetal forces, and the infinite interbalances of all these relative factors.

All of these highly volatile factors, when funneled through the human body, bring about that which we call dance.

Basic Dance

Basic dance is arriving at a balance from which creativity can begin, by first disturbing that balance. Basic dance is that state of balance and totality that is considered a norm or starting point. From this point, style, stress, distortion, and other imbalances can and should be emphasized and employed. Basic dance has no personal characteristics.

VISION OF A NEW TECHNIQUE

The most distinctive aspect of American modern dance was what I have called the concept of the *unique gesture*. Ironically this distinction was also its greatest hindrance: the idea of uniqueness would eliminate the practice of the prescribed vocabulary of the many movement forms, which embraced the numerous varieties of dance. To this day, and particularly during the earlier years, it was often erroneously assumed that ballet technique was a basic requirement for art dance. Ballet technique is contrary to the concept of the unique gesture, particularly when that technique is based on the practice of motional rituals, which stifles muscular liberty or leads to glib athleticism. A modern dance technique is possible, but it cannot be based on patterned motional forms. It can be accomplished by an analysis of human motion as an art and by a practiced study of the aesthetic potentials of that medium.

One of the most vivid recollections I have in my dance study was a moment in a class with John Martin, then the astute dance critic of the *New York Times*, who announced to a class at Bennington College that at that moment of dance history we had at last discovered the full potential of the human body. In 1937 this was, to me, a shocking statement. I had previously believed that this knowledge was centuries old. I had yet to learn that modern dance was based on this new realization—not on past forms— that modern dance in 1937 was a contemporary form, at the beginning of its formulation.

For dance to flourish, it needed a technique that would not impose styles or rigid patterns that would lock the body with motional indigestion, but rather return it to the study of motion as the basis of its art. It is possible that in this way techniques can be established that can bring dance training to the equal stature of the more disciplined arts such as music, painting, and sculpture.

Today, patterns rather than aesthetics seem to dominate. Definitions remain vague and a precise training for participation in modern dance is missing. What approach to dance should an aspiring student engage to ensure a technique for his or her expression of the world? Ballet, jazz, ethnic, or modern dance techniques? Most students of dance try them all, and the resulting smorgasbord leaves only an unrelated assortment of the obvious leaps, splits, turns, and undefined gestures.

The first quarter of the twentieth century found the United States deluged with something it had never had before: professional dance. The deluge was not so much in quantity, but in variety. Ballet began to take hold, and Isadora left her mark. The Denishawn filled the stewpot with morsels from all over the world— Spain, Indonesia, China, Japan, and Mexico, in addition to invented concoctions of styles not heard or seen before.

It was out of the dance cuisine of Denishawn that new American dance arose. Martha Graham, Doris Humphrey, and Charles Weidman toured as members of Denishawn Company and performed everything from glitzy Aztec rites to Japanese sword dances, from fake Chinese rituals to glamorous Broadway musicals. A lot of art mixed with a lot of showbiz, and one didn't know where one ended and the other began. The miracle was that out of this mad stew emerged a single focused idealism. It happened without anyone's conscious intention. It emerged from the morass as clean as Arthur's Excalibur arose from the lake. With incredible innocence a tenet was formed that could serve dance. This was the idea of the *unique gesture*.

Free people and creative minds are not prone to following patterns. Patterns preconceived by others are the security blanket of the unadventuresome spirit whose timidity requires the protection of predigested forms.

In coining the phrase *unique gesture*, I have described a principle that opposed the existing processes that had obliged the creator to pin his dance communication upon already existing techniques and patterns of movement. Unlike ballet, for example, where an arabesque can be forged into the violent scream of a witch or the ecstatic love of a princess, modern dance, at its best, refused to follow a template. It chose instead to mold the motion directly out of the impulses of the creator's emotions, tailoring them specifically to his or her particular view.

This meant that the design of action was not serviceable for other expressions. It could serve only one master.

The idea of the unique gesture was not deliberately conceived; it was simply born. Its only discipline was to envision a pathway into the landscape of the mind and then lead the spectator vicariously into that vision. Individual artists hacked through their mystical forests with their own makeshift machetes and created motions to conform to these individual paths and visions. Each trip was different, and although movement styles were created, these were characteristics of the dictates of a particular mind, rather than generalized techniques. This individualism created confusion, frustration, and pedagogical difficulties.

Fundamentally, technique refers to a method used to achieve an end. Because each end result of modern dance was devoted to unique ventures created by individual artists, a generalized technique was always in a state of flux.

Each artist attempted to create his or her own motional forms, derived directly from the individual's unique sources. It was the marriage of mind and motion. The wide inventory of motion was as infinite as the myriad facets of the mind. Was there a technique? Absolutely. The technique was the skill of releasing the body to the service of the aesthetic mind, by passing the temptations of the narcissistic ego and the pathways of muscular habit.

The concepts inherent in such an ideal contain a key to the meaning of humanism. Mankind had at its service the limitless source of its own genetic endowment. This places the responsibility and glorification of life upon the spirit and vitality of the individual. His motional statement of life is his own unique expression as the forces of life course through him and engage his huge accumulation of personal references. This was not vague symbolism or copied patterns, but gestures of such revelation that one could affirm the very fact of life itself. This was modern dance at its best.

This was also a time when many artists mixed political and social activism with art. Often political protests became significant aesthetic ventures. Some succeeded mainly because compulsions to produce art are also primal moralistic forces.

The idea of the unique gesture, as it was originally practiced at Bennington's Summer Dance programs, changed the whole concept of concert dance. In particular, it separated dance from virtuosic displays pinned upon a skimpy story line. The newest trends in music also made agreeable companions to modern dance. Dissonance and erratic conglomerations of pulse and meter were easily within the comprehension and aesthetics of the modern dancer.

But above all, the concept of the unique gesture is ideally a profound *dance* concept in that it combines the human body, mind, and spirit. This is a most fragile linkage. The challenge is to maintain the moral stamina required to remain wholly faithful to the impulses of the deeper self. Man's attraction toward the easy life—his tendency to fall back on pattern—is so forceful and contagious that it must constantly be guarded against.

All great statements of life emerge from this deep conviction. One can benefit from another's genius, but the genius itself cannot be shared. It is one thing; to halve it is to destroy it.

DECENTRALIZATION

German modern dance was less affected by personalities than was American modern dance, and it was closer to general skill and craft. This was mainly due to the impersonal analyses promoted by Rudolph von Laban. His technique too, however, was a "centralized" one based on precise spatial, architectural orientations surrounding the body. On this he also based his system of notation.

In the United States, modern dance became established as a free creative process. The geniuses of modern dance generated powerful styles, which emanated from their own bodies. In effect, their "techniques" were actually personal styles, albeit ones that were somewhat scientifically based, imposed upon questions of movement.

In the concept of decentralization, the ego is to dance what the anchoring "do" note is to music. Too often the ego becomes the point of focus or centralization, and motion becomes subservient to it. Consequently, the first goal in the practice of decentralization is to contrive methods of releasing the body from the limiting vortex of the ego, the self.

For an art dominated by the exhibition of the human body, this is not so easy. The method for success is to distract the onlooker's eye away from the performing ego by making the body the instrument of other visions through the use of choreographic and performing sleight of hand. This process of shifting the onlooker's attention is what I call decentralization. By this I mean the process of focusing one's dynamic force away from the self and allowing it to reach out and bring other concerns under control. This process presents a hornet's nest of difficulties, and the idea of decentralization invariably cause resistance, especially as our primal instincts forever bring us back to our protective cores, to our atavistic instincts.

A constant state of pulling in, of centralization, can serve as a refuge from the whirlwind of the society that surrounds us, but when it dominates all of our responses, it becomes restrictive. Decentralization becomes necessary to participate in the knowledge of our time, and that means extending out of our center, which had offered us a huge advance in our freedom to experience. It may not offer us secure creative footing, but it does offer an abundance of thrilling, unanchored adventures.

The strongest force in centralization is egocentricity, and the strongest force in egocentricity is sexuality; therefore, I believe it is necessary in a classroom situation to break this down first. We have progressed to a point where we realize that the battle of the sexes is no longer the essential subject for dance.

Breaking down the polar distance between the male and female, for instance, led me to begin using unisex costumes in 1953. This also allowed greater freedom in assigning roles in the dances. In most cases, in my work, the male and female roles could be interchanged. I rarely singled out the sexes.

Relieved of the overemphasis on sexual differences, I concentrated more intensely on the motion itself. Motion could more easily become the subject rather than being an adjunct of the dancer. The most positive result of working from this perspective was the emergence of a stronger definition of dance: dance became the art of motion, freed from literal subjects. Motion was no longer the servant of the individual; it became the master.

I watch carefully as I direct class activity. I implant a motivation and then examine very carefully the route to its outcome. After summarizing the results, I initiate corrective activities to clear the path of psychical interference or unresponsive body parts—all very simple as an idea, but discouragingly difficult to achieve. The centralizing "me" factor is extraordinarily powerful, and performers are reluctant to relinquish the exhibition of self in favor of the act.

In searching for a new technical approach, I gradually developed my definition of dance and began to conceive of a new creative direction for myself. As I explored, my main objective was to identify the role of the dancer and the nature of his motivation. I then sought a manner of teaching that would best develop the technical ability of the body as the instrument.

Unlike painters and musicians, the dancer bears within himself a potent force in the form of his own material presence. It is not only his physical presence that matters, but also his psychical force and the strong tendency to impose his presence upon the onlooker.

The more closely I tried to observe the body's motion, the more impatient I became with the ego's intrusion upon the action. I found myself using all sorts of devices to try to eliminate, or at least minimize, the ego's dominance.

German theories lent themselves well here, particularly Laban's concepts of dimension. Like Laban, I conceived of the body as a three-dimensional entity empowered by the mind. Looked at in this way, a simple abstract motivation, such as forward, backward, up, or down, quickly revealed the failure of any body part or the whole body to fully engage itself. Mannerisms, negative idiosyncrasies, timidities, aggressiveness, and all other hindrances to executing the act were quickly revealed, and corrective processes toward decentralization were initiated. Laban's theories were precise: they stated that specific architectural radiations emanate from centralization. Despite my opposition to centralization, the Laban theories furnished a fine initial corrective for technical study. Their precise architectural design revealed very clearly the student's inadequacies in controlling the union of intent and achievement. Consequently, they offered guidelines for improving one's skill in executing the dictates of decentralization. Laban's system of notation was also a great aid to looking at motion objectively rather than subjectively. Consciousness and clarity of dance structure increased.

By this time in the development of my ideas at the Henry Street Playhouse, Murray Louis had established a large children's division that was attended by hundreds of children. Through him the four- to eleven-year-olds accepted my methods; they were also enchantingly eloquent in their creative expressions. These youngsters had not yet reached puberty, so they were not bugged by sex. Consequently, it was not difficult for them to explore abstract motion as an event on its own merits. Their *direct* doing helped to assure me that primal gestures still existed inherently within us, no matter how sophisticated our society had become. Prepubescent children naturally accept abstraction and nonliteral imagining. Puberty is the classroom of centralization and sexual fixation from which many do not graduate.[1]

Relieving oneself of centralization allowed motion to open up a vast new area of metaphoric expression. Clearly this was my path to travel. I found that this new world of dimensions beyond the seeing eye was truly a contemporary world to be experienced on its own terms. Eventually, I concluded that the message resided in the motion itself. *My definition of dance was now fixed: dance is the art of motion, not emotion, and it carries its own intelligence within itself.*

In 1953 we presented our first concert in this new vein of releasing the focus from self and self-image. The piece was called *Village of Whispers*. It was composed of many dances—group works, solos, and duets—which we prepared in composition classes. The main theme was based on images that rested beyond or behind the façade of a village. The titles were *Glade, Creech, Dark Corner, Styx, Hex, Gemini, Tournament, Tensile Involvement, Evil Eye, Monarch, and Lorilei.* The dance attempted to enact an entire statement via an abstract structure instead of pursuing it through characterization or situation. Its concept was more closely related to a musical elaboration than it was to a dramatic one.

I was aware that this process was a familiar one in acting. But in acting it was used as a device to develop characterization, and I was attempting to evolve abstract choreography. Still, I was not wholly satisfied with the dancers' success in decentralization, which suggested they were just embodying things other than themselves. I wanted them to transcend themselves entirely.

---

[1]Nikolais did not teach children's classes at the Playhouse. His office, however, was on the same floor as my classroom studios, and he would often come in and watch the improvisation and composition studies. Yes, at six years old the students were composing for each other.

Decentralization refuted several early theories of motion, which stated that motion originates in the region of the solar plexus. With the new awareness of decentralization, one could now place the origin of force in or on any surface of the body, even a pinpoint of flesh. The concept quickly developed a new potential for nuance in motional expression. Its main advantage was that it released the choreographer/dancer from the centralized gut action, which had strongly chained the dancer to characterization and situation.

Decentralization attracted praise and interest, but it also received an equal amount of negative response from the establishment. The criticism came particularly from those whose self-identification with modern dance archetypes left them with no other peg on which to hang their egos.

Cries of "dehumanization," "coldness," "puppetry," and "mechanicalness" arose. The outcries were reminiscent of the early days of abstract painting. With no figurative or representational vision offered as a portal into the painting, literal-minded people failed to get the message. Abstraction requires a multifaceted and lively frame of reference from both the creator and the viewer. Depth of aesthetic perception is measured by the degree to which one responds to the abstract. The detail of the abstract components in a work aesthetically define its quality. In this vision of decentralization, the less aesthetically oriented person is left in a dither because the obvious external form, the dancer's personality, is subdued.

Unfettering dance from its centralization not only allowed the smallest kernel of force to appear at any point in or on the body, it could also cause a force to arise from any source in the space surrounding the body. It was not a matter of eliminating the center but of relocating it to other parts of the body or other points in space. When one is released from centralization, one becomes more completely aware of an infinite environment.

No longer dominated by personality and ego, the dancer now was able to merge into an environment of which he was a part. He found himself a contributing member rather than a dominating dweller. Space became more than just a hole in which to kick or spin about; it evolved into an architecturally fluid companion. Time was no longer a metrical, reiterated beat that restricted the dancer's step; it was a malleable measurement adapting itself to the shaping of the art subject, flowing with the subject's needs rather than forcing the action into rigid steps. Motion became the vital pulse of the human structure, not a classical decorative posture or a skillful movement cadenza that merely decorated the figure. Shape, too, was no longer just a static attitude or pose. It transcended its literal function to become whatever the choreographer proposed.

I am well aware that the practice of decentralization seems to contradict the very core of personal assertion. After all, performing makes high demands of the human ego. Yet the artist must go beyond himself. Great performers are willing to transcend themselves to live within the substance of their art.

In decentralization, the dancer goes even beyond this point: his head may not be a head, his arm not an arm. The dancer may have to give up his identity to place himself at the service of something that bears no resemblance to his physicality. By the magic of motion, he will illuminate the poetic substance of something entirely new. Shaking off the shackles of the fleshy identification, the body may become the eloquent motional spokesman of all things within the reach of man's most mystical visions. He may then inform us of things beyond ordinary vision and comprehension. He can tell us of the wonderment of life itself, beyond any thing previously felt or observed, by reaching to the farthest limits of imagination.

* * *

In order to vitalize areas that have no means for self-vitalization, the dancer must project his own neuro-muscular system into points of interest around him. This calls for a strong conceptual ability and a selfless willingness to share. With a fluid generative source, the dancer can vitalize and give identity to spatial and temporal concerns. His designs in space, his sculptural forms, can now exist in their own right, and no longer need to be centrally dominated and ego-infused.

Being able to fill abstractions with their own life force expands the performers' range enormously. It also allows the dancer to achieve heroic proportions. No longer limited to what the body allows, he now can expand to become whatever the mind can imagine. Conversely, he is also able to deal with other areas within himself. The interior is expanded as subject matter, too.

What this did for the dancer was to give him a larger persona. Contemplating his navel was no longer his limitation. His imagination could freely operate, creating landscapes and vistas to challenge him and force personal expansion and growth. The task before the dancer now was to gain the skill and accuracy to enliven these new insights. To deal with space as a living matter, to sculpt and shape the body at will, to both anchor and release time, to sense the nature of motion—all of this gives dance an expanded focus and responsibility, as well as expanded capabilities.

Nikolais dedicated his pedagogical life to the task of sharing a new vision for dance. On stage his creative life was devoted to making dance a visual as well as a kinetic art. As a teacher, however, he was passionately dedicated to the purity of dance.

He provided a core definition of decentralization as a process of "identification with." One could identify with a color, the scent of a rose, a cat's crazy antics, the dawn. Intuition, imagination, and sensory capabilities were no longer self-directed. Decentralization allowed the mind to range freely over a universal canvas.

Decentralization provides a means of dealing with abstraction and is at the heart of Nikolais's explorations in dance and his creative pedagogy. He gathered together the principles that defined the art of dance (space, time, shape, and motion) and directed them toward giving meaning to the abstractions of the art.

There is a sensory process involved in decentralization, a means by which the dancer has the ability to relocate the center of the body to any part of the body or point in space he focuses on. This becomes a matter of concentration. It also involves graining, and the engagement of the psyche to facilitate this displacement.

Decentralization

Centralization is a personal control, a secure home base, which tends to limit the full scope of an action. It is a personal filter, a filter flavored by the ego and thereby limiting and coercing the identity of a movement.

Decentralization releases the central ego's hold and allows the body and mind to freely shift the focus and movement center to any point in the body or surrounding space. Decentralization allows space, time, and shape to relate their contribution to the totality of a movement. Decentralization is the unbiased statement of action.

GRAIN

When we speak of grain in wood, we refer to the various channels of force that visibly show the linear life direction of the wood's fiber. The human body can also produce directional grain, but in a much more complex way. By accentuating direction, grain adds aesthetic colorations to kinetics. Without grain, motion is somewhat bland.

An example of graining is to imagine that we hold a paper drawing of the body horizontally. You sprinkle it with metal granules and then put a magnet underneath it at a single point. All the metal granules will be drawn toward that point. The body and its interior will have, as much as possible, a common visible focus, causing subtle textural changes in the body's attitude.

The principles of grain are fundamental for controlling the quality of motion. They need not be obviously mimetic, but rather directional. For example, an arm reaching straight forward will resemble a dead signpost unless it is imbued "grainwise" with forward vitality. The same arm in the same position can grain downward or upward instead of forward without losing its place in space.

This principle also applies to the arm in motion: one can lift the arm but grain downward, thereby calling attention to the space below; or one can lift it and grain upward, thereby calling attention to the space above. To give the impression of weightlessness, the dancer must grain upward despite the force of gravity. On the other hand, should one wish to give a downward gesture the quality of excessive weight, then one must add downward grain to the body to accentuate the pull of gravity, which will create the illusion of extra weight.

The dancer can project the force of grain into space as well as through the body, conveying to an audience the many subtle and abstract directional qualities of motion. The dancer, by graining toward the intent of the movement, can direct the viewer's eye to the subtlety and direction of an action. He also makes visible the internal continuity and flavor of the choreography.

Graining, by allowing internal fluidity to replace the limiting hardness of a concentrated focus, serves as a major factor in achieving decentralization.

GRAVITY AND VERTICALITY

Of all the physical forces of power, gravity is one of the most significant in dance. Momentum, centrifugal, and centripetal forces are qualified by gravity and the dancer's freedom of action rests within its limitations. The dancer is suspended between two forces, one created out of his own control of energy and the other exerted by physical laws outside of himself.

Through his will to extend himself upward and away from gravity, the dancer counteracts weightfulness and creates a balance of upwardness. The weightfulness demanded by gravity is counteracted by an upward power, which is generated by his will. The dancer calls upon this will either consciously or subconsciously. It is his manner of control and purposeful manipulation of these two lines of energy that give him a fundamental vertical or basic setup.

Downward is a direction—not an emotion. Yet we are so accustomed to associating downwardness with negative emotions and behaviors that it is difficult to sense going downward as simply a motional act. We must separate it from the negative behaviorisms that are often associated with it. Sadness, moroseness, weakness, or other submissive sensations must be set aside and gravity examined on its own terms. When we speak of upward or downward, we are speaking of motion taking place in these defined directions.

With the definition of verticality and its archetypical or primary theory of height—its upward and downward directions of action—we now face the issue of the motion between these two points. The dancer's concern is with the qualities of movement derived from specific time control between the vertical and prone position. What sensitivities occur between these two positions? What controls exist?

The two obvious determinations are those that allow us to rise and descend at a certain speed. We must consider the multiple joints in the body that permit this action, and their obeisance to the two energies involved: human psychical energy and nature's physical energy. One supplies the upward energy, the other the downward. In this journey of up and down, the release of oppositional interest is called into play.

I find it best to explore each direction on its own terms, despite the fact that they are interrelated. In standing upright, we must supply upward force to counteract the downward pull of gravity. In descending, on the other hand, as opposed to falling, we must decrease the upward force at a continuing rate of release. In rising, the muscular efforts are much greater because there is no upward power comparable to gravity. We must supply our own.

The experience of gravity can best be felt through an isolated practice with the extremities (arms, legs, and head). I usually begin with this exercise in the dancers' warm-ups on the floor. I ask the dancers to lift each extremity one by one, feeling its weight against the pull of gravity.

In understanding the complex control of weight, the two words that suggest the oppositional points are *suspend* (hang from), and *fall* (drop, collapse). There are no difficulties with the words *fall*, *drop*, or *collapse*; there are, however, some with the word *suspend*. Take the arm, for example. In holding it overhead vertically, we do not actually suspend it. There is no marionette string or sky hook upon which it hangs. Instead, by a system of muscular leverages, it balances itself in a vertical, upward position. To allow it to fall, we must release all of these muscular leverages so that the arm collapses into gravity. This opens up a large area of technical practice and exploration. Again, I find the extremities the best parts with which to explore this release. I find that at least ten percent of all dancers are unable to release their muscle tensions quickly, thus they resist gravity with tension.

One good test is to ask the student to lay an arm across your extended arms. Direct him to release his muscles as you suddenly take away your support. You will find that the body has developed tension safeguards to prevent injury from falling. Quite a few will be unable to do this sudden release until after repeated trials. This same test can be applied to legs, the head, and even to the trunk. Of course, in the latter, one must be careful that the capitulation to gravity does not end in physical harm. Sequential release of various body parts is an excellent practice and can be pursued during locomotion with interesting motional results. Often, it is preferable to think of downward as a direction rather than as the sensation of weight dominated by gravity.

Although gravity is a directly downward force, it can be used effectively by aiming the downward capitulation into a particular direction. This may result in swing, thus involving momentum and centrifugal force. These motional qualities will be studied in detail later.

It is also necessary to practice the skill of instantaneously releasing muscles and energy to gravity in regard to the restrictions found in the hip joint. Release of different areas of the spinal column is also an essential practice. One area we usually generalize is the upper vertebrae that support the head. Here, the release of the small muscles surrounding the vertebrae close to the skull is quite different from the release of muscles surrounding those more pronounced joints deep in the neck area. One should bring attention to this subtle difference.

When one returns a body part from another position to verticality, it is important to judge how much weight and energy is used to lift that body part away from the pull of gravity, and to ascertain whether or not excess energy for this adjustment is being used to cause undue tension. The body part then becomes stiff and without kinetic quality. Here again, the activity of restoring vertical balance should avoid the sense of lifting upward in favor of the sense of departure or lifting away from gravity. This keeps the sensation within the context of acknowledging gravity.

Referring to earlier statements regarding sensory perception, we are reminded that the mind can refuse certain perceptions so that it can illuminate others more powerfully. It is possible to disregard sensations of *upward* even though we engage in that direction by sensing the motion as going *away from downward*. This takes subtle control, but it is essential to learn how to do this, and it's a skill that can be used in both abstract and representational expression.

High level of upward willpower. Boston dance workshop.
Photo courtesy of the Nikolais/Louis Foundation.

THE PSYCHE

The original Greek word for psyche referred to the soul. Throughout the later centuries it became identified and invested with other qualities. Today we use the word *psyche* to refer to the mind, a complex part of the body revealing more and more insights and motivations—a substantiation of an inner person. We don't know what the psyche is. It's a convenient term for a mystical dimension which psycho-dynamics has donated to us, but we use the term frequently, as if it were something separate from the body. Often when teaching we refer to the psyche as having preceded or having been behind the gesture, rather than being with the gesture. We can only see the physical body, yet we do see the psyche somehow, through the will and interior graining.

In time, medical science will perhaps locate the psyche's specific structure or chemical makeup as it continues its remarkable exploration of the brain. For our purpose, we are going to credit the brain as the container of the psyche with all of its remarkable functions.

The psyche houses the will, guts, and drive: our inner person, motivation, intuition, and imagination.

It deals with all matters of interior space, such as grain and density. It translates the abstract, interprets sentient response, and achieves balance or consonance. It is therefore important to consciously recognize the psyche as an essential entity.

It becomes necessary for the dancer to call this interior person into consultation and action, and therefore he must recognize and strengthen the psyche as an active and functioning part of the body. We try to connect the idea of the mind and the brain just as we look for the dynamics of the psyche at work in the body. These are not black-and-white distinctions; they are all matters of degree. When we are in a state of sensing the distinct quality of a movement, the psyche reaches into the interior of the body and helps us locate the distinction. The psyche also learns and performs choreography. It is an important participant that must be recognized. It is, in a sense, a personification of the outer self without the abilities or the physical restrictions of the flesh. It can set goals, which the body then strives to achieve.

* * *

PSYCHICAL AND UPWARD ENERGY (PRESENCE AND MOTIVATION)

Despite the explorations of the "wild blue yonder," the stratosphere, the space shuttle, and the man on the moon, our everyday engagement with space is basically with the horizontal plane. Man's awareness of this normal level is stressed daily, so he is often unaware of what is above him. Yet man's three-dimensional occupancy of space requires overhead projection and the participation of his sensory presence above him.

A theory of German modern-dance technique taught that from the waist down the dancer should direct himself downward, and from the waist up he should project into the space above. I, however, encourage upward projection from the point of contact with the floor, through the vertical body and penetrating into upward space. Thus the body as a whole, like the arm reaching upward, structurally erects itself and extends into the space above.

When we stress upward motion, we shift our sense of grain. We no longer think about departing from gravity, but rise upward without reference to downward. Here again, the finer sensibilities are employed. If we descend, we do not descend into gravity; we depart from upwardness. Instead of feeling weight, we feel a continued sense of lightness, even though we are descending.

This process of controlling directional sensitivity relates to our physiology. Through open pores and tactile alertness we can focus on specific directions. The surfaces of the body that relate to the direction of our interest become more alert, warmer, and sentiently more attentive to that direction, even though we may be going away from it. An arm descending may feel either the weight of its descent or the lightness of ascent. As described in the previous chapter on gravity, the ascending arm could

seem to go upward away from gravity rather than just rising. These subtle choices are eventually mastered for performance and creative use.

Elevation does not define itself as the joy of elevation. Just as going down is a motion_not an emotion_so, too, going up is an action in itself that makes no specific reference to an emotion. We can qualify it later as an emotion, which can be anything from elation to disgust. But in its initial study, we want to free movement from associations, just as the colors green and red are free before they have been used to paint an asparagus and an apple.

Upward energy is an elemental motional force generated by the will or psyche. Complete capitulation to gravity (insofar as we are able) brings us into a state of passivity and is best accomplished by a prone position on the floor. Gravity compels all body parts downward and toward passivity. Consequently, any motion of the body must be accomplished by a force outside of gravity's control.

The source of this force that compels motion is the will of the individual. The mind in one way or another wills the body to move. The strength of that will counteracts the gravitational force, and motion occurs. It is the vitality of this will that generally characterizes a dancer's capabilities. On a purely physical basis it is will that gets the dancer to achieve feats of air work as well as complete lengthy and arduous rehearsals.

Upward energy, or any energy causing action in any direction other than downward, is highly complex. It is made complex by the state of mind that controls its design. Consequently, psychical energy is a major factor in dance. How that energy deals with gravity can determine where, how, why, and when motion occurs.

The machinery of the mind permits it a vast freedom beyond the confines of the physical body. It often functions independently from the physical body, as in dreams in which an individual makes fantastic journeys concocted by the mind. We also engage in daydreams; the body may be employed in a routine chore while the imagination engages in pursuits outside of that time and place. There is the mind, and there is reality.

In studio practice, the dancer must will his mind to be totally present. The reality is the actual environment and what he is doing in it. Coordinating them requires both mental and physical discipline. He may at other times be required to enact imaginary motions. This requires skill in projecting his presence into those events. He makes an imagined reality into actual reality. Although it may be referred to hereafter as actual presence and immediacy, it is the performer's mindset that creates a state of realness.

In the larger task of technical direction and practice, the major process is correction and the correct practice of the performer's psychical presence in choreographed structure. This process is an abstract one. Here the performer does not imagine an emotional nostalgia (such as love). It is a direct action devoid of any discrepancy among mind, body, and environment. The dancer seeks a balance between himself and what he is doing.

There is more to explain in relation to the dynamics of the space or environment as it contributes to the performer's "presence." We may conceive of the performer's psychical aura as the space affected by the mind of the person present in it. Whether an actual energy is expelled from the individual doesn't matter. Certainly a good portion of this illusion of psychical projection derives from the individual. At this time, it is convenient to describe this aural space as projection.

In effect, then, we can conceive of an active perceptional and/or projectional aura surrounding the body as far in space as the senses can effectively press them. In standing, all focal senses are balanced, with no one energy projecting beyond a normal point of alertness. There is a sense of consonance in this achievement. Despite our lack of knowledge about how we perceive space, direction, and time, we nevertheless know the act of presence must include an awareness of all of these things.

STASIS

Within the three phases of motion, we find the first phase, that of passivity, stillness or stasis, is most closely related to the concept of a performer's presence. In this phase of stasis, we are concerned with the dynamic state of the dancer's bulk, the corporeal instrument.

To the onlooker, this state is apparent in the manner in which the performer stands. It is seen in the textural tone of the body as a whole. This cannot be accomplished with only a correct physical posture. It needs the illumination of the mind, which then activates the fine detail that will not be present otherwise. On the other hand, if the state of mind is correct for the event but the body fails to possess the thought, due to physical weakness, nerves, or to devious subconscious antagonism to the act, then the state of stasis is jeopardized.

Since early civilization, man has recognized a surrounding or nonphysical volume to man. Out of this emerged a multitude of expressions characterizing behaviorisms. Among these are phrases such as "beside oneself," "narrow-minded," "shallow," "big-hearted," "small-minded," "reduced to a pulp," "depths of despair," "bursting with joy," "self-contained," and so on.

These descriptions are partly hyperbolic but also curiously real. We can say of the physical build of man that he is so high, so wide, and so deep. We can also say, in the nonphysical sense, that he is a shallow person, one lacking breadth of concept, or that he is high- or low-spirited. A wholesome man is well balanced in all directions. He is a well-rounded person.

The body as an instrument is mainly axial in structure. However, like a marionette whose strings have been cut, it can be a tumbled mass of flesh and bones, heaped upon the floor. It will inevitably capitulate to gravity unless some motivation causes it to stay upright, and rise to its full potential height.

There is no motivation which science, anthropology, psychology, and other "-ologies" have found acceptable regarding why man stood upright.

At this point, we must establish a beginning posture from which the dancer may depart into motion, be it sitting, standing on one's head, in shoulder stand, or lying down. We must have a beginning, no matter what form it might take. The most convenient form is the posture of standing. We must then describe the nature of stillness out of which motion is born.

Standing in stillness is no easy accomplishment. It is, however, a basic endeavor that needs to be accomplished. In the practice of stasis, we must conceive of a status quo out of which we will depart into action.

In scientific definition, stillness is labeled as inertia. In the dancer's case, however, this stance is far from lifeless. We might better call it either stasis or a state of standing presence. Standing presence implies the dancer's awareness of his existence in a defined space and time. Space and time are constant energies transpiring through and around him. To be present within them, the dancer must constantly adjust to them. Somewhat like Alice in Wonderland, he must keep moving his state of awareness to stay in one place.

The quality of stasis is one of immediacy. Immediacy in stasis means to perform stillness with all the vitality of presence. The dancer, through his imagination, can thoroughly imbue stasis with the aliveness of presence.

Presence is not only a physical reality. The performer must draw on his imagination to fully focus himself into a state of presence. He must do this with such force that his faculties are undivided. They are there and nowhere else.

The inability to achieve presence in standing stasis can be due to an endless variety of both physical and psychical deficiencies. The physical ones, for the most part, can be corrected. This is so, particularly if the psychological causes that created them have disappeared, but the muscular habits remain. Physical habits can be corrected; but on the other hand if the psychological conditions are still active, then correction becomes much more difficult. I have found, however, that frequently, if the physical stance is corrected, it in effect leaves no room for the psychological detriment to house itself. If the psychological condition is not too severe, it is likely that it will release itself in time and the physical slate will be cleaned.

Within his perceptions, the dancer must acknowledge the action of space and time; otherwise, they will outdistance him and fall out of the range of his immediate awareness. Part of his act of stillness is the balancing of his energies and perceptions so that they ride upon time, neither exceeding it nor falling behind it. The same is true of space. As one stands, there are the three-dimensional radiations that keep one alive to the presence of self in space and time. Stasis, in this sense, is multifocal. It is part time, part space, and part self.

The dancer stands open like an Aeolian harp as time and space pass through him, leaving their nature in their wake.

The space surrounding the body also serves as an atmosphere for the mind. There is to the human, in stasis, an implied volume far beyond the confines of his actual physical shape. The dancer is capable of achieving a physical size of greater proportion when his projected psychical volume is added to his corporeal dimensions. This additional extended dimension is, in effect, a psychical aura.

The common accord of body and mind is essential. A mind intent on a vision that is not in agreement with the body's activity can only create confusion.

Most technical direction and training is a process of correction meant to achieve this accord between body and mind while performing. This particular process is abstract, classical, and balanced. The performer does not imagine an emotional state or conditioned environment such as fear, hate, nostalgia, love, or the like. It is a direct action devoid of any disagreement between mind, body, and environment. The feedback from the movement supplies the nature of the movement.

Immediacy is not a normal state, but is made possible by a super-charged projection of self. This requires the skill of projecting one's presence so strongly that it becomes a reality. Although this immediacy may seem like actual presence, it is in reality the performer's mental control that creates it, and consequently, it is an imagined state of performed realness.

The word *emotion* is a confusing one. All human motion is to some degree embodied with it. What we more commonly refer to as emotion is related to the inability to act as a direct result of sensory stimulation. This takes on overtones of frustration, discontentment, or other forms of displeasure, even to the extent of rage, fear, hate, or more passive states of longing, nostalgia, or the like. One may also be in a state of excessive passions, stimulated beyond the body's capacity to cope. This, too, will cause imbalances. The classical aspect of motion is free of these conditions; instead, it demonstrates consonance between mind, body, environment, space and time. It is a state of balanced presence.

The force of the mind reveals its life through the body. The body is the conduit between the mind and the surrounding space. The body, by physically expanding or contracting, reveals in space the measurement created in the mind. The greater the conception of height in space, the taller the body. And so, too, with other physical spatial projections.

As an added note, there is also a relationship between sanity and sensitivity, and insanity and insensitivity. Sanity is related to a reasonable participation in an environment. This requires sensory perception of that environment and its effect on us. If we recede, or "drop out," for any unintentional reason, our ability to live with full vitality is interrupted. Totality is not resumed until the moment when we reestablish contact with the environment.

The significance of this to the dancer, from a technical point of view, is in his control and skill in manipulating the body as it reflects the mind's relationship to environment or space.

It is easy to imagine how a conflicting mental dimension can affect a dimension of the physical body and disrupt the clarity and totality of stasis.

DYNAMICS AND ENERGIES

In dealing with dynamics, the total art experience must be considered: the choreographic manipulations of the body, the fullness of the dancer's performance, and unimpaired viewing on the part of the audience. All three participants must be focused on a mutual achievement. Here, we are concerned with the choreographer and the dancer, whose clarity and skill will help direct the audience toward a kinetic experience.

Dynamics are the kinetic energies created by changes of other energies, which include time, shape, and their juxtapositions. They are determined by how one chooses to use the energy and forces available and how to contrast these energies with each other. This makes for a great many opportunities for dynamics.

Dynamics also call for a bit of surprise as to what is to be contrasted and when that contrast is made. Dynamics are necessary because they keep the audience alert with expectancy, enlivening the choreography with the unexpected. Dynamics are the surprising tastes of good cuisine. They are the energies derived from change.

Although inertia has often triggered more reaction than a violent approach, mobility is still a dominant principle of dance and must remain in sight.

* * *

The nonverbal or nonliteral artist is primarily concerned with sentient response. His job is to control the dynamics of energies—not only real energy and force, but illusional and metaphoric energy, as well. For example, there are certain reflected vibrational energies that emanate from the color red, and its juxtaposition to another color may add additional dynamic relationships to the eye and to the mind that do not exist in actual, factual energy.

The word *green* can never be as effective as the sensory experience of the color itself. Even when qualifying words seem to give exact definition, the word is still an inexact communication requiring interpretation. While the work of the nonrepresentational artist requires interpretation, it is for the most part directly received through the senses rather than routed through symbolic form. Nonverbal communication reduces or eliminates the process of translating the object into a symbol and then the symbol into a subject, thus it prevents the loss of meaning that occurs in circuitous translations.

Through the process of familiar symbolic representation, pictorial and literal representation tends to alleviate a good portion of sentient responsibility from the onlooker. One need only be subjected to the guided tours through great art galleries to realize how much of the aesthetic dimension of a work of art is generally neglected in favor of its external literal or representational channeling.

When painting and sculpture become abstract (nonliteral), they drop the representational image and state themselves directly through sensations of color and form.

Of all nonverbal communication, music has been the most successful. The sound itself is the communicating source, and there is no need for intermediary translation.

The arts of poetry and literature, which are dominated by literal symbolism conveyed through words, arrive at a level of sense-response communication by other means. Sometimes the writer destroys the specific by treating it absurdly, by reordering the written connotations to form controlled nonsense. In this way, meaning is destroyed, thus bringing verbal symbols into the realm of direct sentient communication, as in Gertrude Stein's works.

Nonverbal communication is concerned with free flow rather than pictorial or verbal representation and imagery. Ideally, it involves a direct contact with the audience's sentient experience. This condition is possible when they have a finely tuned and basic realization of dynamics that allows them to experience the essences and powers of relationships and change.

A musician strikes a succession of notes, and in doing so he controls the initial amount of effort applied. This is energy in the real sense,

and its control is essential. Beyond this energy is a juxtaposition of sounds and silences devised by the composer, which is then interpreted by the musician; this results in audio stimulation, which in turn causes a response in the mind of the listener. Thus, from composer to musician to listener, there is the involvement and communication of psychical energy.

Although scientifically we know little about the reality of psychical power, in art various forms of action occur which cause dynamic activity in the mind that goes above and beyond common, tangible definitions of energy. An obvious example is that of a painter's relatively small canvas, which may call to the onlooker's mind a cataclysmic event. By no means does the canvas hold the energy of the actual event, but it does hold the potential of creating an illusional, dynamic happening in the viewer's mind. Implications of time and space, the power of metaphor, the suggestions of events, and fantastic excursions into the imagination are all potent potentialities within the mind of the observer.

Since the physical energy is restricted to one's mind, this power remains safely at a physical distance and minimum. We can thereby experience a cataclysmic macrocosmic event vicariously, without fear of any personal danger.

Art deals with microscopic vision as well as macrocosmic imaginings, and it reveals and reacts to the dynamics of minutiae as readily as to gargantuan vistas.

To the mind that is open to abstraction, the force of abstract art is dynamically powerful. Within a literal work we often find that it is the abstract suggestion that gives it its power.

Dynamics, then, in the general sense, refers to degrees of energy, either real or implied, imagined or caused to be imagined.

Dynamics include everything that is opposed to the stillness of stasis. We have within us a source of energy that can propel us to move out of a state of passivity. We also have the dynamics of space and time, as well as of gravity, momentum, and centrifugal and centripetal forces. We have the human psychical responses and the compulsive energies of motivation as well as the ability to create illusions of energy.

The dancer's motivational drives activate his sources of physical power, thereby bringing his body into action. He combines these motivational energies with the coursings of time, space, and gravity, all of which exist around him, and the other phenomena that govern the laws of motion. The artist designing all of these varying dynamics is what triggers the illusional energies to occur in the mind of the observer. Therefore, the artist's skill rests primarily in the manipulation and design of dynamics.

Dynamics are realized by means of our sensory meters. Sensation is brought about by relativity and change. If we place ourselves in a room entirely colored red, we will find that after a while the sensation of red is lost and there is a suspension of color sensation. Dynamics are not only actual energies, but are also forceful as a sensing of change. The sensation of dynamics may be real or imagined, factual or illusional. The artist attempts to govern both the factual and the illusional, to control real energies as well as those that are implied or projected. His artistry is greatly determined by his skill in manipulating and causing the phenomena of change according to his aesthetic dictates.

Dance employs a dynamic range that, with the exception of actual physical energy, is perhaps not different from other arts. But the definition of its range of forces arises from its emphasis on motion, which reveals a highly complex use of energy.

Energy is the backbone of aesthetic involvement and is the primal reference of all art.

In his spiritual history, man has been driven toward a metaphysical utopia where all his efforts have been devoted to a release from corporeal pain and bondage. Within this striving rests his reason for being. His greatest moments are those of the spirit. Art is the triumph over the physical. As science is to the body, art is to the soul, and the ecstasy of man's moral evolvement to a higher plane rests in art and in his response to it. At the moment of art, there is mystery only to the conscious mind; in the inner self there is assurance and clarity.

Both science and art begin in mystery. Science dispels mystery insofar as it is able to; art treasures it. Art eliminates even the concrete fact so that the underlying mystical forces beneath may be more accessible to primal sensory perceptions. When it resorts to conscious reason, that art is apt to err.

Although we do not know the actual nature of man's psyche, we do know that it is the psyche that dominates man's behavior. The energy of the psyche, whatever that may be, and the power behind it, which drives it in directions unique to man, are art's first dynamics. They are defined as "motivation." Dynamics are, therefore, a primary force, which includes man's instincts. It is the artist's sense of this force and its direction that qualifies his art. The artist's creation must fall into the stream of this force, and it is his reference to it that gives his work validity and depth. This force compels him. He must make constant reference to it, consciously or subconsciously, during all of his creative endeavors.

Next to the force impelling the psyche the power of the imagination serves the artist most. Imagination is also a form of dynamics, for it is out of imagination that the artist makes his creative choices. In the mind, one can split atoms with no undue physical disturbance. It is also in the mind's eye that the artist may experiment and predetermine his work. It is in the mind's eye of the beholder that the artist's work is retranslated and where communication takes place, whether through empathy, metakinesis, or aesthetic interpretation.

From the preceding dynamic forces, the dancer proceeds to physical energies, the actual movement of his body according to the dictates of his aesthetic premises. Here it is easier to measure the forces; however, it remains necessary to manipulate the body as an abstract instrument rather than in a physically recognizable manner.

Once physical entities are set into action, the external laws of motion come into play: gravity, momentum, and centrifugal and centripetal forces.

In summation then, we find that dynamics occur through several processes, each involving either real energy or a psychical suggestion of force.

Dynamics represent the motivational power that drives man toward his idealization and impels him to expose these ideals through art.

They represent the psychical power that derives from motivation, which in turn drives the imagination and causes the decision to act.

They represent physical energy, which is motivated by psychical power.

They involve laws of motion, including gravity, momentum, and centrifugal and centripetal forces to which the body must cohere in order to stay within the good graces of external natural forces.

They involve the dynamics of time and space, which qualify laws of motion but which extend beyond them in implication and, eventually, into aesthetics.

Art pursues its judgment through specific demonstrable determinations. The control of dynamics is by no means a wholly conscious act. A work is composed largely through the artist's sensitivity to dynamics, through equating sentiently rather than by conscious mathematical judgment.

We are concerned with the artist's skill in controlling the dynamic happenings and implications within his medium or media. The medium is not the art message. The message derives from what the artist causes to happen dynamically through the medium.

With the contemporary art scene, the tendency is to eliminate the pictorial or literal image: the painter must make sense out of his colors. With no trees or boats or portraits, he is obliged to create with colors. If he is not sensitively eloquent in this respect, his communication will be limited.

The dancer's medium is his physical body, his instrument. His artistry arises from the motional values he causes his body to enact.

Dynamic values also exist within the medium itself. For example, Brancusi's *Bird in Flight* would be far different if it were sculpted in wood or marble rather than polished metal. And, certainly, the high development of sound and acoustical properties of musical instruments today are a part of the dynamic value of the finished works themselves.

The dancer's body is the most complex medium of all. In addition to its direct, live, energy value, his physical characteristics can determine the nature of some of his roles. Nevertheless, the dancer's power of "transcendence" and transformation can magically change and redesign his actual corporeal image. Here, the dynamics of illusion can have more significance in the production of art than the dynamic values contained in the dancer's body itself.

The artist must correlate all these forms of dynamics. Each successive step derives and evolves from the composite forces assembled to reveal his subject or intent. To create his dance like the seed of a plant, his initial noumenon contains the nature of the matured product. He must sense how that seed wishes to grow and what energies are involved. Then he must construct an itinerary in space and time that will allow this evolution to take place without interference.

In essence, the artist's progress is determined by his judgment of dynamics, and it is the artist's refined sensory perception that makes that judgment. Through his sensory meters, he controls the degree of dynamics necessary to create a choreographic structure or form, representations of his aesthetic thought.

The great performers of the traditional modern dance period often combined the arts of dancing and acting. Ballet also uses literal and nonliteral devices. Many of its early choreographers, instead of mixing the abstract and the literal, deliberately stopped a section of abstract dance and proceeded to a wholly literal mimetic action, only to return again to purer dance. Here, each level supported the understanding of the other by sequential rather than simultaneous exposition.

Any process requires the dancer's faith in the communicative force of motional abstraction.

SENSORY PERCEPTION

In an oversimplified way, we can say that a performing art usually comprises three components: the medium, the instrument, and the message. First, it is essential to establish some precise definitions as to what is the instrument, what is the medium, and wherein rests the message. In music, these three components are easily discernable: the piano is the instrument, the sound emanating from the piano is the medium, and the nature of the sound, caused to happen by the aesthetic manipulation of the performing artist is the message. In dance, however, there are confusions and also irrational concepts about all three of these factors. The one great difference, and certainly the most complex one, is that the instrument and the artist are one and the same. The task is to distinguish the boundaries and domains of each. The human body is a complex array of bones, muscles, tendons, nerves, and sensory origins, as well as a morass of other biological material. All of these communicate with the brain, which forms the center of the nervous system and the seat of consciousness and volition.

In trying to bring a change in the technical and aesthetic practice of dance we must deliberately guard against admitting into our brains sensations beyond those that promote the understanding of motion. The brain has enormous powers of selection and rejection. It can diminish some avenues of receptivity or it can overemphasize others. It also stores behavioral habits that intrude inadvertently upon motional events. This placing of unwanted debris onto the motional path confuses kinetic definition.

A central purpose of the teaching process should be the clarification of motivation and the clarity of its motional result. That is, teaching makes clear the reason to move and the motional identity that results from this experience.

It is through our control of sensory perception that we can refocus motional intentions. We can redirect the senses to focus on motion as a basic, abstract, self-contained statement rather than on the performer's personal emotional condition or circumstance. Motion, in this process, erases reference to the dancer's ego or personality and redirects all sensitivity to the motional event itself.

Recently, I happened to tune in to a television program about one of the most brilliant pianists I have ever heard. He had so completely attached himself to the musical sound that both he and the piano seemed to have disappeared. The sound emerged seemingly without restraint, and existed on its own terms. Of course, we saw the pianist play. But his body and fingers showed no effort as he passed through extraordinary musical phrases. It was as if the physicalities of the act were invisible mechanisms focused toward a greater end—the music. His aesthetic dexterity and control in passing from one chord to another and his changing of speed, density, and color made the flow so flawless that one was carried into the brilliant context of the sound itself.

With dance technique, the intent is not to eliminate characterization or to depersonalize, but to readjust one's thinking for the purpose of focusing on a far greater insight, the practice of motional investigation. This serves to enlarge dance's aesthetic scope, not only as a destination in itself, but also as a much broader, more substantial artistic base for whatever form dance takes—literal, abstract, or any combination thereof.

Can the dancer do this? Can he restructure his focus into the direction of isolated value of motion and make this the basis for his skill? Fortunately, human beings have the most complex and extraordinary equipment to do so through their sensory perception.

Kinesthetic perception lies primarily in sensory organs located in the muscles, tendons, and tissues. These organs respond to the degrees of flexion, extension, twisting, and placement of all body parts. But this, by no means, is the limit of our perceptive potential. It was only a few thousand years ago that we began referring to the Aristotelian five senses: sight, hearing, touch, taste, and smell. Science now acknowledges the existence of many more sense perceptions, perhaps as many as 30. To mention a few, there are the "sense of" space, time, direction, balance, gravity, body temperature, velocity, and pressure, as well as kinesthesia and many others that determine the quality of motion and presence. All of these encompass the full participation in the awareness of action and being.

There are senses that inform the body of its physical condition: blood temperature, carbon dioxide content, hunger, thirst, pain, etc. Our brain also houses certain obscure senses for which no special organs have as yet been found. In some of these cases, there may not be a specific organ relating to a specific event. Various perceptions derived from more than one organ are automatically coordinated to report the particular circumstance, such as seeing and hearing at the same time.

This abundance of perceptions cannot be consciously dealt with simultaneously. We must select those that serve our immediate purpose and relegate the others to a secondary or sub-conscious state of storage from which they can later be drawn. This does not mean that they do not function, but rather that their function is momentarily inactive. The skill to repress is not the skill of temporarily hiding the unused perception, however; it is that of making certain that perceptions that contribute to the desired action are proportionately and appropriately present.

The key to all this is that the dancer, while dancing or in a state of dance study, should not allow himself to make any motion without having the experience of sentient perception. There is no meaning to a motion until a particular perception is realized and focused on. The lifting of an arm, for example, can be sentiently manipulated in many different ways, such as sensing the upward or weight, or lowering, or graining outward as it lifts. Because the body is so volatile and fluid, perception may be changed quickly and at will.

Sensory organs are like a television camera that receives messages and records an event. Behind it are the mechanisms that transmit these results to the observer. These, in turn, are not received unless the performer and the observer are tuned into the same channel. Awareness is the key factor. Perception does not occur unless the mind is focused on the event via its sensory organ. One may look but not see, listen but not hear, move but not be aware of the motion.

The human instrument contains a multitude of sensory organs that indirectly participate in various experiences. For example, taste for food is greatly affected by sight and smell, as well as the sensations derived from our taste buds. Eating green-colored mashed potatoes or sweetly perfumed garlic is hardly a gustatory delight.

We often mistakenly conclude that a perception derives from a single organ or type of organ. We may credit the eyes with a perception that actually involves contributions by the ears and nose, as well. Many of our perceptions, while predominantly derived from a particular kind of organ, receive support from other organs, which add verification, understanding, and depth to the event.

So it is with dance motion. Dance primarily involves human sensitivity to motion. Perceiving and interpreting the impressions of motion through the senses is imperative to the dancer. Since most of our kinesthetic organs are located in the muscles, tendons, joints, and tissues, they only inform us of our physical actions: flexions, extensions, twistings, and placements. They do not inform us of the condition of the space through which we move, or the time, direction, balance, gravity, and visual and auditory aspects of environment; they do not inform us either of the numerous other factors needed to qualify and identify motion in detail from the aesthetic point of view.

It is the nature of the details of the action that gives dance its aesthetic legibility. Without this sensing and performance detail, only a gross outline is apparent, which communicates very little other than the visual structure. Motion demands, by its definition, the detail values of its itinerary. This means that, where movement implies the form of action, motion implies the manner in which the action occurs. Many dancers move with brilliant physical facility, but aside from the interest which acrobatic dexterity may provoke, the communicative level is very sparse. The dancer's failure to transmit the motional values, first to himself, and then to his audience, is the fundamental reason for the inability to communicate.

It is, therefore, within the sensory processes that we find the sensitivities that distinguish the artist.

The process of refinement, however, requires awareness and judgment. The mind has considerable control and fluidity within the process of perception. We can stare into space and perceive nothing. The eye may be full of impressions of the space but the brain may choose to ignore them. The brain may choose to detour the impressions through the subconscious, which can censor them and call to consciousness only those pertinent to its present need. Parents frequently have this experience. Engrossed in a particular task in which most surrounding sounds are ignored, they are alerted by the child's crying. In this instance, the subconscious mind, with instructions from the conscious mind as to what to call to its attention, acts as a sort of alert.

Sensory efficiency can be increased by actual physical maneuvering. A good illustration for the dancer is the turnout of the legs. By means of turnout, one gains a greater three-dimensional mobility in space. Although the leg is not a sensory organ, within it are discrete sensors that distinguish spatial orientation. The opening of the thigh exposes a greater surface of this sensitive area. One has only to place the legs in knee-front, parallel position to feel the tactile difference in space. One can recall the common expression of embarrassment in which the thighs turn in as if to deny presence. Nevertheless, how many dancers practice to attain turnout to the extreme without perceiving the difference in feeling toward space derived from the rotation?

The leg turnout is a gross example compared to the myriad, minute body positions and actions that can place parts of the body into advantageous sensory attitudes, the results of which will lend expressive detail to a gesture.

Much more complex is the skill of the mind to vary its perceptive dynamics in relation to a sensory organ or organs. A particular sense may receive the impression of the scene as a whole. The mind, however, may choose to target or pinpoint its perception on one detail within the total picture. It can intensify the perceptive experience by deliberately blocking out of consciousness all unwanted areas. This can be noted readily in such senses as sight, taste, hearing, and smell.

The tactile (or touch) sense organs have a multitude of receptor organs serving them. These are distributed throughout the body, and separately or together they can reveal the tactile landscape they encounter. Again, the mind can focus on single parts of this landscape. It can block out of consciousness the touch perception of one part of the body to intensify the experience of another. This process of perception is highly significant in kinetics, where one can highlight or diminish certain aspects of motion in order to make others more evident.

The mind is the coordinating center for the senses. It can group the senses in cooperative action for a given task. Often, this takes on the form of deliberately subduing the function of one sense to give greater dynamic power to another. Watch someone's eyes during a moment of concentrated listening. You will find them out of focus, if not shut, so that there will be no visual interference with the listening. On the other hand, the eye may assist the ear in its interpretation by giving it visual evidence. Very often the dancer must deliberately employ the technique of subduing one sensation to enhance the values of another. Perhaps the most obvious example is that of ignoring the sense of weight and gravity to give the illusion of lightness.

By the coordinating senses, we arrive at what we often call "a sense of." This "sense of" has no particular receptor organ of its own. We speak of "a sense of" motion, but, in reality, this requires the cooperation of several senses. Similarly we speak of "a sense of" justice, a mechanical "sense," common "sense" and even "a sense of" good taste. We can speak of "a sense of" shape, or time, or space without necessarily referring to the reactions of a particular organ, but rather to the coordination of many powers of perception that permit the most acute acknowledgement of the desired factor.

We are apt to consider consciousness and subconsciousness as sharply divided, black-and-white areas rather than a unit controllable to a degree. We speak of the mind's facility to darken certain areas of perception or intensify others. In addition, we have the ability to confine areas of perceptions to the subconscious with instruction to alert the conscious when those areas are desired. This control of degree of consciousness is of particular value to the artist. It is of inestimable significance to the dancer who, in addition to the sense of kinetic, relies on the support of many other senses to give dimension to his art.

While the dancer is mainly concerned with motion, he must also have a strong sense of the sculptural form of the body in action. He must have a concept of shape. Because his action occurs in space and time, his sense of these, too, must be acute. In his art, he will find that there are times when one of these will dominate the other, when the values of time, space, or shape take on greater significance than the others. Sometimes motional concepts will dominate. The dancer must have the skill of subduing the sense of one to enlarge the value of another. The control of these sensory subtleties is a major part of his artistry.

We cannot assume that all senses operate in the same fashion. Each one has unique values that add particular dimensions of understanding. Not only do the various organs have different physiological structures, but they also vary considerably in their psychological imprint on the mind. They function on various communicative levels. We can easily see this in the differences of psychological perception between the senses of sight and hearing.

"Seeing is believing" and "Show me; I'm from Missouri" emphasize the common feeling that the sight of something gives credence to its existence. There are qualifications to this; still, by and large, the eye tends toward a much higher degree of reality acceptance than the ear.

Hearing promotes a more active interpretive and imaginative process. Relieved of the responsibility of visual reality, the ear gives the mind a stronger invitation to abstract levels of action than does the eye. It has the potential of plunging the hearer into a freer associative level. It is no wonder that music always has been and still is a much more abstract art than the visual arts and dance.

The eye is capable of provoking the mind to a similar level of abstract acceptance. When it encounters something that cannot be contained on the realistic level, it automatically attempts another facet of understanding. Often, however, a mind strongly oriented toward material reality cannot shift to or cope with an abstract level of reality. The "seeing-is-believing" fixation demands the literal, and this criterion becomes primary as all other levels of communication are lost.

Here, we must consider that each of the senses has its unique and particular psychological entrée into the mind.

A single sense may have several routes of psychological entrée. The eye is the most vivid example. When we look at a painting, the psychological stimulant refers predominately to our color and pictorial experiences. Kinetic sculpture invites the eye to engage in both form and motion. In dance, the psychological input is routed mostly through motional and kinetic sensation.

One aspect of dance I have creatively explored places strong emphasis on sculptural forms and color. It is not that this has not been done before, or that it does not ordinarily take place in dance; it is rather a matter of degree. In my own creative work, I have often raised the appeal of color and sculpture in dance to an equal, and sometimes greater, communicative importance than kinetic values. Any departure into such different dynamics tends to confuse the eye of the purist. Yet this is not an artist's concern. If the onlooker fails to join the artist's dynamic scheme, he is left without a framework of reference to judge that artist's work. His sensory perception and psychological paths are not open and free to function fully within that milieu.

Although the kinetic movement sense is a major one for dance, it is the sense of motion that is more significant. Motion includes, in addition to kinetics, feeling, hearing, balance, gravity, sound, and response to light and color, as well as shape. Together they add support and semantic dimension, without which dance as an art would be meager indeed.

For the most part, dance training revolves around gross physical coordination devoid of sensitivity toward inner motional detail. Dancers do refine certain kinetic values, but very often they will only touch on space, time, and gravity to the extent that they are necessary to support their kinetic interests. The other perceptions are left to accident or subconscious experience.

Dancers should persist in concentrating their focus on whatever sentient experiences and resulting perceptions may occur within a particular scheme of motion. Dancers can deliberately focus on pertinent and particular senses so that they can explore the greatest range of experience. In training, the skill of quickly shifting perception from one exploration to another can develop a fluidity of awareness. For example, the arm can draw a circle in space in a multitude of ways, each one having its own particular value. The periphery may be stressed so that the outer circular line is emphasized or awareness may shift to the line as a boundary to the space it encloses. In the periphery of a vertical circle, the gravity sweep of the lower arc or the high upward suspension may be emphasized. These examples only begin to suggest many possible variations, each distinguishing itself because of the difference in sensory and perceptual focus.

The possibilities are considerable and need not be induced by literal situation. As a matter of fact, it should be made clear at the outset that the dancer's art is motion, and dance training must stress the communicative values of motion—not those of mime or emotion (in its unusual meaning). Basically, the dancer does not practice sadness, madness, gladness, or the like. The dancer's language is instead the textures of light, heavy, thick, thin, soft, hard, large, and small. Out of these components, the dancer weaves a motional itinerary inviting the onlooker to travel along vicariously. These movements can give both the dancer and the onlooker the sense of anything within the universe that is of a similar motional nature or that can be communicated by metaphor.

We do not know the range of our perceptual faculties that may be of significance to dance. The dancer needs to allow the perceptive powers of the body and mind to function so that they become responsive to the most minute details of the artist's intent.

Although we cannot, to any great extent, refurbish our senses, we can greatly increase our skills of perception. We know that sensation occurs as a response to change in the body or environment. The senses register differences in degrees, which, in essence, are dynamics. The artist's skill in perceiving and in responding are two of his primary functions and should be practiced daily in class through total sensory involvement.

MOVEMENT RANGE

There are three kinds of movement that the body, because of its physical structure, can perform comfortably. These all deal with how the body operates within the space it occupies and the space that surrounds it. They are simple to identify and simple to perform, and therefore create a key vocabulary for both dancer and teacher to share.

LOCOMOTOR

The entire body or entire body part moves as a unit into a new space. Nothing lags behind: all parts depart and arrive at their new destination at the same time. The motional quality rests in the traveling and the arrival into a new space.

FLEX AND EXTENSION

Joints are usually found wherever body parts are attached to the torso or to each other. Flexion and extension condense and extend the body or body part in space. They also change the space the body occupies. Space goes from in to out, from bigger to smaller, from close to far away. In dance this change of size is one of the major functions of the joints.

PERIPHERAL ACTION

The body or body part is anchored at one point and the furthermost part moves freely in the space around it, describing all sorts of linear designs. The extremities make considerable use of this movement range. These extremities include the head, shoulders, arms, elbows, hands, legs, knees, and feet.

Peripheral action makes great use of the surrounding space as a canvas to draw on. Writing on paper provides an apt analogy. In order to make a mark, a degree of pressure must be applied, so too with peripheral action of the body. One has to extend the body point into space so that the design

is seen. We witness not the body part moving as a body part, but the body part as a peripheral marker, etching its design into the surrounding space.

The hip when it tilts (tucks under) is performing a peripheral movement. The top of the pelvis is the hinge while the lower section is allowed to swing forward and back. A major criticism and clarification to make in the hip setup is to emphasize the hip moving forward as a unit into place as a locomotor action versus the peripheral swing "tuck under" implies.

Because of these hinge attachments, swing action is a common form created, but swing is only one movement possibility and its circular design should not obscure straight and other intricate linear designs that are also possible.

In performing peripheral action, focus and grain direct the viewer's attention to the pattern and design being made by the furthermost point. The focus and grain direct the audience to see the design, not the body part making the design. The written word, not the pencil writing the word, is made visible.

A spatial line can be continuous, as one indicator leads into another, or it can be transitioned through the body and picked up by another indicator. The transitional line through the body can be made continuously visible.

It is important to understand that peripheral action is linear and continuous and needs to be in constant motion. If it stops moving and the line ceases to be, the eye will go to the shape of the body or the identity of the moving part rather than the peripheral action. With the cessation of movement, the stop can also register as a pause in time, and time becomes visible.

ROTARY

Rotary refers to rotating within the space occupied by the body or body part. Rotary is prominent in turning actions, which are defined in Week Six of the Class Manual.

THREE CONDITIONS OF ENERGY

We understand conditions of energy by the terms *tension*, *relaxation*, and *release*.

To demonstrate this we take, for example, an arm extended forward. We have now:

the arm,

the forward extension as the movement, and

the energy flowing within the arm, to keep the form alive in space.

With **tension**, the lifted placement of the arm in space is visible, but the energy within the arm is locked and no interior motion is visible. The arm is rigid, lifeless, and tense.

With **relaxation**, the arm releases its tension to gravity, and as a result drops downward, thereby changing and destroying its extended form in space. Relaxation changes the movement.

With **release**, the locked energy is released to allow an interior flow of energy within the arm. The form, however, is still maintained, visible, and defined, and the life within the arm can grain itself to whatever direction the dancer chooses.

Usually, in their haste to ask for a release of tension, teachers just say, "relax." By doing so, they jeopardize the form of the movement. When the state of release is understood and attained, it balances the interior performing energies with the exterior design of the body or movement without sapping the energy needed to support the movement from within.

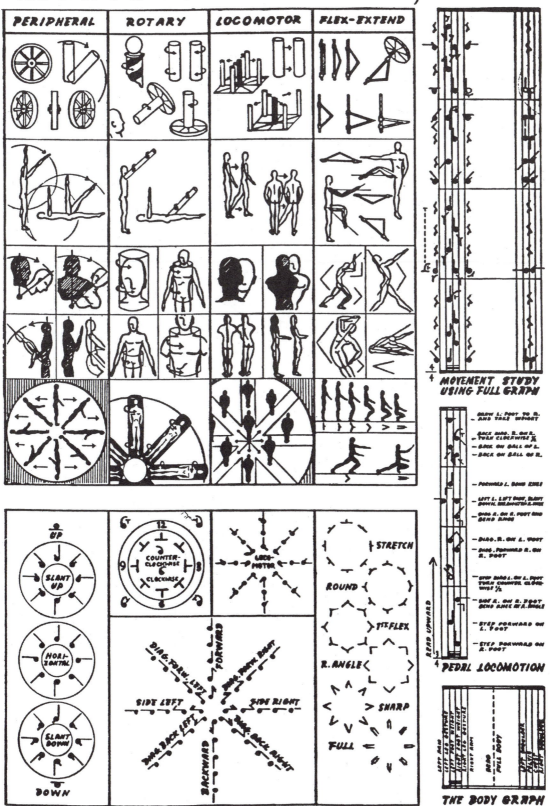

Alwin Nikolais's method of dance notation.

SECTION II: CREATING—
Improvisation and Composition

DEFINING IMPROVISATION

The Nikolais/Louis technique is a creative technique, and as such it is strongly based on the practice of improvisation. In all of the creative arts, improvisation is a major means by which one can deeply explore the materials of the various arts. It is an in-depth investigation not only of the material, but also of the artists' originality and imagination.

Nikolais called the improvisation class "theory." Its purpose was to theoretically investigate, through improvisation, the many facets of the principles of dance. Eventually, skills develop to explore these intricacies and depths, and lead to the development of a strong and sensitive performing technique.

Improvisation brings the intuitive component of the artist into play. Intuition guides the skill of invention and marks the uniqueness of the artist. The intuition makes instantaneous judgments. In dance, improvisation is both instant choreography and instant performance. It is the dancer's skill to open all his receptive channels and listen to the dictates of the body and its sensory network. This intuitive judgment is a remarkable asset. It dictates structure, invention, and performance and marks creative distinction.

Verbally critiquing movement in technique class is relatively simple in comparison to "crit-ing" improvisation. In technique class, the movement challenge is stated and tangible. It is also visible, clearly demonstrated, and described by either the teacher or other dancers in the class. In improvisation, the movement is unique and does not have a prescribed form with which to judge deviation. The major handicap is that the dancer cannot see what he is doing. If he is watching himself in the mirror, he is not improvising the movement fully. He must therefore call on other sensibilities to direct and guide him as he improvises. He is guided mainly by his intuitive judgments. These judgments are the body's means of evaluating itself and its interior action.

A strong inner person directs the development of creative material. This is not as mystical as it may sound. The inner person is generally a physically unfettered version of the outer person.

The inner person supplies the will, the invention, the flavor, the mystery, and the magic that bring distinction to creativity and performance. The inner person has his own sensory language of feelings. It is the means by which the harsh, literal language of the outer world is translated into the ambiguous, abstract language of art.

When I undertook this manual, I had a major concern. How does one verbalize the nonverbal? How does one critique intuition; especially when, while improvising, dancers rarely know what they are going to do? The heat of the movement is over before the dancer can realize what has occurred. Listing improvisation premises to develop skills was simple. But how could the teacher direct the ongoing improvisation when very often the dancer did not know what he was doing until it was over? And how could I describe the movement when so much was happening at the same time?

My solution to this dilemma was to divide the class in two, so that half could watch while the other half performed. I would then direct my comments to those who watched. While half the class was improvising, I would say, "There, did you see that?" urging the viewers to see those moments when "it" happened, when everything drew together and the premise was transcended by a unique aesthetic moment.

Unfortunately, the dancers on stage had no idea what I saw and was talking about. They simply relished the compliments, when compliments were forthcoming, from the observers. They knew they were successful, but did not know the specifics of why and when.

So how, then, does one critique and direct an improvisation when the dancer doesn't know where he's going with the movement until it is almost over? When he does not know what his movement looks like? Aside from very general directions, such as "use your arms," "change your time values," "get up, you have been on the floor long enough," all of which hardly reflect a creative directive, the gift of verbal imagery becomes important.

A teacher learns very quickly that when dealing with criticisms the major obstacle to overcome is the dancer's ego. "That's what I wanted to do, that's what I felt," dancers will say in defense. Before their egos turn to hostility, the teacher's gifts for words and analogy have to be applied. The teacher must constantly remind the dancers of the premise, if it is not a free improvisation, and if possible make them aware of any opportunities they may have missed. Since the dancer doesn't know what he did and what the teacher saw, the teacher's facility for description comes into play. The challenge, again, is how to deal verbally with the nonverbal.

In going through a half dozen different notes taken by students, I realized that they used either Nikolais's or my "crits" as a way of describing the improvisation for later recollection. Therefore, I used the same device in this manual to describe various improvisations. These critiques describe the studies as well as the general flavor of the class.

Presenting beginning improvisation to new students can be both a traumatic experience as well as a moment of thrilling accomplishment for both student and teacher. These are murky waters we are about to enter. As an introduction, a teacher should explain the depth of intuitive judgment being asked of the students.

Within the students' genes reside thousands of years of experience and knowledge; it is now their job to penetrate that wellspring of richness and to tap into what their bodies already know. The teacher should then urge them to try to get their body and body parts to respond to internal sentient stimuli, without any restraints or fears or self-consciousness. For example, if the dancer uses an arm in a body part improvisation, encourage him to let the arm respond to its internal sentient stimuli, and not to prescribe its form intellectually. There may be only the slightest gesture to begin with, but encourage the students to see that the arm has a mind of its own, and to go with it in whatever spatial and temporal designs it might wish to make. This is a major first step toward students trusting themselves to move.

Beginning improvisation is a great challenge for both student and teacher. Not only are there no rules for success, but there is also a distinct invasion of one's privacy and insecurities. I begin with everyone seated and relate the story of the 10,000 years of heritage within them and how they are going to tap into their uniqueness, their psyche, their imagination, their intuition, and their sentient abilities. All the things that determine who they are and how they think will be called into play.

Then get everyone up and onto the floor. In numbers there is security. The dancers must become aware that they are going to make contact with and be guided by the aesthetic intuition that exists within them. They will begin to understand the two people inhabiting their body: the "pedestrian person" and the "artist person." Begin the improvisation by having the dancer assume a body shape that is unfamiliar to them. Let them twist the body somehow to effect a sharper taste within the body, but one that is not gripped or locked.

Have them listen to the body and wait for the first movement to begin. Sense and see the first body part move. It could be any part, and the first movement can be almost imperceptible. They are now becoming sensitive to how the inner person wants to move. It will not necessarily be what the students expected. Let the movement lead and take the body with it. It won't develop very far. Then start again with a more interesting shape beginning, such as standing with an arm extended in a design before them. Wait for the first movement to begin. Tell them, for example, not to intimidate the arm by saying to it, "Well, show me where you're going if you're so smart." The arm will freeze up and do nothing. Wait for the shy inner person to gain courage. The arm may lower in some direction, or raise or bend, or the elbow or the fingers may begin to move. Feel other body parts begin to relate to the arm.

This preliminary exercise is the start. Then have at least half the class watch as the other half performs. Watching and seeing are the best teachers of improvisation. The teacher guides the viewer's attention to what is successful.

Now half the class goes to the center of the floor. The half that sits is going to learn to see when the first movement begins the journey of development. The standing half begins. Some simple steady percussion accompaniment fills what may otherwise become an ominous silence, but does not lead them rhythmically. The dancer moves and feeds the development by adding other body parts and moving out into space. The teacher can now call out possibilities the dancer has failed to see.

Invention is closely related to originality, which in turn has its base in creativity. The skill of improvisation offers a pipeline to invention, and I don't believe there are many choreographers who do not watch their dancers keenly when they are choreographing to see where the movement "wants to go."

The dancer is called upon now to listen to his body, to let the body dictate the terms and guide him. The dancer begins this process by first recognizing and respecting the wisdom and capacity of the body.

Children's comp class.
Photo by David Berlin.

Group improvisation with half of class watching.

Class Viewing

In showing dances, usually the part of class sitting out and watching gains more from the critiques than those dancing. The viewer can see what is being done and what the teacher is critiquing, whereas the dancer needs to siphon the connections through his intellect, slowly and carefully, before his body senses what to change to make the corrections. The viewer can be stimulated and challenged by what successful examples are performed as well as profit from the less successful attempts.

Teachers should present this material at their students' level, choosing the verbal imagery and degree of technical challenge that they see fit.

Because of the necessary integration of aesthetic, creative, and technical aspects of this technique, finding an order in which to present the various materials becomes important. Building confidence and coherence in a student is as important as developing a strong technical base and creative imagination.

All criticism should be of a positive nature. It should indicate success and achievement as well as pinpoint where the study went astray and where it can get back on track. Faulty efforts arise mostly when students lose sight of the premise and other factors are allowed to become more dominant.

The class will usually contain different levels of skills and different innate abilities. Those dancers with physical skill and no fear of moving will excel. However, those with any hesitancy due to ego or inability will need more coaxing and guidance.

When Nikolais introduced theory as a class definition for what became improvisation classes, so much of the work was without the basis it has since acquired. Improvisation with its instant choreography and instant performance would later become another feature of this class.

It is at this point that I would like to make clear a basic distinction between technique, improvisation, composition, and performing. Briefly, in technique class the teacher sets the rules and is the boss. In improvisation, the dancer's intuitive judgments set the rules; the body is the boss. In composition, the form itself dictates how it wants to grow, and the art is the boss, and in performance, with the addition of the audience's contribution, all the factors are combined and the dance is performed and delivered. The performing artist, in this total sense, is the boss.

In improvisation, the dancer, understanding how much all his sensibilities will be called upon, assumes the responsibility for evolving what is unique to himself and works to reach his creative boundaries. Knowing that he will not be called upon to remember or repeat anything he does in the heat of improvising, he can let loose as long as he stays within the premise of the improvisation and doesn't use this as an opportunity to indulge himself.

Improvisation and composition usually followed the across the floor portion of the technique class.

IMPROV CRITS

Improvisation has few rules. It is a free-swinging experience and the results are wide ranging. More than anything else, it is a journey to the source, a revelation of one's inventive capacity. Here are a few comments of the sort the teacher should offer during early experiments with improvisation:

Begin at a starting point, and follow your movement. In other words, just go with it.

Wait for the body to make the first gesture and go with it. Listen to the movement as it speaks back to you. Perform the movement sensing what qualities it contains, sensing the motional flavor. If you do a movement and you don't know what it says, it will speak for itself if it is done fully and finds its own identity. Don't arrive before you sense where you are going.

See how much every detail matters. The wisp of hair falling over her face . . . suddenly you found your mind becoming alerted to other details about her. But be careful of flying hair. Hair has a motional value of its own that can interfere with the dance. Put it in a bun so that it won't move. Unless, of course, you want it to move.

Improvisation is the naïve, trusted doing. It is of such an elemental nature that it can be easily overlooked. It is a passion that imbues the body and senses. It is the oxygen to the respiratory system of motion. It does not come into focus unless the dancer understands and trusts the capacities of art. This oxygen might be manufactured in the body biochemically because it varies in different bodies.

First group, come and sit down and don't despair. You have to start somewhere.

There are thousands of points of view for improvisations. Practically every criticism I give you on what not to do is a basis for what to do in a new improvisation.

To a dancer improvising enthusiastically but outside of the premise: "It was very nice but it had nothing to do with the premise. My job is to see that you understand the premise. Try it again but stay with the premise."

The speed of reaction is essential. Things are happening quickly all around you. Keeping up with them and relating to them is primary. The mind must be clear and alert, and the body facile and responsive. With beginners, the teacher should provide a lot of effective encouragement and verbal direction. In time, after watching and learning to see the success of other beginners, things begin to flow.

Other improvisation crits are distributed throughout the manual with given lesson plans. The crits are relevant to specific premises, and hopefully will impart useful ideas and imagery.

After warm-ups and the technical challenge of the movement patterns, the dancer's body was usually warm enough to move freely and follow the improvisation as it chose to lead him. The spontaneity of improvisations left little time to anticipate and prepare for movement reaction, and so it was necessary that the body not be taken by surprise; the dancer could possibly hurt himself if he had not warmed up sufficiently.

Depending on the size of the class, I usually split the class into two or three groups. As one group is "on stage," the other watches and gets the rare opportunity to practice watching and "reading" dance. As there is *choreography*—literally dance writing—there also should be a word for dance watching or reading.

When "crits" are made during improvisation classes, they are made for the viewers who have been watching and can see how the criticisms relate to the movements. The students who have just danced sit and are amazed at the conversations, remembering little about doing what is being discussed of their performance; they remember the inner workings, not the outer physical representations.

During improvisation, there should be no elaborate accompaniment to coerce the dancer with a time structure. The dancers supply their own temporal quality.

You cannot teach creativity, but you can create an environment in which students can sensitize themselves to learn the processes of creating. Invention in improvisation depends as much on the verbal and critical astuteness of the teacher as it does on the facility and inventiveness of the student.

Improvising in Duets: Contact Improvisation

The premise, improvising in duets, was always a problem with beginners. Nothing would happen. They were shy with each other and neither dancer knew when or how to begin. When beginners went up with a new partner for the first time, they usually just stared at each other. If one started to move, the other awkwardly repeated. However, when they were in physical contact with each other, they related. When they separated, both stopped. So eventually, the idea of keeping some point of contact and making the contact inventive became an early improvisational tactic. Keeping a point of contact somehow focused the students' minds on how the body made decisions for itself.

Partnering

Partnering is basically a situation of trust, of identification with each other. We must know where our partner's weight is, his breathing and timing, the common choreographic goal, and the necessary energy control.

Partnering also means just that—two people assuming equal responsibility. I have seen such exquisite partnering that the rapport was more moving than the choreography. I have also seen naïve support work with one partner offering no resistance to his partner's pressure for support. No one had explained to this dancer that his partner's pressure against him was how she supported herself. His unfortunate partner had to balance and support herself throughout the dance.

GESTALT

The word *gestalt* as used in this technique derives its meaning not from the behaviorist Gestalt psychology, but rather from its definition as "the total or the whole as it is reflected in its parts."

Gestalt is the recognizable and sensed nature of a totality, the identification of an ineffable entity. This new identity is sensed and imparted into every part of the body so that everything speaks of it. The feelers of all the nerve endings, and the taste buds of all the sentient equipment in the body, and the mind's synapses work concurrently to guide the motion toward the revelation of the new life. Once established, this germ will then serve as a creative and compositional guide in extending the seed to its fruition.

In contemporary terms, one can think of the recognizable gestalt of an abstraction as its DNA. It is a commonness that links all the parts of an entity. This involves both the outer physical and the inner psychical participation of the performer.

Student notes from class best describe gestalt here:

Sense that moment when something you do becomes identifiable, when, out of the mass of material you create, something becomes an entity—an identity—a life.

Leave it free to find its own growth. Use anything you like to allow its growth. Watch it.

You have designed something that falls into perfect cohesion and order. It is whole, complete, and total.

Gestalt relates to organic choreography. You are letting a seed take life. It has a life distinguishable from your own: an identity so powerful that with the first gestures it makes its presence known. Work toward a definite sensation—some feeling of identity. Often a composition has to be worked on over and over again because there is not enough identifiable subject matter to deal with. Work for an aesthetic Rorschach test that will provoke imaginative reaction and association from the viewer.

You can start this from any one point of view—time, space, shape, or motion. But in the beginning, it is easier to see form from a *shape* point of view. The body is a malleable vehicle of motion. Through our imagination and ability to transcend, we can become other things.

Up until now we have worked on motional visibility—now we come to the aesthetic aura. This is hard, and involves astute performing skills. Transcendence is the making of something that pulls itself out of you. Or pulls you up into it. It is bigger than you are, and consequently you must become bigger than yourself to fulfill the thing toward which you've aspired.

The choreographic prerogative allows for one to obstruct the coherence of any organic development. Deliberately ignoring logic or gestalt and redirecting development, when it is deliberately done, is often the choreographer's distinction or signature. But first be able to achieve the logic of gestalt, before you practice "playing" with it and reforming it.

NATURE AND ART

Nature and Art

This story is about Isadora Duncan. It has been told in various versions. Earlier in my life, I met two people who witnessed the story (so they said).

When Isadora performed in Boston at the beginning of the twentieth century, she was very young, beautiful, and danced in revealing clothing. Obviously this combination divided her audience, and her performance drew very cool, reserved applause from the old guard and wild applause from the students. Much annoyed by the reservation among the audience, at her finale curtain call she walked forward and addressed them. After a few words of admonition, she exposed one breast and announced, "This is art," to which a voice from the audience returned, "No, dear lady, that is nature."

Today some degree of nudity is commonplace on the stage. Exposing a breast on stage is not as earth-shaking as it once was, nevertheless its form and beauty is created by nature. It is nature's composition and expression. Nature gets the credit for its composition.

However, my respect for Isadora will accept anything she said as the truth.

There is a marked difference between what is natural and what is artificial or manmade. Nature makes her beauty with natural materials and according to her own rules of composition. For example, she may fashion a mountain range over eons of time or cover everything with ice age whiteness: her white-on-white period.

Whereas man, with his limited time on earth and his mechanical resourcefulness, has, out of necessity, had to accelerate his abilities to create beauty. Nature calls her efforts natural and man calls his efforts art.

To create his art, mankind evolved the craft of extending his abilities. Musical instruments were skillfully crafted to serve the musician, who for the most part creates his art through an extraordinary development of his fingers. Artists use paints, canvas, and sculptural materials such as metal, glass, concrete, and so on, which are, for the most part, manufactured. The printed word, in addition to an alphabet, needs an education to decipher the language and a press to print it. The voice and body are developed and trained to exceed their natural capabilities to an unnatural degree.

The dancer's instrument redefines itself. The body alters its capabilities and functions to a more than natural range, in a sense; it distorts and develops skills, which are now manmade. Leaps, leg extensions, balances, and inordinate flexibility become part of the dancer's abilities. The col-oratura and the G above high C, the thirty-two fouettés, the geometric *Nude Descending a Staircase*, the detail of a Fabergé egg—all of these must press the natural into an unnatural range and hence into the realm of art.

The instruments to make art are not natural ones. They are manmade or man-altered—and so, too, is man's instrument for dance, the body, altered.

The dancer begins his evolution by transforming himself into an instrument of exceptional strength, flexibility, and motional range, and enhancing his sentient, tactile, and conceptional abilities.

The dancer will also, in this training, be asked to expand his creative abilities through constant challenge. One learns the skill of dancing by dancing. One gets stronger through repetition.

By doing, and doing, and doing, the body will gain strength and skill, allowing the dancer a versatile instrument to reveal intuitive judgments in all their subtlety. By repetition, these artificial skills become natural to the dancer's body. All these performing skills can become natural through repetition, rehearsals, and performing. An artificial, manmade naturalness is created. To the performing artist, the skills he forces can become natural to his life function. He creates a new manmade, selective naturalism, very much in line with Darwin's theory of selection and survival. We can alter and restructure nature by altering our bodies with what were once "unnatural" skills and abilities. In other words, a dancer's training is a preparation for artistry.

The dancer will now undergo a period of training to reshape and develop the body. This period will stress endurance, concentration, and the ability to metamorphisize the self into abstract imagery, among other transformations. The dancer will now shape and craft an instrument to deal with and perform the art of dance.

When the body speaks, it makes itself heard only as clearly as it can articulate movement. In the same sense, there are movements and reactions that are natural and others that are devised with skill and quality. Belching is natural and the coloratura voice is an acquired skill. A sculptor cannot sign his name to a beautifully weathered piece of driftwood and claim credit for it as his own. Nature has a great many movements that are hers. Choreographers must find their own invention. This is not to say that skillful choreographers cannot employ natural movement in their vocabulary, but if the movement is not altered to sufficiently communicate a new identity, then nature should get credit for it, not the artist.

Creating is different from discovering. Discovering means finding what already exists, whereas creating is the ability and skill to give life to something that did not exist before. Nature already exists; art is created.

THE LANGUAGE OF CRITICISM

The Nikolais/Louis technique is a creative technique. It is intended to simultaneously develop technical skill and aesthetic judgment regarding movement.

Finding a suitable verbal language to deal with as complex an activity as dance is a formidable task. Choosing words that will say more than their specific meaning and mixing them with other definitions is our challenge. We aim to create an environment of imagery that resonates. In the manual portion of this book, I have listed the critiques made in class to give a picture of the diversity of the creative presentation and also to recreate some semblance of the studies presented.

Dance teachers bear a greater responsibility than just teaching steps. When a student stands before them, the student presents more than arms and legs; he presents a total person. The teacher must deal with the entire inner person as well. The harsh reality of this profession is that only a small percentage of people training to dance will actually dance professionally. A larger number will dance under nonprofessional circumstances, but most students will benefit from training in multiple ways. Most important, their lives will be enriched to respond aesthetically to the world around them, which is a benefit of inestimable value.

In preparing the class plans for this manual, I found that I was often presenting the same points but in a different manner. Reiteration is a big part of teaching and learning. As any teacher knows, each class presents an entirely different environment. The weather, class attendance, day of the week, events in the teacher's life—any number of occurrences can influence the class and affect the presentation of a premise. Certain vocabularies are more effective on certain days, and students are more receptive to certain imagery at certain times.

Stimulating the inner person to participate with the physical action is an essential part of this pedagogy. Presence, totality, sentient awareness, and imaginative richness are constantly called into play to complete the fullness of action, and it is the teacher's responsibility to constantly prod the dancer into this total participation.

In technique class, the critical vocabulary is usually specific and tangible, whereas in the improvisational, creative, and performance portions of the class another more metaphoric language is employed. But more often the two languages are intermixed, so that the metaphoric becomes specific and the technical becomes ambiguous. Both languages are necessary for clarity.

VERBAL CRITICISM FOR ABSTRACTION AND THE NONVERBAL

Criticism is generally left in the hands of the choreographer or teacher, but the dancer's ability to correct and improve himself is equally important. Dealing with what is often an intangible area can be a misleading experience; it can be as confusing as the diversity of languages at the Tower of Babel. Literalness is expressed by words while abstraction is communicated through sensation. One uses both exact definitions and verbal imagery to express oneself.

Since teaching dance is part verbal, part demonstration, and part awareness, the choreographer and teacher must be particularly eloquent in all areas. In order to be able to impart the fullness of dance, the teacher must also teach the language of abstraction to his dancers. If this area of language falters, then the teaching becomes limited and choreography can be incoherent.

To best deal with critiques and definition of creative aspects such as improvisation and composition, I have included the critical comments that were made in those classes. I thought these comments gave varied and sensitive descriptions and best defined the qualities of the studies shown. Somehow these comments evoked the flavor of the improvisations performed in the dance class. Once the studies ended and were wiped from our vision, criticism seemed irrelevant with nothing to relate to it. Nevertheless, the critiques did paint a verbal impression of what was performed.

I felt that if students remember dances by these descriptive criticisms, perhaps the same crits would evoke within the reader a semblance of the improvisations and dances, as well. The same crits can serve from dance to dance. Words are relative; reactions and responses to movement are relative; personal reactions to dancers, as well as what they are dancing about, are relative. This leaves us with very elastic definitions.

The unfortunate thing about presenting successful studies is that there is little to criticize or comment on. Consequently, too much time is spent correcting the faulty dances, while the deserving ones are passed over hastily. Being aware of this oversight, I spend equal time with praise, sometimes to the point of embarrassing the choreographer. It also helped develop my vocabulary for praise. In mixed-level classes it should be understood that criticism is relative to the technical and creative level you're dealing with. Criticisms become relevant to specific examples. There is no definite right or wrong. A phrase of movement that might be perfect for one assignment could totally miss the mark for another. That is why a continuity of classes is important. Over a period of time many examples will be observed and many different criticisms and verbalizations will have been made, giving an insight into the wide range of creativity and individualism that exists in a premise and within a class.

Abstractions need more than one verbal description to make them specific. It takes several descriptions to flesh out an abstraction.

Teacher–Student Contract

Showing compositions in class is a simple contract agreed upon by both the dancer and teacher. It goes like this: You're going to show me what you can do, and I'm going to show you how you can, perhaps, make it better, stronger, or richer.

COMPOSITION

The intent of composition is to arrange the materials of dance in the most coherent and articulate manner possible for the communication of the choreographer's intention. The choreographer guides the artist in arriving at a consonant structure that includes an intuitive sense of order and timing.

There are musical structures such as ABA—theme and variation, which can serve as basic guidelines in practicing form; however, the success of any choreography will eventually depend on the originality of the thematic vocabulary created by the choreographer.

Compositions are judged by these simple standards: first, invention; second, structure; and third, performance. Very often one standard is more successful than another. Creative invention of movement is primary. This does not in any way lessen the importance and effect of the skillful structuring of the material. Structuring the invention into a choreographic whole and then bringing it to life with a sensitive and kinetic performance rounds out the definition of composition.

Motion, time, space and shape, dynamics, energy, the dancers' instrument, the body, psyche, emotional and motional ranges, intelligence and control of ego, among others, are principles that comprise the dancer's creative art. Mobility is the glue that binds all these factors together. Mobility is the state of going, of motional possession. It is a state of easy, ready participation.

The elements of composition have a common base in all the arts. The principles of all of the arts are somehow bound together. The sculptor uses shape, the musician time, the poet alliterations, and the painter space and color. The choreographer, who has limited his aesthetics only to dance, has divorced himself from an enormous insight, perspective, and experience in compositional methods by not being familiar with the other arts.

One thinks, "How would Rembrandt or Picasso have painted this, or, How would Beethoven or Debussy have composed that?" Indeed, Bach and Mozart were not revolutionaries. They evolved their art from the materials of their past. Their compositions basically used standard choreographic methods for their time, but what a wealth of invention and imagination they produced! Again, there are no rules for creativity.

The intent of composition can vary: from specific to vague, from narrative to abstract or nonobjective. What will determine success is its degree of communication with an audience. Therefore, the sensitivity of performance is essential to revealing intent. At this point there is no need to answer the common question, "What does it mean?" We are going to assume we have an intelligent and sentiently aware audience.

What we would like to do is to present you with the possibilities of your identifying your work, and try to give you a technique with which to do so.

Composing for a group. Columbia College, Chicago, 1974.
Photo courtesy of the Nikolais/Louis Foundation.

46

If the mind is at fault, then the body is at fault. It's the job of the teacher to try to identify discrepancies and to either make corrections or devise other ways to bring about the union of the two so that what you have in your mind takes place in the body and vice versa.

Dancing is an activity where one derives sensations, feedback from the movement, and it is the clarity of these sensations that gives dancing its logic.

When we use the word *content*, it means a summation of sensations, of feelings, which somehow through the structure that you have created delivers to the onlooker a vision of life.

Imagination? The audience brings the imagination, and the artist brings the stimulant to release the audience's aesthetic vision. Abstract narrative is a nonverbal exposition, in this case an evolvement of choreography or structure.

There are no definite rules for composition, only those relative to a specific creation. *Rule* is a terrible word because it implies right and wrong and codifies originality. However, there are directives that can be applied to make a choreographic work more lucid and available to an audience, as well as offer basic structure for a legibility of viewing.

Stringing random steps together is, unfortunately, a common idea of what constitutes choreography. Modern dance has by now borrowed so many things that are superfluous and meaningless to its definition. Generalization tends to weaken, not strengthen.

Some of you will have greater success with your studies than others. You will produce studies that are bolder and more provocative. All of you, however, have a particular affinity for some aspect of vision that will make you shine. But this basic substance has to be valid in itself before you can start decorating it with overlays of sound and light. You learn to strengthen your vision by watching and seeing how the material falls into balance when an art moment occurs. If it works, it is right. No rules.

Create from a germinal point of view. Discover what lies in your material and let it grow. Create an entity . . . a gestalt, a seed. This seed you've created will indicate the way it wants to grow. You have to sense what you've given life to and how it needs to grow and form itself. Who knows what you may have spawned. Always prepare yourself

for what you may have given life to. A palm tree in a flower box can be a big, unwelcome surprise.

Every dance bears within it the seeds of the next dance. Don't get sidetracked and compose both dances simultaneously. Leave the new seed to be developed at a later time.

Studies are a prelude to the composition of longer dances. In a study, the teacher usually defines the premise and the boundaries of communication are set. But with a dance the student must identify the premise and formulate all the necessary structure to reveal the intent.

Improvisation is achieved on the spur of the moment, but composition allows you the time to set and reset the dance. Space in which to choreograph is usually at a premium. Dancers learn to work anywhere. This patchwork continuity tends to fragment the strength of a continuous motivation. It is important to have a strong gestalt to "hang" onto. Wherever you find the space to work, you will have to bring along the quality and flavor of your study. Then, like a performing artist, you will face the challenge of reproducing that same quality each time you perform the study or dance. The best artist doesn't vary in quality from practice to performance. Being consistent is part of the definition of professionalism.

Composing must eventually become a habit, a second nature. Set a period for creating every day and stick to it.

Watching gives the viewing dancer a special opportunity to see what he himself might look like if he were dancing the role. In all other arts, one can view or hear the work others create, over and over again, but in dance, performances never allow an in-depth or repeat viewing. There is no rerun button. One viewing of a stage busy with action is all you get. Once the dance is over, it's over. Learning to watch dance is a very special skill, which only regular viewing can develop. Composition showings are immeasurably valuable.

Let the dance find its own voice, make its own sense, find its own beauty, sing its own song. Make something that never existed before. Find the space, shape, time, and motion that will qualify the dance. Find the logic and reason for moving. Everything you create has its own life. So your job is to live up to yourself.

You learn how to create the right kind of water, sunlight, and fertilizer inside yourself to nourish and make your seed grow. You just never know what kind of seed you're going to gestate. Whatever it is, you must trust it and go with it. Once it has identified itself, then you can mold it, or discard it if you choose to do so.

Think of yourself as a bit like a director with a camera. Say to me, "I want you to see this right elbow . . . this left elbow . . . all of me . . . the space behind me." There is an editing machine within you that can actually take my eye and tell me where you want me to look and when. You know you can handle the viewer by graining and sensitively selecting where you want them to watch.

You still have to deal with the idea of material selection before you choreograph. Everything still has to be translated into the vocabulary of dance. Inherent in you is a sense of consonance. It knows when things are balanced. It knows when what you intended is total and unobstructed. For the viewer to perceive a thing for its intrinsic beauty is to exercise aesthetic judgment. Beauty is part of an eternal line; beauty stimulates the sense of consonance. It involves the judicious use of materials.

Creativity is a very private affair. Penetrating and rummaging through that world of accumulated memories, thoughts, and sensations to motivate a creative act cannot be taught. At most one can be urged through a process of dealing with the imagination.

Words and their definitions are the greatest obstacles to comprehension. Even the most literally specific definition can be misinterpreted. [It is no wonder, then, that when dealing with poetic definition one is walking on very shaky ground, a ground quivering with misconceptions.]

The language that the artist responds to most is the language of sense response. There is even a phonetics for teaching choreography. Dancers have a dancer's language. It's a jargon of sounds, clicks, rhythms, melodies, noise—anything that distinguishes and explains movement or how the movement is to be performed.

How the dancer wishes to use these sense responses is a matter of choice. As long as the dancer knows these are his choices, fine. As long as he knows how to deviate from basic practice, fine. One can deliberately sing off-key as long as he knows how to sing on-key. Singing off-key deliberately takes a considerable amount of skill. However, we are now practicing singing on-key.

POSSIBLE MATERIAL FOR COMPOSITION STUDIES

Pulse

Meter

Rhythmic interplay

Touch body parts

Peripheral drawing on space

Close space volume

Dynamic line

Twist and focus

Suspension points

Circular action

Treading

Space fixation

Momentum motifs

Exits and entrances

30-second dance

TEXTURAL DYNAMICS

Effect of the body on space

Effect of space on the body

ENVIRONMENTS SPATIAL STRUCTURING

Linear: one-dimensional

Planar: two-dimensional

Cubic: three-dimensional

GESTALT

Subject

Object

SUBJECT SOURCES

Nonsense sounds

Literal words

Associations

Self-sounds (clap, stamps)

Kabuki

Insults and adulation

Adjectives: outrageous, abandoned, etc.

Metaphoric personal story translation

Dada

Symmetry

Unison

ABSTRACTIONS AND ILLUSIONS

Thick–thin

Heavy–light

Fast–slow

Large–small

Wild–tame

SUBJECT SET

Animal general

Animal specific

Atmosphere: carnival, haunted house, etc.

Concepts: Witchcraft, monarch, miser, etc.

Pairs: Old age/youth, etc.

USE OF VERBAL MATERIAL

Newspaper ads

Poetry

Word phrases as titles

CHOREOGRAPHING FOR EACH OTHER IN CLASS

To introduce choreography into improvisation time:

Invite everyone upon the floor to experience the nature of the improvisational premise for the day.

Assign duets. Select third dancer as choreographer for each duet. Ask who wants to choreograph. Eventually everyone will choreograph. This choreographing assignment will eventually develop into quartets.

Allow thirty minutes for the choreography to be set. Studies generally are one or two minutes in length.

Give them a five- to ten-minute time warning to review material for showing.

Inform everyone that the choreographer is the boss. No arguments with him. Suggestions are permitted if they are asked for.

For the performance of the study, the choreographer can beat a tempo on drum or clap or count.

We are going to look at the choreographer's creative ability and the dancer's performing skill. Both must bring their skills to the fore. Choreographers will demonstrate their skill in transferring movement. The choreographer is responsible for bringing out the dancer's skills and learning to verbalize as well as evaluate his own abilities at constructing a form. Choreographers prepare to receive the blame and dancers the glory. That's life! Audiences empathize with dancers, not steps.

During the period of setting the dance, the teacher walks around the room and helps where there are problems by urging dancers on to fuller performance value and by pointing out what details the choreographer may have overlooked.

The last ten or fifteen minutes are for showing the studies. Everyone watches. Teachers point out where success rests or falters. Corrections are made and the dances are repeated. Hopefully the corrections will improve the studies.

Don't expect too much. After all, consider the limitations and time limits. Use these choreographic sessions whenever you see fit but wait until both parties have some vocabulary under their belt. Begin at about the eighth week to use some of the improvisation creative time for choreography. Make sure that everyone gets to choreograph. Ask who has not choreographed and assign them, but don't force anyone. They will come around to it in their own time.

Change means growth, and growth means stretching, and stretching, in the beginning, often hurts. There is always something discomforting about change, but change is growth and achievement is about growth. Stretching both your mind and your muscles is a challenge that causes change. No matter how you put it, you are going to outgrow yourself. You are going to change.

Keep in mind that the development of technique, improvisational skills, and choreographic capabilities always mean a development of some sort. Improvisational skills dig deeper into the very personal psyche, and the resulting exposure is both penetrating and acute. Choreographic abilities expand judgments and performance by putting one on display before an audience. All of these challenges are going to stretch the dancer to some degree.

Each lesson plan goes into detail through twenty-five weeks. By constantly repeating basic material, the dancer's technique will grow considerably and will help the teacher in developing challenging across-the-floor patterns.

"Reading" a Dance

In structuring a dance, the choreographer and performer must concern themselves with the audience's accessibility *to the work.* Legibility *has to do with that accessibility. Articulation and clarity of intent are the dancer's concern in this operation. Within the piece there are also factors of phrasing and pointing and punctuation, which further help the audience to "read" the structure. Long, convoluted sentence structure may work in a novel, but onstage the dancer does not have the luxury of this indulgence.*

Dance does not allow replay. The dancer must know what he is "saying" (dancing) and he must "say" (dance) it.

Privilege of Failure

Let's at the outset confess that no one has actually succeeded in mastering all of the challenges of creative dance training. Some have excelled in one area and struggled with others. Let's realize that every artist has his area of failure—not necessarily failure, but rather weak spots where his congeniality does not respond to the occasion, where his area of congeniality is too small. We will soon recognize that every artist has his limitations and in turn his weaknesses.

Dance creators can be likened to growing plants, which are also expected to produce every season. And as with flowering plants, sometimes the harvest is poor and sometimes spectacular.

Creative artists should be able to enjoy the occasional privilege of failure. Their track record of success should assure their future achievements.

CRITICISM

There is no specific order to the crits below, rather they evoke a tapestry of what occurred and what was commented on in class during the showing of various studies.

- The piece could be clearer and stronger. I can see where it wants to go, but you are interfering with it and confusing its development. Why don't you step out of the picture for a moment and listen to it. If you don't like where it is going, change it. Don't coerce it.
- "Identifying with" is knowing who you are to begin with and how to invest that knowledge into the movement you are performing. You can't identify with a movement until you put yourself out and sense it fully. Anything does not necessarily go.
- You have this immediate job of transplanting yourself into an act, which at the moment you might not prefer to do. But simply, by your orientation toward dance as a lifework and as an art, you will yourself to do it, as an actor wills himself to become the role. This builds the strength of discipline, a skill vital to the practice of any art.
- There is too much material in this dance. You've got to know when to stop stimulating yourself, or you'll just go insane! Just chaos . . . so many unresolved points of view going on, one right after the other. Chaos means many strong things are going on and not enough resolving to make them coherent. You're like the dancer who got up to show his dance and said, "I've got a fabulous dance I want to tell you about," then talked his way through it at great length.
- Think, "I've created it. I'm responsible for the life of that movement. This is my offspring, my baby."
- There are NO rules—none at all. The work itself dictates its form. It is essential that you make yourself available to your art. Join it.
- Your entrance is too long. You do too many things too long and in the same way.
- If you are going to work in these very pale tones, you need a structure to hang it on. As it stands, it is too undefined. It needs a more substantial basis.
- It didn't resolve itself. It didn't come to a period. You didn't end the phrase. You left us waiting for the other shoe to drop. Remember your audience is only human. So humor us. Or should I say, human us. Drop the other shoe.
- It was a wonderfully contained macabre piece. Beautiful distortion. The beauty of hideousness. It was contained; it never struggled. That beginning had within it all the materials to develop into something distinctive. Thank you. Wow.
- Have a general sense of how you are going to begin and end things.
- You have to become intimate with your material. You become totally obsessed with your material, and your material becomes totally obsessed with you. Become one with it. Don't hold back. No matter how strange it feels.
- Don't break out of things so quickly. Get the awareness of how long it takes for the shape to travel through space visually, to reach the viewer. If you rush this, your sense of time is faulty.
- You have to have a dynamic germinal thing going or nothing is going to happen. It's like trying to bake a cake in a cold oven. No matter how many ingredients you put into it, it needs the heat of performance.
- What you brought in was the first thing that happened. The whole process of choreography is basically one of selection. You simply settled on your first sketch. When you become as skilled as Picasso, then everything you do is gold, at least on the commercial market; you can present your first sketch as the finished product.
- Before you can sing a song, you should know the notes. See if you can learn the notes more quickly . . . memorize faster.
- Isn't nature wonderful! You told me nothing new.
- Don't hold out your hand lifelessly like that. It looks extraneous.
- Repetition becomes dull . . . then monotonous. Then you wonder when is it going to end. Then it begins to say something to you. Monotony. If you want monotony, you have to suffer it through the dull stages.

- I don't think you can give a good performance if your choreography is not good. Set it. Reach into it and develop it.
- Don't use technique class shapes and stretch positions. Identifiable positions bring commonplace images to the viewer's mind, which is unfortunate.
- Your transitions were so long, they were practically movement phrases in themselves.
- I don't care what you do if you do it with dignity! For example, you cannot subjugate a cat's dignity. Function with animal dignity. Don't play around, don't play house and diddle around. You demean yourself.
- Too long. I began to look for other meanings.
- To an advanced class: "In composing, one of your skills is knowing how to punch up the best parts. Always know where the best parts are! Remember, you are training to be professional dancers as well. Give yourself some juicy challenges."
- You set a series of predigested materials. It's like following Arthur Murray charts on the floor. If you were really waltzing, you would rarely ever do what the charts say.
- He hit on whole areas of just going. Now he must learn to pause and select.
- Curiously, you can fall out of the state of dance, if your concentration on the material is stronger than your sensitivity to it.
- You overdesigned it. You did a lot of designs that had nothing to do with the case. It was interesting, it was nice to watch, but a lot of things had absolutely nothing to do with your opening statement.
- You're playing at the problem rather than doing it. It doesn't have the full volume of aesthetic dedication.
- Once you've done it, you've done it. You should have made the design with such marvelous neon intensity that once you've done it, you can stand away from it and say, "See this line in space!"
- Good. This was more provocative.
- Don't try to do it—do it!
- You repeated each thing too much; you tend to lose our interest. You made the statement and then you made it over and over again, as if in writing an essay you repeated a sentence over and over.
- Make sure that, if you do repetitions, they are needed. You'll find much of art and design is limitation. What not to do. What to leave out. What excess to take away.
- This is the closest so far. It's a good, strong design, and pretty well narrated. Abstractly narrated, not story narrated. The time structure seemed to help, and even the motional aspect seemed to help. I would like you to look into shape a little bit more strongly, but generally this is closer to what we should be seeing. Thank you.
- The structure was there but she wasn't technically skilled enough to perform it. But you could see how a stronger dancer would dance this beautifully. This is why we work early in composition, so that when the body skill catches up to the creative skill, they are both ready to do justice to each other. The creative skill should not be held back by a technically weak instrument.
- In abstraction, emotion is inherent in motion.
- That was nice to see. It's a thing that also is very often used in new areas of dance choreography—particularly in circles where you have nondancers. A very natural kind of movement . . . not so highly technical—quite, quite valid. We can accept that as an exploration.
- This was interesting. You have a good structure, choreographically, but I think you threw the material away from the "time" point of view. You might have elected to do some things a little slower—a little more sensitively, tasting it as you went along. It was too glib. This is one of those instances where you have to distinguish between the structure of the piece and the performance, how you sense the movement and how you "play" it.
- The finesse of the body is so extraordinarily minute in its possibilities.
- Basically it was insensitive, tight, awkward. You have to be very skilled to do natural things! To be consciously awkward, deliberately, is very difficult.
- Do not call an audience in to see something you know is going to be unsuccessful.

- That was more ghostly than ghost. Unfortunately, you didn't take advantage of it. Try to visualize in your mind what the viewer is seeing. It's a skill you must develop especially if you're going to compose for yourself, which you all eventually must do, hopefully, successfully.
- How do you know what you're doing? Say to yourself, "What's being seen?" and simply picture it in your mind. Be less centralized, more open, then it becomes more objective, clearer.
- Shape, space, and time will no longer be the mysteries they used to be, and motion and shape no longer attitudes and movement.
- The choice of where you go to next? I'll be darned if I know how to tell you how to do this. Somebody will make a choice of how to go from one point to the next to the third and we'll be fascinated by it. Somebody else will do the same thing and it won't work.
- Do not get comfortable when you are down on the floor. Keep the shape kinetic.
- The simplest thing is the most innocent one, going directly to the problem.
- I bet you shower with your shoes on. You're so insensitive to what your feet are doing.
- You put obstructions between you and your sensations.
- Watts Towers, in Los Angeles—go to see them. The creator of Watts Towers said, "In all of history you are only remembered if you are "good-good" or "bad-bad." This quartet is "good-good."
- Mannerisms are very subconscious. They exhaust the audience's eye. It shows the dancer didn't know what they were doing. As a teacher, don't teach your mannerisms, which are often unconscious. Instead, teach principles. Don't cover up and avoid the issue.
- Nikolais had twenty-five students do thirty seconds of very intense movement with five entrances and exits. Juxtaposed, it was very funny!
- This is the Theater of the Absurd. It speaks through the language of irrelevancies, of banalities, of absurdities. Juxtaposition gives them their irrelevancies. We're laughing at relationships. It's hard to verbalize about irrelevancies.
- You know how a kitty just gets bigger and bigger when you scratch its belly. Makes you say, "Where'd all that kitty come from?" Give me that quality of expansion.
- Your sense of height was very good. You kept your vertical beautifully. You never let your neck hang out of weakness of will. Very pungent material.
- Reach the top, as far as you can go . . . relevé . . . elevate.
- Ira, you hung on to too much of Ira. Give yourself totally to what you are doing.
- You can only know by seeing, by sensing. Since you can't see yourself work, count on sensing. You've got to get that basic generative energy going all the time. Be sure it's energy you use . . . not your personality.
- It began to get too dancey. Began to get a polish, a veneer. Keep those raw aspects you started with.
- You are creating a metaphorical language. She transformed herself. You didn't see a physical body anymore. The archetype, the superhuman, the witchdoctor, the artist all speak in metaphors. Keep your ambition beyond what you can achieve so that you are always reaching. The unknown tantalizes artists. They have incredible curiosity . . . an insatiable delight in incredible experiences. The unknown hooks them—they're restless, probing, nuts!
- You've got to know what to chuck out from all the stuff you've learned about dance. Get a big shovel and throw everything you think dance is out of your mind. Your image became too shallow and superficial. Not rich with substance. Here you have a body that has such expressive power, you can't demean it. You demean it when you do certain little things. There is not enough inner dignity.
- Good! There was an underlying itch and an underlying necessity to move.
- It is a misconception that you have to dance all over the place, all the time. Lots of people think if they aren't straining every muscle, sweating in every pore, knocking themselves out, they aren't dancing.
- She transcends her whole physicality. That was highly imaginative. Bravo! How can you think so fully?
- You must understand that shape, time, space and motion are ingredients that are simultaneously present. They constitute the whole.

- Even though all four major principles are simultaneously present, you can stress one and eliminate the others from our seeing.
- Go to the problem directly, not indirectly. Have no extraneous attitude toward it—don't try to interpret it . . . let it be its own statement. In other words, it delivers its own message—you do not have to deliver a message on top of it.
- You go as simply, as cleanly to the problem as you can. You put that one thought in your head, and start working. You let no other thoughts interfere with that one manifestation.
- Do not make any other thing more important than the thing you want us to see. You have to be the judge of what you do.
- Don't be so inventive that you invent yourself right out of the problem. Stay simple for a while. Stay simple so that you can get used to it. Try to get to simple designs. Later you'll have plenty of time to do all the kooky designs in the world, but for the moment, be simple and direct. Let me know, you know, what you're doing.
- There is a big difference between art and artsy . . . between dance and dancey. One is doing it, the other is playing at it.
- Don't think that niceties solve anything in art.
- Principles are meaningless if you dissipate them.
- To an intermediate level dancer: "You are too developed to go back, you don't have the professional skill to be able to go back. You're trapped in your path of growth; however, the good news is, you're growing. Forward is your only direction."
- Habit is so easy! Challenge yourself! Get out of your complacency.
- While dancing "full out," one has to learn to fill their lungs and take deep breaths without heaving and destroying their vertical or alignment.
- Don't let me see all your transitions occur with a gut impulse; don't make everything spastic.
- The best thing about that was that your jaw was soft. That was a great stride forward for you.
- I never saw your motor kicking over. I saw only you pushing the car up the street.
- It's as if you're saying, "If you don't like this mink coat, how about this ermine?" You add layer after layer . . . until it becomes a mound of furs. And we can't see you buried in them.
- Student: "I lost my balance." ML: "That's all right. You could have done that movement lying on the floor. Should you fall again, be inventive. Perhaps your body was telling you something about how to develop the phrase."
- You have to overcome this sense of drama you create with everything you do.
- I say, "stay simple," but that doesn't mean you have to be dull!

SECTION III: THE CLASS MANUAL

INTRODUCTION TO THE CLASSES

Dancing and stretching have now become part of almost all physical training and body toning regimens, from the yoga discipline to aerobic dancing. With so much crossover, it becomes important to give dance its unique identity. This identity involves its purpose: presenting the aesthetic values inherent in movement.

The purpose of dance is basically the fulfillment of the act for its own sake; it is not movement given to satisfy another function. In sport, for example, the movement is generally focused on another objective: hitting a ball, operating a machine, riding an animal, arriving at a goal, competing in a speed competition, and so on. These objectives help define the various sports. The relaxing, contemplative,

slow stretching, mind-discipline activities serve yet another purpose.

Aerobic activities dedicated to accelerating the heart rate and calorie burning are based on gaining certain health balances. In addition to those major physical activities, there are offshoots of dance as well. It is only natural that people who teach will be stimulated by what they have learned and what they excel in, and if they teach, they will teach those specifics. Variations, offshoots, and elaborations are all tributaries of the main source.

Ideally, dance training should occur without the ego intruding; however, there is the danger of removing all ego and intrusions only to arrive at a colorless result. Purity does not effectively

"Make a big chest."
Murray Louis teaching class in Eugene, Oregon.
Photo courtesy of the Nikolais/Louis Foundation.

stimulate the senses. What is known in the arts as "working on the edge" is important in engaging the audience.

Beginning classes serve a number of purposes, one being the opportunity for both instructor and students to get to know each other. The energy of the class, the creative temper, and above all the rapport between instructor and class should be established in the first few classes.

The wealth of information to be presented and the vocabulary necessary to deal with that information have to operate simultaneously. This technique demands that both the mind (psyche) and kinetic sensibilities be present and participate with the development of the physical skill necessary for artistry.

The material to be presented in the early classes may seem considerable, but then so is learning the ABCs of any craft. In the beginning it can seem like too much to grasp, but during these beginning weeks, technique, improvisation, and composition soon begin to teach themselves and the class moves along quickly.

Just be assured that the brain will teach the body and the body will clarify things for the brain. The senses and the muscles will further clarify things, and you will soon experience the unlocking of the complexity and richness of movement.

There is no single definition for anything except perhaps an exact scientific fact. Since the human body is not a fact but an amalgam of infinite variety, we find that dealing with students' individuality becomes a major factor in teaching dance.

There are hundreds of languages spoken on this earth, and the English language has no end to the annual admission of new words into its domain. As classes progress, the definition of some words will have to bend a little. Trying to verbally translate an abstract achievement can be a nightmare. Describing sentient experiences and aesthetic reactions can be daunting. But in class, seeing, doing, and feeling all contribute to a three-dimensional elucidation. It isn't necessary to be exclusively verbal: physical and sentient eloquence will do as well, if not better.

One must consider the complexity of the body and acknowledge the fact that several entities occupy and use the single body known as "you." Among these entities there is the "pedestrian you" and the "dancer you." In charge of the body is the "you you," the one who regulates and makes the final decision as to who uses and controls the body at different times.

The "pedestrian you" and the "dancer you" think differently about many things: about food and rest, discipline and disorder. And frequently the "you you" must step in and settle conflicts as to who uses the body, and when, and especially how.

The dancer senses the vertical, the pedestrian slumps; the dancer keeps weight forward, the pedestrian walks on his heels. The dancer keeps his hips forward, the pedestrian lets it all hang out in the rear. Eventually through persistence and discipline the dancer can triumph and train the body to move and appear to its best advantage. With persistence, the dancer can even make the pedestrian shape up and look decent.

In charge of all of these decisions is the psyche, that central control lodged somewhere in the brain. It is essential that the pedestrian and the dancer learn to cooperate so that the body can move and execute movement with a sense of totality.

In undertaking the study of movement, the dancer is primarily concerned with two areas. The first is the "steps" or the form: the technical, physical reality of the movement itself. The second is the motional quality inherent in that movement and how its nature transcends the physical form. That is basically how Nikolais defined his theory of dance, movement as the outer form and motion as the inner experience. In his role, as a purist, he went further and separated the two events. In the classroom he dealt with motion, as it would be experienced as a sentient part of art dance. He simultaneously explored the use of the body in defining other principles of dance. These included the variety of space, both inner and outer, time and its range from stillness to speed, sculpting as well as creating the necessary physical instrument of movement. To manifest the psychical intent, he challenged the mind and psyche to motivate and function imaginatively to feed the body the energy it needs when performing the complexity of a given choreography. All this, dancers practiced in the technique class. The creative class brought other sensibilities into practice. Once these technical essentials had been made clear and the choreographic purpose defined, the teacher was responsible for evolving a vocabulary of his own so that he would be comfortable with developing and directing the class as well as offering guidance and criticism.

Space became a canvas. Time was sensed and its duration calibrated. The body itself had to be malleable and transformable to any shape demanded of it. All this lent students new identities and defined the nature of the motion. Motion, that volatile life that rested within movement, was motivated.

How the dancer focused his sensibilities toward these abstract principles demanded a release from strong centralization, upon which the ego insisted. In order to divest himself from this self-focused limitation, the technique called upon the dancer to decentralize his motivations and to operate with a fluidity that allowed him to experience the depth of a wide range of movement.

The classroom was the place of learning and its challenges provided the means to enlarge the performing range. In a sense, the Nikolais/Louis technique is a performing technique as well as a creative technique because the classes focused on bringing movement to life.

The goal of technique is to coordinate movement to arrive at a totality of execution. Creating is not necessarily an orderly process, nor is learning. This manual reflects the juxtaposed logic that teaching implies. One thought can lead to another, adding to its complexity and mystique as it develops.

The training at the Henry Street Playhouse and later at the Nikolais/Louis Dance Lab usually covered a three-year period and lasted four hours a day, five days a week. It was a comprehensive creative dance training. The material in this book covers this concentrated course of study, which often included a four- to six-week summer session as well.

It has to be assumed that understanding a premise or principle intellectually is not the same as being able to perform it. The brain can make instantaneous conclusions, while the body often takes weeks or months to absorb material. In the same sense, one can read through this manual in a matter of hours, but it may well take months or years to be able to apply it to dance.

There are four areas to be responsible for in each class. The first is **the teacher** who is in a sense, "the boss" during technique class. The teacher determines the premise and bears the responsibility of providing lucid criticism in accomplishing corrections.

Second, one must consider **the body**, which during improvisation is "the boss." The dancer, whose range of sensibilities and sentient responses determine how and what movements evolve, has an acute and vivid imagination and an immediacy of response. Much of the intuitive response rests with the psyche.

Third, with structure, **the art** itself is "the boss." During choreography, the inherent order of the choreographer comes into play. The evolution and structure of form and continuity rested with his choreographic skills. Within his conceptions the showcase of the art rests. It is his responsibility to make a dancer who is already good look better. His theatrical skill is needed to blend all the elements of production into a total stage event.

And finally, that mysterious and unidentified body called the audience plays the ultimate card. How the stage and the audience blend together suggests the magic of performance. The **performance** is the focus of all of the elements. The performance is also "the boss." Broken down to these four areas of consideration, from class to performance, the art of dance covers a broad spectrum of responsibilities and input.

In class the warm-ups can vary, but it is recommended that they have a familiar pattern and rhythm so that the purpose of warm-ups, which is to warm, stretch, and limber the body, can be achieved without too much intellectual interruption.

The basic warm-ups were developed in the 1930s by Hanya Holm and Joseph Pilate, both of whom knew and understood the mechanics of the body. Those warm-ups, with modifications, are included in this manual. Although they are best described on video, I have presented them here in photographic and written form. The daily classes include and introduce gravity, dimensions, flexations, rotary and peripheral action, body isolations, swings, succession of movement, time values, and sculptural subtleties. Once the dancers learned them, together with pliés, they comprised one continuous, roughly forty-minute performed sequence. The teachers stressed the motional values of the warm-ups when they were similar to the technical premise of the day. These similarities lent additional depth in performing the stretches.

During this warm-up period, the dancers could keep their sweat clothing on if they chose, as their bodies warmed up and broke a sweat. Then the class stood up unencumbered by warm-up clothes, so that the teacher could observe their bodies and make corrections and the dancers could better sense their own action and line.

Since the dimensions of the body were the first principle to be explored, it was essential to establish a "room architecture" and forward orientation, and to maintain this throughout the class. The forward orientation of the body and that of the room were not always the same. The room's (or eventually the stage's) forward orientation could be changed but the body always maintained a constant forward direction. Once the architectural forward orientation was established, the body could then be related to it. This was also the beginning practice of stage directions. The room had a down and upstage depending on how the teacher wished it to be.

After the in-place alignment, the teacher reviewed the plié and relevé series. The dancers performed the movements radiating out into the dimensions of the room or stage and projected them through the forward wall and out into the imagined audience and further out to the back of the auditorium. Open pliés were pressed out into space, and closed positions were performed from the "in place" positions. The dancers followed the pliés with plié position jumps. At this point the teacher introduced the premise of the class and the dancers explored it technically. Swings, turns, under-over curves, and any areas that needed careful analyses were clarified before developing them spatially across-the-floor.

Across-the-floor dealt with the premise of the day. The teacher explained and clarified this, and developed space, time, shape, and motional qualities while the dancers were moving across the floor. The teacher introduced grain during pliés.

The class was divided into lines, depending on the size of the class. Leaders changed every day. The rhythmic count of the phrase determined when the next groups began. The phrase began on the right foot going one way and on the left going back. These simple directives helped the coherency of the class and pulled together some of the more undisciplined minds. It also made it easier for the teacher to see where basic orientation corrections were necessary.

It was advisable, I found, to learn each student's first name so that I could make corrections while they were doing the movement. I often called them by the color of their clothing or some other distinguishing sign when I couldn't think of their name quickly.

A very important thing to remember is that students do not know what they look like when they are dancing. They do not know what others see. Corrections are much more pertinent if they are made while the dancer is moving. It helps to alert the dancer both to what they are doing wrongly and how they can correct themselves while they are moving. Making corrections en route can be more effective than thinking about them afterward.

A movement was wrong only because it was not applicable to the premise or was contrary to what was called for. That same wrong movement might be perfect in another context, however. Right and wrong are relative.

The movement phrase is developed with basic locomotor action. Directions, levels, and under-over curves, turns, circles, air work, stop and go, and rhythms and variations of body parts are all added for challenge and interest. These across-the-floor patterns grow in complexity as the form develops and as the teacher introduces material. Finding the kinetics of the movement phrase is an important objective to pursue.

Going across-the-floor in every class acclimates the student to the sensation of moving through space, so that space becomes an automatic concern as the movement phrase develops.

In the beginning, before they have gained skills, dancers will feel a bit shortchanged with only walking as a test of their great *terpsichorean* abilities. But let them know that repetition and the clarity of execution makes for clarity of communication. I should also remind the teachers that the classes should be challenging on every technical level.

Generally, classes ended with runs, leaps, and jumps, leaving the students with warm, flushed, and exhilarated bodies.

Unique Gesture

This is not a "how-to" book. It is an in-depth investigation into the mysterious amalgam of physical and sentient factors that comprise the instrument of the dancer. The investigation is layered. As each layer is reached, the results allow the search to go deeper.

Unique means exactly that: one of a kind. All the factors that comprise the identity of an individual—physical, psychological, emotional, imagination, upbringing, social and so on—combine in various degrees to create a singular person with a singular mind and imagination.

THE BODY AS AN INSTRUMENT

Long before man developed language, before he began to travel the road from artifact to art, before he talked about the meaning of life, rationalized his gift to create beauty or advanced his higher, sophisticated theories of art, he was already functioning as an artist. The life within him was already creating miracles of abstract beauty.

The cell, that marvel of logic and beauty, was operating on a nonverbal course of abstract achievement.

All of man's arts are extensions of himself, either knowingly or instinctually. With music, the course of blood through the heart valves is the basis of the most complex rhythms and of the simplest blues line. The dance is also there, urgent and restless, along with the painter's need for colors, both garish and soothing. The chromosome instinctively enacts a ritual as awesome and complex as any religious ceremony.

The brain, that poor latent development, has been spending its time since its tardy ascendance to prominence catching up to the wisdom of the rest of the body, and making such a hullabaloo about it that it has often obscured many of the things the body already knew about itself, both sentiently and inherently.

Let us say, to make a point, that the body is 1,000,000 years old. The brain began its distinguishing development about 100,000 years ago; recorded history began about 30,000 years ago and the science of the mind about 5,000 years ago. A person reaches some degree of intellectual maturity by the age of twenty-five. How meager is our lifetime of experience when compared to the 100,000 years of experience imbued within us, and how presumptuous to think we know more about anything than our body does. We must,

therefore, think of our body as an entity that is entitled to its own identity. The history of man is written in his cells. This represents an enormous individual computer bank of experience to draw from creatively.

Man's fears, instincts, pleasures, wit—his potential personality—lie within him waiting to be formed and developed by fate, chance, and society. Both the known and the unknown reside there as well. In class, all this will be investigated in some form and to some degree.

The body comes equipped with a skeletal structure, which is not without flaws, but is nevertheless a remarkable engineering feat.

The body has a nervous system that allows man to communicate with other living matter, within himself and outside in other things both visible and invisible, known and unknown. It motivates the brain as well as confuses it. The body's muscular system provides maximum mobility at minimum effort, once man learns how to use the bodily machine. This system allows him to provide for himself and others. And buried deeply within all these, lodged mostly somewhere within the cellular structure, are the senses. Our human uniqueness lies in what our perceptions have gathered from the senses. Each person has embedded deeply within himself a heritage of sentient history as old as life itself. A person, who thinks and responds through his senses, is a sentient person.

His mistrust of the night, his confidence in the day, his recoiling from an unfamiliar sight or touch, and his reaction to color and sound, are basic sentient responses. Most of his pleasures and dislikes, and much of his confusion with life, often rest in the discrepancy between his intellect and his perceptions.

* * *

It is said that no machine has ever been invented that does not imitate the mechanical facility of the human body.

Specifically, the human body consists of a basic nomenclature. There are the chest and hips, which constitute the central and powerful torso. From this center emanate the extremities of the head and the neck, which provide its fluency;

the arms, which are joined at the shoulders to the torso; the arms as the sum total of the upper arm, the elbow, the forearm, the wrist, the hand, and its digits; and the legs, which include the thighs, knees, shins, and feet. The legs begin from their lodging in the hip socket.

This is roughly the general physical material that the dancer has to work with.

Rounding out these body parts are the next layers of muscles, ligaments, bones, organs, and the brain.

Lending further richness to this is the imagination housed in the brain and in the memory banks, which are buried in the muscles and cells. We can dig deeper still and find the artistic and aesthetic potential that rests within the body. In dance art it is this deep area we are concerned with.

The suitability of the body for the art of motion is greatly dependant on its structure as an axial instrument. The body, with its hinges and axles, enables us to carry out most of life's functions. Rudolph von Laban roughly classified the mechanics of these hinges and axles in three categories: peripheral, rotary, and locomotor.

In the peripheral, the body unit attached at one end allows the outer end to describe a periphery in space. In the rotary, the axle structure of the body and its other units allow rotation like a barber pole_that is, rotating within its own space. In locomotor action the whole body may shift to a new space, or in isolation, can shift from side to side, or forward and back. So, too, the chest and the hip. Labanotation analyzes movement on this basis using symbols to record them.

Yet this is only the bare beginning of aesthetic motional involvement. Dance is considered a kinetic art. In the joints, tendons, and tissues, the organs of kinesthesia sense and inform us of the degree of flexion, extension, and/or rotation of the body parts affected. This may not seem so astonishing except when one realizes that a great pianist playing a Beethoven sonata lifts, strikes, and presses keys at not only great speeds but also in various degrees of pressure, bringing about subtleties of tone that transcend the gross term *mechanics*. But how little the dancer practices such nuances. Even here we have only begun to explore the body as an instrument of aesthetic motion.

Obviously there is an intercommunication between mind and body, which we mostly take for granted: the mind sending the dance instructions to the body. Less often acknowledged is the reverse process: how a physical action sends a sentient response back to the brain. It is this process that is usually neglected in dance training methods.

The mind stimulates the body to action. It can also impede action by reservation and social censorship. Just as important, however, is the reverse process in which a strongly sensed action made by the body, or by any of its parts, can stimulate the memory bank of the mind, causing a revelation which might otherwise not be released.

Between these processes, mind to body and body to mind, there is a vast network of senses and controls. In order to fathom this complex network, we must recognize that the mind is a huge warehouse and storage place of the memory banks, not only of the input of the individual's experience and knowledge but also of his genetic heritage. All this knowledge and experience shapes his actions and general behaviorism. The dance artist must have access to this memory bank, perhaps in even greater depth than those in other artistic professions. We know that entry is made possible through numerous recall processes. But access is one thing and the selection of material from the memory bank and its arrangement on the body to communicate aesthetically is another.

We can be in awe of the human body in recalling how Isadora Duncan, in a dance performance of *La Marseillaise* at Carnegie Hall, progressed from a reclining position on the floor to a standing position with arms upraised. As the curtain came down, the audience roared and rushed to the stage to be near the miracle—to be close to and absorb the last moments of her incredible performance. We wonder what degrees of bends and rotations she coordinated in such a way as to lift a whole audience to this ecstatic response.

Obviously, many other factors were involved besides anatomical ones.

THE DIMENSIONAL CONCEPT

The human body comes in all shapes and sizes—some tall and thin, others short and wide, and so forth. Except for extraordinary deviations, we can usually describe bodies somewhat roughly as being so high, so wide, and so deep (meaning forward to back, not depth). We can say the same of a milk carton, a house, or an ocean liner. These designations applied to the human body, however, offer the student and teacher a mutually understandable vocabulary and a means to correct and add to the dancer's technique.

To remain erect and achieve his height dimension, the dancer must furnish an upward energy that counteracts gravity. The dancer must project himself above the gravity pull by imaginatively devising an upward force. He has a built-in mechanism—an innate sense of well-being, a spirit, a vitality—that he can use to accomplish this height. This need not be thought of as a mystical power but rather as a status quo that aids him in fulfilling his height dimension. I have already referred to the body's aura, which involves the realization that the dancer must project himself into the area above him.

This projection needs to be accomplished through the sternum, which holds up the body's skeleton: if the sternum does not fulfill this task, then it is likely that the shoulders will take over. When this happens, negative posture occurs, which will cause difficulties in the mobility of the arms. Most important is the projection of a vertical line beginning from the balls of the feet and continuing through the legs, hips, chest, and head, and up into vertical space above the head.

At this point, the dancer should begin to sense linear body line, a very simplified form of the sculptural body line he will later enact. This is an imaginary line, which does not exist until the dancer establishes it. The significance of the space above the dancer's head cannot be overemphasized. Failure to project upward causes upward space to go dead, and a great loss of kinetic projection results.

This height dimension is fundamental to the dancer. If it is not given importance, it is likely that gravity will take over. The dancer must learn to use gravity as a push-off and helpmate rather than as an anchor and a detrimental force.

The dimensional concept does not stop at verticality. Horizontality also comes into play. We refer to its dimension as width and depth. Width involves sideward right and sideward left. Depth concerns itself with forward and backward.

In the stasis standing position, all of these directions are equalized. If any one direction becomes more powerful than another, restraining tensions develop, or the figure is pulled into that direction. The dancer's control of these multiple directions contributes to his technical development.

In a vertical stance, the dancer radiates equally in all directions. In locomotion, he purposely releases opposite forces of radial energy that cause him to move in any direction he may choose.

Dance as the art of motion is, among other things, the architectural design of directions.

The simplest directional control is the act of going forward. Forward is a horizontal venture into space. The following is an example of how easily horizontal can be confused by conditioning. I had a young student in class who was rather tiny. When supposedly going forward, she persisted in turning her head upward and looking into the space several feet above her horizontal destination. It took me days to discover the reason for this discrepancy. This tiny young lady was a talented, aspiring organist who spent five hours daily practicing on a huge organ console, where the music rack was set at a considerable distance above her head. Five hours a day of such a visual exercise convinced her brain that upward went along with the direction of forward.

Any misalignment in the vertical stance by any body part is visible. We can approach correcting this by using a method that refers to our ordinary language of dimension. The body may be roughly conceived as a rectangular three-dimensional bulk having height, width, and depth. This rectangular form has a front, mainly because of the placement of eyes, nose, and mouth, and sensitive areas of the trunk, which also give a psychological determination to front and forward. These dimensions and directions provide a specific frame of reference for relating to both the physical form of the body and to its surrounding space.

Because the physical body is also the instrument of the mind, we can begin to check on the performer's capability of agreement in these dimensions. That is, one can now ask, does the concept of height in the performer's mind agree with his actual physical state of height? At the beginning of training, such agreement is rare.

The other dimensions may be checked in the same manner. The failure of agreement in one dimension usually takes a corresponding toll on the others. A failure in height will affect width and depth, as well.

This is the basis of a performer's abstract script—abstract, yet specific. One must acquire the skill of matching or tuning the body and space to the mind.

Much more rests within this concept of dimensional tuning, which will be extended considerably in later explanations. At the moment, we are concerned with a status quo, a selected neutral point from which specific measurement can be practiced. This neutral point is a standing stasis.

When standing in stasis, we strive for fulfillment of dimension. We avoid narrow vision, one-sidedness and the like, and search for wholeness. Wholeness implies the full projection of height, width, and depth, by the mind and through the body into space. In terms of the performer, it means full presence of mind in a fully enlivened body in a three-dimensionally enriched space. This full projection actually radiates in all directions—not only deep, high, and wide, but diagonally and tilted as well. The dimensional terms are the most convenient to use as a framework of reference.

More needs to be explored in relation to the dynamics of the space or environment as it contributes to the performer's "presence." We may conceive of the performer's surrounding space as a psychical spatial aura because it is a volume of space that is affected by the mind of the person present in it.

The mind that practices this spatial control is stimulated far more precisely by the thought of outward projection than by the thought of inward receptivity.

In effect, then, we can conceive of an active perceptional and/or projectional aura surrounding the body as far into space as our senses can effectively penetrate.

Despite our lack of knowledge regarding how we perceive space, direction, and time, we know that the act of presence includes an awareness of all of them.

ALIGNMENT

TOTAL BODY ALIGNMENT

The body is a three-dimensional object. It has height, width, and depth. The purpose of alignment is to maintain the fullness of these proportions. A weakening of these proportions indicates a weakness of inner strength. The mind or psychical participation is necessary to enliven the body fully. Throughout this aligning process, the interior factors, such as the will, constantly feed the body to gain its full three-dimensionality.

THE LEGS

For a quick alignment, let us start with the legs. We must sense the difference between parallel and turned-out legs, the distinctive sensations that rest in the degree of thigh rotation.

The placement of the feet in parallel position is, granted, the natural position the legs would assume if they hung freely from the hips. But since we are preparing the body for an artistic venture, we must prepare it artificially and rotate the thighs or turn them out to facilitate a wider base on the floor for additional balance and for higher extensions of the legs. This turn-out degree will allow the dancer to work either turned in or out. This outward rotation also allows the hips to press further forward and to open further.

The "turnout" is a rotary action of the thighs. The legs reach their furthest degree of operable rotation with the first turn-out gesture. The feet do not continue forcing turnout after the thighs arrive at their capacity. It is through persistent practice and eventual strength, that the thigh is gradually forced to turn out further.

From this point on, the knees, arches, and ball of the feet assume the responsibility of the leg action. The knees direct themselves over the ball of the foot, and the arches are lifted as a result of the knees turning out.

To sense and strengthen the arch muscles, practice the knees rolling in and out as the toes press the floor, and see and feel how the knees control the lifting and lowering of the arches. The teacher should constantly remind the students to lift their arches.

THE HIPS

The hips are a major and vital part of the modern dancer's power and torso strength. In modern dance the abdomen and hips were once claimed as the seat of the emotions. In Shakespeare's time, so was the liver. Times obviously change.

The hips, because of their structure, do not have a clearly defined forward and backward, side and side. What constitutes the bulk of the hip should first be determined and sensed by the dancer. To define the front of the hip, I ask the dancer to place the heel of his hand on top of the pelvic bone and stretch his fingers downward. Where the fingertips end constitutes roughly the front of the hip. The area the hand covers includes the hip thigh joining, which with training is stretched, lengthened, and "opened" to facilitate the fullness of the forward hip.

When the hip is fully pressed forward, a turned-out rotation occurs, which relates the hip to the thigh rotation, so that the rotation of the thigh and the opening of the hips occur simultaneously.

The back of the hip requires an awareness of another sort. Here the lower vertebrae create and control the backwardness of the hips. To sense and isolate this lower spine area, you should spend a bit of time daily in isolating the lower vertebrae (lumbar area). Begin this isolation during stretches, while lying on the floor, by pressing the lower spine down without tilting the hips up. The lower spine stretches so that the hip vertebrae can be isolated. This can be practiced standing against a wall as well. Gaining a fluidity of pressing the lower area of the spine backward without tilting the hip is essential in isolating the back of the hip. Lifting the abdomen can also facilitate lower spine isolation.

In moving sideward, the dancer should be careful not to break and lift the hip from its placement and tilt backward and up. To ensure accurate sideward movement, the hip always has a forward pressure, so that the hip can easily shift within the front side-to-side slot while pressing forward.

In the forward diagonals, the hip presses both forward and sideward to achieve the in-between diagonals. The same is done for the backward diagonals.

When the hips move backward, the muscles in the abdominal area lift and allow the hip its limited backward locomotor range. The hip does not tuck under; it locomotes as a unit into a backward space.

THE ABDOMEN

The abdomen connects the chest to the hips and as such must be regarded as equally important.

As the hips are pressed forward, the abdomen lifts, swelling the chest.

The abdominal muscles help support the chest lift.

The "abs," as the connection of the hips to the chest, because of their elasticity also help to separate these parts so that they can both move independently of each other.

It is important to use these muscles without locking them. Breathing is still essential. The premise here is "lifting the abs," not holding the breath. Dancers, in their attempt to contract the size of their stomachs, often squeeze the stomach muscles instead of lifting them.

THE CHEST

The dimensional identity of the chest is fairly simple compared to the head and hips. The back of the neck and head contain certain tensions, and the lower spine, which constitutes the back of the hips, contains other baggage. Both ends of the spine have to be stretched and lengthened and the accumulated tensions at both ends released to let the body have a clear, linear, and open voice.

The front of the chest and the sternum have other responsibilities. The sternum, in particular, has to supply the spirit and willpower to keep the body lifted. It cannot collapse and yield to the downward power of gravity. The sternum suspends the body, and the willpower, part of the psyche, is reflected in this upward thrust.

The dimensions of the chest are identified by the upper rib cage, not by a protruding lower rib cage. This upper area is crowned by the sternum, which pinpoints its upwardness, and in locomotion its forwardness. Backward is spread evenly across the whole back surface outward from the upper spine.

The diagonals forward are a little more complicated. Here the pectoral muscles come into play. As the sternum lifts, the "pecs" roll out or open to present a broad sounding board of the chest—on which many nuances of action will later be played,

particularly during diagonal action—and suspension points.

Sideward going requires the arms to lift a bit and expose some space so that the sides of the chest can be seen moving sideward without the arms interfering or covering the action.

THE HEAD

The head has the most difficulty in overcoming directional orientation because it houses the eccentric nature of the face. One has to ignore the intrusions of distracting emotions and tensions, and think of the head as a body part, with the spine and neck on which it balances as supporting features.

The eyes are not the top of the head, nor are the forehead or brow. The top of the head is the top of the head. The lengthening of the spine as it enters the skull helps to identify the top by giving the head a sense of its backward length. To demonstrate this, release the back neck muscles and let the head fall back, which raises the chin a bit. Then lower the chin, as the back muscles lift, and the head returns to place. The eyes play an important role in the clarity of head placement. Let the head fall back again and feel the eye looking forward down the nose as the eyelid lowers. Again, lower the chin to place and feel the eyelid forced to lift to allow the eye to look forward. As the eye opens, feel the whole face open and the sides of the temples pull back. Strengthening the lifted eyelid is essential to an alert face.

The ears represent the sideward of the head, and with the face front we have the dimensional setup of the head. Balancing the head is not a simple matter of directional alignment, however, but more a challenge of balancing the mind and spirit within the head. Throughout his years of training, the teacher will constantly be reminding the dancer to "lower the chin," "lift the eyelids," and "open the face."

For a tactile sense of the top of the head reaching upward, the long-prescribed act of balancing a book on the head helps to identify this direction quickly.

To keep the eyes and focus from thrusting the head too far forward, form an image of the eye starting from the back of the head and looking through two long corridors to reach the front of the face. This image gives the eye something to do so that it doesn't get stuck in place and stare.

Although the vertical position appears upright, in reality there are three possibilities offered:
1. *Standing with the weight on the heels is a pedestrian position, where there is no concern other than simply standing. The body is resting, slightly backward.*
2. *Standing with the weight equally balanced between toes and heels—in place.*
3. *Standing with the weight forward, ready to go.*

Physically oriented people, such as boxers, dancers, or tennis players, have to be primed to move quickly and are acutely aware of timing and speed. To shift the weight from the heels to the toes can make us lose as much as half a beat and put the dancer behind the beat. Keeping the weight forward demonstrates an alert body, ready to release itself instantly into any direction.

To lift and "open" the face, relate the arches of the feet to the face. As the arches lift, so do the face muscles. This also gears the entire body as a unit toward opening and presenting the front of the body.

WEIGHT PLACEMENT

With the body aligned and in vertical we come to an essential factor in dance preparation: the matter of weight placement.

In vertical posture, we conceive of the sternum as the point on the upper body that holds up the spine like a string of beads. This sternum point holds itself up and if you imagined a plumb line hanging from that point, the line would drop right over a point midway between the balls of the feet.

Think of the foot as having three areas of placement: (1) The front (ball and toes), (2) in place (weight centered), and (3) back (weight on the heels).

Simple as a shift of weight might be, it's the difference between a car with the ignition off, turned on, or in gear waiting for gas. The shift of weight from back to forward can greatly influence timing. With the weight forward, one can step on the beat; with the weight back, half a beat is lost shifting the weight forward though center, before one can take the step. The mind is also apt to fall behind the movement if the weight is not forward.

The weight is kept forward with the heels reaching downward. The body is primed and alert and waiting to move.

This is why dancers, boxers, tennis players, and other athletic people who depend on timing keep their weight forward when engaged in their activity. When they are in a pedestrian mode, as people generally are, they walk with their weight on their heels. Pedestrians are not concerned with time or stepping on the beat. Dancers are.

Once a dancer understands the complexity of rolling the legs out, pressing the hips forward, lifting the abs, opening the chest, reaching high with the head: all of these directions should be achieved with one word: 'turnout.' The body radiates in all directions and the dancer says, "This is me." Aware, alert, clear-eyed, and ready to go.

After the teacher presents this detailed arrangement of the body, the class should quickly make a daily review to prepare the body for pliés, dimensional fulfillment, and locomotion into space.

So as not to overwhelm the student by this complicated placement all at once, each class should offer further insight and detail about the range and pliancy of the body. The steady understanding and achievement of the motional range of the body is perhaps what dance training is all about.

Dance training depends on the rate and speed of the body to grow and the mind to mature. A degree of forcing is necessary. This is called persistence. Dancers, like musicians, are noted for their discipline.

With pliés, the dancer will begin to move into space, pressing into the space around him, which is defined by extending his physical dimensional size, up and down, sideward left and right, and forward and back.

REMINDERS

It is advised that you read the entire lesson plan through to grasp all of the ramifications of the premise. Notes in each week can apply similarly to technique, improvisation, and composition. The totality of all three of these aspects unites the Nikolais/Louis approach.

Once a pattern of movement is set, adhere strictly to it. Accuracy in time, space, and shape will be a constant technical challenge for the class. Performing a phrase repeatedly will develop skill and sensitivity. The teacher should repeat crits and suggestions from class to class.

If the teacher does not demonstrate, they should point out students who have success with a movement phrase. Visual demonstration is important and can expedite explanations.

THE STRETCHES

The purposes of stretches is to warm, limber, and stretch the body in preparation for dancing. The dancer's mindset differs in this endeavor from the one he has when he is coming across the floor, improvising, choreographing, or performing. The focus here is generally directed toward the body parts and how they function. Afterward, space, shape, time and motion play a more significant role in coloring the movement and decentralizing the thinking.

Hanya Holm and Joseph Pilate originally designed the stretches; however, through the years as the technique was defined we added to and reordered them. We have also elaborated on them.

What is presented here is the most recent version of the stretches. Again, they are presented for the purpose of warming, limbering, and stretching, and their order can vary for whatever purposes the teacher chooses.

These stretches do not constitute the nature of the Nikolais/Louis technique. The technique is defined by being able to bring totality through shape, space, time, and kinetic motional fullness to movement. A characteristic of the stretches in this technique is the lengthening process: legs out of hips, reaching and lengthening into space, and in always considering the space in which the stretches occur.

The material presented in this stretch section is flexible and should serve whatever technical and performing style the dancer might be involved with.

The stretch warm-ups are the first part of the technique class. Bear in mind that dance classes

Lengthening into space. Artist-in-Schools, St. Louis, 1968.
Photo by T. Mike Fletcher.

are bound by a time frame and the stretches and pliés should not exceed more than forty minutes of an hour-and-a-half-long class. If the stretches become lengthy, then the class becomes a stretch class, which is occasionally perfectly valid to explore the shape and motional details of the exercises, especially on very hot days when the muscles are warm, relaxed, and the spirit is a bit laid-back.

Stretching involves various tempos. Some are slow and sustained and others ride on a persistent beat. Nik's classes were accompanied by percussion sounds, primarily drums. The teachers played them so that they could better control the tempo of the class. They could stop quickly to allow for criticisms and give new directions, and they could be insistent and drive and push the class. They could be rhythmically compelling and concise without the necessary harmonic overtones and phrasing of the piano, which tend to soften energy values. I, on the contrary, talked out the stretches and clapped my hands for pulse, as I walked through the room and made physical corrections and reminded the class of the subtleties within the stretches. I did not get to the drums until pliés.

Warm-ups deal with strength and stretch. Some people are muscularly tight, while others are released. Released and muscularly loose people must work for strength to control their stretch, while muscularly tight dancers must work to gain muscular release. Tight dancers work for an ability to release tension and with steady doing, do gain a greater stretch capacity.

It helps if both teacher and dancer share a basic anatomical vocabulary. *Abdominals* (abs), *pectorals* (pecs), *sternum, Achilles tendon, gluteus* (gluts),

and so on. Those who teach introductory students may wish to review this.

Lengthening out of the body: legs should always be reaching and lengthening out of the hip socket. Arms and head long and reaching out into space. Think long muscles, not thick, chunky, tight muscles. This long and out thinking suggests decentralization as opposed to the thick centralized focus. Always consider the space around the stretching body.

These stretches were executed on the floor so that the dancer did not have to deal with the ever-present forces of gravity that come with standing. Nikolais began his series with an awareness and release to gravity: lying on the back, beginning by lifting the body part away form the gravity pull and releasing to it and sensing the totality of the body part. Then he proceeded with the longer stretch series.

Lying on the floor was also a way to sense how the downward pull of gravity was evident on the entire body surface. It allowed the lengthening grain of the vertical through the aligned body to flow uninterrupted from head to toe through the spine. Spinal corrections were also easier to make and the stretched toe was constantly applicable.

I began more simply and more physically. In a beginning sitting position, we began with slapping the face, head, neck, torso, and the inside of thighs to awaken the body to focus on movement and the class, calling the bodily sensitivities from their pedestrian concerns to their presence in class.

These stretches come to as much of a warm-up series as I care to state. Some classes began with running, some with a swing series. The order of the warm-ups was considerably varied.

WARM-UPS—THE STRETCHES

The stretch series is a complex one. Introduce and explain stretches gradually. Keep in mind the warm-ups and plié series have a forty-minute time limit, and be judicious as to how you divide the time.

We begin by sitting with folded knees to the side—soles of feet touching. (Illus. 1)

Slap face, neck, chest, and so on, to awaken the sensitive parts of the body and draw focus and attention of the mind to the warming-up process.

Illustration 1

Each gesture in three counts:

1. Lower spine tilts back and releases to gravity, back rounds.

2. Lift torso up into vertical and then over the feet.

3. Keep low while pressing the lower spine through, rise up to vertical.

4. Arch back—squeeze shoulders back, forcing front of chest to open. Return to vertical.

5. Round the spine to the R.—return up to vertical—and round to the L.—return to vertical.

Repeat (4 sets)

Whenever the foot is free, keep the toes stretched.

For most stretches, return to vertical between directional change. Vertical is your point of departure and arrival. Vertical in all instances means lengthening out of the head, whether in an upright or horizontal position.

BOUNCE SERIES

We use the word *bounce* here to define the rebound action of the gesture. Bouncing returns the body to its beginning position so that the action, whatever it may be, can be repeated. Bouncing as such does not stretch a muscle but can, to a degree, warm it.

As with all physical action, a certain degree of intelligence and precaution must be applied to stretches. Violently wrenching any part of the body can injure it. Forcing a cold muscle into an extreme physical act is sure to result in injury. The warming-up series must be done carefully and intelligently.

Each gesture in three counts:

(1 set) Head bounces forward—side R.—back—side L.—Head swings forward and around. Repeat left side through each point.

(1 set) Upper back drops forward and bounces—rise—up to vertical—R. pectoral presses up—sternum presses through—L. pectoral presses up—upper body swings a full circle passing through each point.

Reverse to other side.

(These points are also the chest suspension points.)

(1 set) Whole back drops forward from waist, with weight three bounces each point—R. lower side (R. arm overhead to L. side)—body arched backward—L. lower side (L. arm overhead to R. side).

Reverse to other side.

Whole torso swings R. around in four counts. Passing through each point—and arms swing as well—throwing weight forward to gain centrifugal force.

Reverse to other side.

Sitting up, lengthen arms overhead—slowly release torso forward. (Illus. 2)

Illustration 2

Two counts each position:

1. Drop forward with rounded back.

2. Swing arms up and straighten back from lower spine to head with straight arms overhead.

3. Pulse arms up and open and arch back, hands behind on floor. (Illus. 3)

4. Head back forcing sternum through and up (repeat 4×).

5. Arrive in opening position.

Illustration 3

Swing hips under and forward with weight on feet and hands—swing hips back and under—stretching rib cage. (2×) On last swing under—keep hips under and lower back down to floor. Lower spine carefully to floor, each vertebrae lowering separately up through neck. Arrive with arms to side—knees to side—soles of feet together. Gently bounce knees, keeping lower spine pressed down.

FLEX-EXTEND SERIES

Keeping back straight, extend legs down and rotated out. Lower spine to floor, toes reaching long and out. Flex and reach with whole body (in 2, out 2). Understand where all the flexors and joints are: ankles, knees, hip joints, arms, and elbows. The quality is feeling the motion flow from flexing in and graining into the body to extending and lengthening out and reaching into space. (4×) (Illus. 4)

Illustration 4

With body long and lengthened, stretch the right side long then the left side, exaggerating torso sideward curve. Assemble. (Illus. 5)

Extend legs out and long and rotated out—back flat to floor.

Pull R. knee to chin as L. leg keeps its length.

TUGS SERIES

Preparation: pull R. knee to chin as L. leg keeps its length. (Illus. 6)

Illustration 5

Be aware of the pulling from the hip joint continuously throughout entire series.

Illustration 6

Each gesture in four counts:

1. Tug R. knee up to chest.

2. Tug leg across chest keeping the lower spine down against knee. (Illus. 7)

3. Tug knee out to R. side under R. arm, against L. leg rotation out.

4. Place R. bent leg across the L. leg above knee height and bounce. (Illus. 8)

5. Continuing bounce—lift L. knee up. (On the walk) Continue bent R. leg bounce. (Illus. 9)

6. Press hips up—continue knee bounce through series.

7. (Change time to sustained four counts.) Extend R. leg up to straight—kick leg back over head. (4×) (Illus. 10)

8. Surge up with R. stretched, lengthen it down and forward in circular peripheral to low—while hips are pressed through and up (tap stretched foot 4× to floor). (Illus. 11)

Raise R. leg up to ceiling, two counts. Lower back to floor through the spine, two counts. Open R. leg to side, two counts, and reach out strongly into a peripheral quarter-circle down to place, four counts. Feel the stretched legs new length.

Lift L. knee and repeat series on the other side.

TWENTY-FOUR

Alternating legs twenty-four times—knees to head and extended out. (Illus. 12)

Extend the leg stretched off the floor, one count.

Both knees up to chin, two counts, and extend long, two counts, on extension both hands behind head, supporting it as leg beats, four counts. Repeat

Illustration 7

Illustration 8

Illustration 9

Illustration 10

Illustration 11

Illustration 12

four sets. On fifth set, arms, head, and upper back lift so there is no contact to floor and abs carry the weight for sixteen leg beats. (Illus. 13)

Big breath and collapse. Roll over to R. side in preparation of hip-leg flex-extension series.

Prepare hip-leg series. (Illus. 14)

Weight on R. side—body long and flat. Bend both legs at knee.

Turned-out L. leg, bend at knee with foot in front of R. bent back knee.

Illustration 13

HIP PRESS SERIES

1. Hips pressed forward. Upper body maintains length L. hand on floor in front to keep balance.

Illustration 14

2. Eight counts, hip presses forward. Eight counts, L. knee presses back and open forcing hips further forward. Eight counts, both press, open with leg—forward with hips. Eight counts, slow steady press to open hips still further.

3. L. arm swings forward and over head to touch sole of R. foot. Body twists proportionately, four counts. Arm swings back over head and back to place—L. arm defines peripheral curve low to floor, four counts. (2×) (Illus. 15)

Illustration 15

4. L. knee turns in and bounces off R. knee, two counts. (Illus. 16) L. knee turns out and knee is lifted up to head, two counts. (Repeat series 4×) (Illus. 17)

5. L. leg lifts from knee and extends up sideward, four counts. L. hand holds turned out L. leg and tugs straight leg in 4× while pressing hip forward.

Illustration 16

6. Repeat seven-count series double time, one count each gesture.

   L. leg bends and toe touches R. knee. (Done to exacting pizzicato pulse.) (Illus. 18)

   L. leg extends (up).

   L. leg bends toe to R. knee.

Illustration 17

Illustration 18

L. leg turns in bent and knee to knee.

L. leg rolls out bent to the back.

L. leg extends turned out backward as L. arm reaches forward.

(Illus. 19)

L. leg bends knee to knee.

Repeat.

Remain on the side. Hold the extended L. leg up by holding the ankle area to force the leg lift and height. Make sure the leg is turned out in the hip socket. (Illus. 20)

This is a simple way of demonstrating the hips and leg joint relationship in the turnout of the leg:

> The pelvis bone has slots on both sides. Try to place the leg in those slots so that the raised leg does not hit the pelvic bone and tilt it. With the leg operating freely in the slot, it can be raised to a considerably higher degree.

> Move the leg around until it finds the slot and allows the leg to fit into and lift higher effortlessly.

> Anatomically, the *acetabulor tossa* (hip) and the head of the femur (leg) are involved.

Tug the straight leg, eight counts.

Illustration 19

Illustration 20

DROP KICKS

Release the straight leg down (drop) and kick (throw) the leg up. Maintain the sideward torso placements. (4×) (Illus. 21)

Arm and leg swing in opposition.

Maintaining sideward position,

> L. leg drops across to forward—L. arm back. Torso twisted—leg swings down to back (Illus. 22), four counts.

> Leg bends behind and swing continues forward as L. toe passes R. knee and extends to forward (repeats). L. arm starts back and swings down to forward arrive overhead to back. (Repeat 4×, emphasizing the 1 count as a throw.)

Illustration 21

Illustration 22

FLEX-EXTEND IN SIDEWARD SERIES

Preparation: Flex knee and, as the leg extends, press the hips forward. As a general rule every time the leg extends sideward, it is pressed outward by the hips pressing forward.

Do four sets then four sets double time. (Illus. 23)

Illustration 23

BACKWARD SERIES

Roll over in four counts onto the abdomen with the L. leg continuing flex-extending. Flexed R. toe tucked under for back kicks. (Illus. 24)

Illustration 24

Kick the straight L. leg up four times—bend the knee and kick the leg four times as the upper body arches back. (Illus. 25)

Try to touch toes to head. The hands press the upper body back. (Illus. 26)

Upper body faces floor—arms flat in sideward R. leg keeping extended length. Twist and tap the L. toe to R. extends hand. (4×) Twisting deep in lower back.

Illustration 25

Transition—roll back onto back, aligning the body and roll out extended L. leg up and reaching out from the hip.

FORWARD SERIES

Flex-extend leg up. (4× then double time 4×) (Illus. 27)

Illustration 26

Bend up R. leg, on the walk and drop-kick L. leg.

Drop-kick. (4×) (Illus. 28)

Catch leg inside of lower calf area at end of series. Keeping leg high open out to second, extending R. leg.

In sideward flex-extend L. leg—extending through the toe (4×) at end of fourth time hold the L. leg extended while both arms open in second and head lifts off the floor. (Illus. 29) Support the extended leg with abdominal muscles and the thigh rotations of both legs.

Illustration 27

Hold in this position, four counts. Leg slowly straightened and descends open and out to meet other leg, lengthening out of the hip, four counts, and when it touches R. leg it should be about an inch longer.

Shake legs out and roll to L. side.

Repeat reversing the whole series to L. side.

Illustration 28

LEG SWINGS

The swing is a three-count action.

1. On the back with arms in second to keep the upper body from moving too much during swings—raise R. leg. The extended sideward arms indicate the beginning and end of swing.

Illustration 29

2. Let the straight R. leg drop across the body, touching the extended left arm. (Drop.) (Illus. 30)

Illustration 30

3. The leg drops down and around and open into a swing to touch the R. hand, keeping the hips steady and open. (Swing.)

4. From the arrival point creates a peripheral quarter-circle line as it rises up in preparation to repeat the drop. (4×) (Lift.) (Illus. 31)

Repeat L. leg.

Make all three swing actions distinct: (1) Drop raised leg, (2) swing around, and (3) lift to arrival point. Leg up.

Repeat: change legs to other side.

Reversing the swing

    R. leg drops open to R. hand

    Swings to L. hand

    Lifts to prepare for drop. (4×)

Illustration 31

PREPARATION CHEST LIFTS

Body aligned on the floor, arms in second.

The chest is very pliable but try to concentrate the lift from sternum not lower rib cage.

With a sharp gesture, lift chest to the top of head off the floor. Let side arms support lift (Illus. 32), two counts.

Illustration 32

Lift body and starting from the lower spine, lower chest down to floor, lengthen back of neck. (4×)

Hold last lift and swing arms down across chest then over head high and wide. (4×) (Illus. 33)

Straighten out and align body on floor.

Chest lifts torso over legs (each action in three counts).

    Back rounds down to legs. (Illus. 34)

Illustration 33

    Arms and chest reach out to forward, lower back presses through. (Illus. 35)

    Back rounds down.

    Three counts, lower spine pulls torso down to floor—each vertebra presses floor on descent. (4 sets) End in sitting up position.

Stretch lower back over legs.

Illustration 34

    Round back bounce forward, four counts.

    Straight back forward—lower spine pressed forward—arms reaching out, four counts.

    Gently bounce round back over R. leg. Stretching diagonal L. back. (4×)

    L. arm reaching out diagonally stretching straight back diagonally. (4×)

    Swing over to L. side and repeat steps 3 and 4, two counts.

Illustration 35

Repeat each direction twice, then once with lower back getting more fluid with each repeat.

Feel stretch in lower-back diagonal muscles.

Hips remain on floor and lengthening begins from lower spine forward.

Illustration 36

LOWER BACK TWIST

L. arm crosses legs and holds knee as R. arm swings forward up and back, twisting against lower back. Hips stay on floor offering resistance in a four-count gesture.

Drop. (Illus. 36)

Swing up, arm open chest to ceiling. (Illus. 37)

Press chest up.

Illustration 37

Arm and pectoral open sideward—flat chest—reach side. (Illus. 38)

Change sides. (2×)

SPINE RELEASES SWINGS

Both arms up to R side. On drop for swinging to other side, spine releases down and lifts from lower back up through the spine as arms arrive on other side ready to swing back to other side. (In three counts, 4×) (Illus. 39)

Illustration 38

BREATH RELEASE CONTRACTIONS

Preparation: in sitting position arms in second.

Sharp spine drop—drop, back and down, allowing audible exhalation of breath as back remains low.

Lift torso up—repeat drop—drop, etc.

Time: Drop, drop, and lift.

Repeat 4×.

Illustration 39

SHOULDER STAND

Roll back—round back—throw legs up into air and arrive with hands at each side to support lower back, torso, and legs straight up. Hips pressed forward over head. (Illus. 40)

Those students with extended back or neck-bones should use a towel on the floor to cushion backbones.

Both legs slowly lower down over head to touch the floor (Illus. 41) and up to arrive in vertical. Hips pressed through with legs up. Legs remain down on last descent. Take hold of ankle region as spine pulls itself

Illustration 40

Illustration 41

down. (Illus. 42) The hands keep the legs low and press the spine down as well (this is called the washboard; a towel under spine helps).

Up into shoulder stand.

Repeat washboard position. (4×)

Illustration 42

Throw legs forward. Lengthen over legs, reaching out. Four pulses. Leads to next stretch.

ROLL OVER AND TOUCH SERIES

Roll back and touch floor and roll forward with straight legs, arms reaching forward and out (2×). (Illus. 43) Over and touch again throw forward—legs in second—arms reach out forward (2×). Hold last forward throw and adjust body into position arms and legs in second. Flex and pull wider.

Illustration 43

Hands on floor behind seat—flex just the ankle joint and push the hips forward as foot stretches toe and extends legs wider. (4×)

Pause to stretch into capacity stretch.

Adjust torso between legs. Settle for a moment, then tiptoe forward with fingertips. Keep the width between legs as the torso reaches low and forward. Reach maximum stretch. Relax into stretch, then down on back again. Fold legs up at each side.

Prepare for bridge.

BRIDGE

Preparation: Start lying on the back. Legs bent at the side. Hands if possible holding the ankles, otherwise palms pressed down on the floor as close to ankles as possible. (1) Press the hips and thighs up, four counts. (Illus. 44) Making sure the rib cage does not release itself upward, descend with lower spine leading and press vertebrae successively down to the floor.

Illustration 44

Floor stretches—hips through.
Artist-in-Schools, St. Louis, 1968.
Photo by T. Mike Fletcher.

(Repeat 3×). (2) On fourth time, release and stretch the rib cage pressing up as far as possible (Illus. 45). (3) Bring hands up and place on each side of ears. (4) Shift weight on hands and feet and arch body up. Shift weight from hands to feet. (5) Center weight and lift right leg to the ceiling. Flex at knee—extend twice (Illus. 46)—put leg down and lift left leg—repeat. (6) Lower body to floor—hug knees to chest. And lengthen lower spine. Stretch long forward and roll over face down.

Illustration 45

This stretch is a dance step inscribed in an ancient Egyptian tomb/ temple. Do you realize how many centuries of dancers have been groaning over this stretch?

INTO ROLL OVER AND TOUCH, SWING AROUND AND REACH SERIES

Begin body facing floor legs stretched. R. leg lifts ready to roll over and touch.

Illustration 46

Eight-count series—each gesture in two counts.

1. Roll over to sitting with R. leg on the walk. Torso drops close to bent leg touching the floor with the bent R. elbow. Hips pulled back. (Illus. 47)

2. Swing around and through. R. arm swings out into peripheral circle as hip press up supported by L. arm on floor. (Illus. 48)

3. Hips pull back to sitting position stretching abdomen and chest and bringing elbows to floor before R. knee. (Illus. 49)

Illustration 47

4. Roll over and change with torso low and hips pressed forward. As hips and torso face floor. Change legs and L. leg bends back for rollover.

Repeat other side and repeat series 2×.

Repeat series 2× double time. Persist in exact execution at speed.

Make sure the whole torso is active during this stretch, particularly the hips, and that the elbow reaches forward enough to touch the floor in front of foot of bent leg.

One might think of this stretch as: hip back sitting—hip through push through—hip back sitting—hip through roll over.

Illustration 48

R. leg is folded back and torso faces left leg. (1) Arms reach forward. (four pulses) R. arm swings forward, up and back as L. arm slides out sideward. (2) Lowering body to floor, hold there eight counts. (3) Roll over and reverse. (4) Roll over into second with torso centered. (5) R. arm overhead. Touch L. leg—L. arm crosses body—bounce up to vertical. Repeat 4×. Repeat tiptoe with fingers out and into forward. Keep fingers glued to floor and lengthen torso and spine. Hold position and release tension from hamstring muscles.

Prepare for long side stretch.

Illustration 49

LONG SIDE STRETCH

Legs in second rotate L. leg up and over toward the R. leg. Place R. arm inside of R. leg and hold R. ankle, turning body flat over R. leg. Place L. hand behind head. (Illus. 50)

Illustration 50

Eight-count phrase—each gesture in two counts.

1. L. leg and hip rotate out and down to floor.

2. Chest and L. hand and head twist open to ceiling. Elbow opens to stretch chest. (Illus. 51)

3. L. leg and hip lift and rotate in. (Illus. 52)

4. Torso and head turn back to down position. (Repeat 3×)

5. Transition—rotate L. leg carefully out and into second position. Prepare for other side stretch. Repeat stretch—open into second prepare for torso and arms swing around.

Illustration 51

Do this stretch allowing enough time to achieve the complexity of action, particularly chest twist to ceiling.

SWING AROUND AND REACH

Sit with weight evenly divided between both open legs. Parallel arms reach long over R. leg (Illus. 53) and swing forward around to L. leg. Pull torso up in vertical and swing out and around from L. to R. leg. (Illus. 54) Keep torso low. Two full sets. Two counts.

Illustration 52

Flex and push wider.

Legs in second—hands on floor behind torso—flex ankles, and as they stretch through the toe use the hands to press the hips forward. (Illus. 55) Repeat until the legs are as wide as possible. Be sure thighs are rolled out and torso weight is lifted and forward, not resting on lower spine. Pause here, then shake legs out as they come together by pulling seat back between hands.

Illustration 53

Illustration 54

Illustration 55

LEG STRETCH IN SITTING POSITION

Preparation: Sitting up—straight lifted back, legs folded in front. Round the back and take the R. heel with R. hand. (Illus. 56)

Illustration 56

Eight-count phrase—each gesture in two counts.

1. L. hand behind back of head—simultaneously lift and extend R. leg and straighten torso. Leg is stretched up forward and sternum is lifted as L. hand lifts back of head. (Illus. 57)

Illustration 57

2. Round out and shift weight over L. knee. R. hip is lifted, and R. leg opens into side and rolls in. (Illus. 58)

3. Lift chest and leg again as leg rolls out. (Illus. 57)

Illustration 58

4. Fold in. Repeat forward and side leg stretch. (2×)

5. Place both hands behind head and repeat the leg and torso stretch without hands supporting legs. (Illus. 59) (4×)

Change legs.

Repeat the whole series on other side. (Illus. 60 & 61)

Illustration 59

Prepare for next stretch: roll over onto knees—class all facing the same direction.

Illustration 60

Illustration 61

BACK UNDULATION SERIES ON KNEES

Round back—sitting on heels—head on knees—arms long at side.

(Illus. 62) Do this series as a continuous undulation of the spine, although there are several accented variations of this stretch. Try to maintain a continuous hip flow.

Illustration 62

Each gesture in three counts.

1. Hips under and pressed through forward. Hands adjust to take the next weight. (Illus. 63)

2. Press hips and upper thigh forward. Hands on floor. Lift body up. (Illus. 64)

Illustration 63

3. Break in hip and sit on heels. Keep the head and upper back in place and stretch the ribs to capacity.

4. Round back and down to opening position.

(Repeat 4×)

JACKKNIFE SERIES

Illustration 64

On hands and toes. Toes stretched with insteps pressed through, raise hips up and press into insteps—come down to knees. (Make sure the instep is stretched and pressing through. Weight over big toe.) (4×) (Illus. 65)

Flex toes under with weight on hands.

Illustration 65

Tread into heels for Achilles and calf stretch. (8×) Follow with *accerando* treads. (8×) (Illus. 66)

Walk hands back until body weight is over stretched legs but torso still bent forward. (Illus. 67) With legs together, bounce to touch heels to floor. (4×)

Illustration 66

Illustration 67

Bend knees, take hold of ankles, and touch head to knees. (Illus. 68)

Lift seat up and straighten knees. (Think of lifting seat and taking stretch in hamstrings.) (4×) (Illus. 69)

Release legs and rise up sequentially into vertical with arms up over head. Stay there until you gain a balance and equilibrium.

DROP SWINGS

1. Release body down, swinging back arms with small lift in elbows.

2. Released body swing. Arms forward as body and arms lengthen out reaching long. (Spine pressed through into straight back.) (Illus. 70) Repeat 3×.

3. On fourth repeat—lift up into air with back elbow lift (Illus. 71). Repeat 3×. End on last lift in relevé with arms high.

   Shift weight to R. leg and hold balance (Illus. 72)—shift to L. leg, hold balance. Come down. In balance exercises, leave time open. Challenge length of time in holding relevé. Make one-legged relevé balance alignment.

Illustration 68

Illustration 69

Illustration 70

Illustration 71

Illustration 72

LEG WARM-UPS

Facing forward—right side—legs turned out.

Illustration 73

1. R. foot flexes over toe—heel up and down (8×)—forced toe—all action over big toe and ball of foot. (Illus. 73)

2. Press toes off floor and force instep through in flicks. (8×)

Illustration 74

3. Toe flicks up to L. knee—and down. (Illus. 74) (Stretch toe as far as possible.) (8×)

4. Knee lifts side up (8×) as leg kicks up. (Illus. 75)

5. R. leg descends back and stretches in Achilles. (8×) (Illus. 76)

Illustration 75

6. R. leg kicks up sideward (Illus. 77)—throw for height—hip steady. Press backward into heel and Achilles tendon for each preparation. (4×) Last press off from back diagonal, preparing to kick forward.

7. R. leg kicks forward. (Illus. 78) Arm in second to present height. (4×)

8. Body falls forward over R. leg. Kicking backward straight leg. (4×)

Illustration 76

Change to other side and repeat series.

Illustration 77

Illustration 78

LEG SWINGS

Stand securely on L. leg, R. leg lifted back with bent knee. (Illus. 79) The challenge throughout leg swings is to keep the hips steady. The swinging leg lengthens out of the hip on the downward. Each time the leg is released into the swing, it should lengthen further and pull out of the hip. The swing rhythm is three-quarter time.

1. Drop: release leg to gravity.

2. Swing: release to swing.

3. Lift and suspend: arrive at high point.

R. leg swings forward and backward with bent knee. (4×) (forward and back = 1 swing) R. leg swings (Illus. 80) open side R. to close front side L. (Illus. 81) (4×)

1. Step side R., change sides, and transfer weight.

2. Lift L. leg, two counts.

Repeat on L. side L. leg swings.

Repeat series with straight swinging leg.

Preparation for pliés. Dancers should remove sweat clothing so the body can become tactilely aware of the space around it and make visible its dimensional graining.

Illustration 79

Illustration 80

Illustration 81

CHEAP WARM-UPS

There were days when doing all of the stretches seemed unendurable, so I had the class do a cheap warm-up, especially in place of the pliés. This warm-up involved keeping the arms bent at the elbow and swinging at the side while running in place as the tempo increased. The only direction I used was the word "faster, faster!" About a minute of this was enough to break a sweat and we went on with the class, across the floor. Sometimes the body has to be indulged.

The discipline of imbuing stretches with the necessary quality motivation is, in a sense, a preparation for the professional task of repeating performances over and over again with quality.

UP AND DOWN—VERTICAL—THE PLIÉ

Warm-ups and pliés constitute the basic preparation for the dancer as a physical instrument. Up and down are two major directions that define the vertical dimension. In pedestrian action we let our bodies behave comfortably as we perform these directions. We let our hips tilt back, ribs fall out, knees roll in, and in general we don't think of how we are doing the action but are grateful that we've gotten down and up without falling or suffering too much strain. This is a far cry from the dance "plié" and the mechanism it involves.

Let us first deal with the new space we are going to journey into and occupy so as to not see it as a void and empty area, but as a distinctly flavored environment.

We begin with the body standing in place in a lively state of stasis. Stasis presents the body in a state of balanced stillness, alert and vibrantly alive, totally and immediately responsive to motivation but in a still position. There are two strong energies involved in the plié: gravity and the human psyche's willpower.

Gravity is a physical force, which is elemental to our existence on earth. Its downward pull keeps us from flying off into space. It also has a host of other beneficial attributes. Unfortunately, we have given downward a negative connotation: sadness, despair, defeat, dejection, and so on. From the onset we must re-see gravity as a directional force and not as a negative condition.

The other strong energy is the human willpower. This willpower not only motivates us in all our daily actions, but it also serves as a strong counter upward thrust against gravity's downward claim. Willpower is also part of motivation, which is

Free improvisation. Dancers: Lynn Levine, Frances Tabor, Michael Balard, Raymond Johnson, and Sara Shelton. Photo courtesy of the Nikolais/ Louis Archives.

housed in the psyche as well. It provides the necessary energy or force to trigger action.

These two energies are employed in the plié: one releases to the downward and one the will to rise up. Obviously we must work harder to rise because there is no physical force to help us up, but with gravity if we don't control the descent, the floor becomes our destination.

It is evident that the dancer must supply the energy to control the descent and the energy to rise. This calls for the proper muscular use of the legs, in particular the thighs.

The plié is a basic exercise of the dance. It contains almost every principle for preparing the body to dance. During the plié series one can introduce the premise of the class, for example, dimensions, body parts, shape, flexations, space, and so on.

To further help us to distinguish dimensional directions, we employ the principle of graining.

Grain is the use of a conceptual imagery to design a motional distinction within movement. Imagine the body as being hollow and filled loosely with particles, all having a directional arrow pointing outward. In a normal unconcerned state, these particles float randomly without any concern for direction or destination. But once the mind focuses on a direction or point of concern, then all of the arrows aim toward that focus and the body as a total unit grains, or moves internally toward it.

In going downward, the knees flex outward to allow the body to descend between them. The particles or molecules all direct their arrows toward the downward direction.

After arriving in low level, the mind shifts its focus and wills itself upward. The arrows swivel around and aim upward. To supply the energy to go upward, the mind tells the will to rise. The body not only rises, but also needs to rise properly in dance terms.

There is no break in the torso. The hips press forward, keeping the knees out and over the ball of the foot. As the will forces the body up and the knees force the legs open, the thighs straighten the legs and achieve the mechanism necessary to accomplish the rise. This procedure manipulates only the physical body. Here the performer-artist comes into play.

The breath and lift of upward movement, and the muscular release into descent and gravity awareness, are occurring within this form. The dancer should make visible the change of grain from physical gravity to psychical upward-will. This change of direction is clearly visible if the graining from down to up is achieved. It is an extremely exciting thing to see a class rise and lower together and the space in the room lift and descend. It becomes a moment of transcending the body as the direction of the multiple auras lift and lower the room, stage, or space.

The time value employed is strictly fulfilled. All the eighth notes in the 2/4 time are accounted for. There is movement during all the time allotted for the down and up. There is no arrival on the first beat and holding for the rest of the time. The time value of the plié and rise is legato and continuous.

The form and the directional going within the form are now the double intention of every plié series. Once the dancer understands the technical structure of the act, it is his responsibility to fill it with its appropriate flavor. The movement is then imbued with its motional identity: the going, the arrival, and the change of direction. The compatibility and control of the descent and the breath and lift of rising are imbued into the plié. The dancer rides these two directions with ease and balanced energies.

The practice of motional identity will later help in understanding and recognizing the gestalt and totality of other movements. This distinction between the overt movement and the internal motional identity is one of the major contributions Nikolais made to the clarity of the art of dance.

PLIÉS

The plié series is based on the dimensions of the body and their extension into space. First position: in place vertical up and down, second position: width sideward R. and L., third position: in place diagonal, fourth position open diagonal, fifth position: in place, sixth position: depth, forward–backward.

Between open positions, return to vertical (in place) with proper arrival of arms and legs in closed positions, so that the action goes from in to out—closed to open, in place to spatial. The body weight is centered between both feet at all time, with hips squared off to forward.

The plié is done with the weight equally divided on both legs. The tendency in fourth, fifth, and sixth positions is to shift the weight on to the back leg. Correct this imbalance.

Do four pliés in each position.

FIRST POSITION— VERTICAL DIMENSION— UP AND DOWN

Thighs continue their rotation outward with the knees directed over the balls of the feet. This knee rotation over the ball of the foot raises the arches. The rest of the torso maintains its placement. Hips press forward during the journey of down and up. The back of the knees should be fully stretched at arrival in up. Be sure to arrive at each point of destination. Lengthen arms out from the shoulder.

Motional—The in place dimension is released and the interior motional flow goes downward. It reaches its low point dictated by the technical ability of the dancer's body. The limitation is the stretch of the Achilles tendon and then the reverse occurs. The downward ceases and the flow releases upward. You must stress this motional visibility within the form during the plié series. The deep plié in first, third, and fifth positions places the weight evenly on the flexed toes.

Do not let your face reflect your inabilities. You may be struggling inside, but the viewer doesn't want to see your problems. Don't forget your face. You will always have problems with something. Don't let the viewer see them.

SECOND POSITION— OPEN—EXTENDING THE BODY INTO ITS WIDTH DIMENSION—SIDEWARD RIGHT AND SIDEWARD LEFT

On second and fourth (open, deep) plié positions, the heels keep in contact with the floor to challenge the Achilles tendon.

As you release the focal projection into forward and backward, the body now reaches into its fullness of width. Maintain the position of the hips, knees, and arches as they were in first position, and the sideward step allows for an extended reaching to a wider encompassment of width as the body descends. The arms, which opened into sideward, when in place, now reach further out into space with the descent.

The grain is directed through the sides of the body, particularly through the fingers and knees. Release the forward focus of the eyes. One seems now to be looking out of the ears. On rising into the vertical in-place position, the grain shifts from sideward out, to the top of the head rising upward. This transpiration of energy shift is very noticeable, and the student should see and recognize the wonderful phenomenon of motion traveling sideward outward in plié and then upward in rising.

TECHNICAL CHECK

The height and depth dimensions are released to allow the sideward going. Be sure to reach the end of each sideward movement before the journey upward or downward begins.

Don't force the turnout, but persist with the rotation in the thighs. Turnout rests within the capacity of the thigh and knee, not in the feet and ankles. Don't consider an ankle swivel a turnout of the leg.

The student thinks and gestures, "I am this wide," and then achieves and possess that width with authority.

**THIRD POSITION—
CLOSED—PREPARATION
FOR DIAGONALS**

Third position is achieved by placing the heel of the right foot snugly against the arch of the left foot. The right arm curves forward, the fingertips in line with the sternum, and the left arm curves slightly in its sideward position. This is now an in-place closed diagonal position. Continue the technical challenge of chest, hips, and legs: challenge the hip to remain forward by pressing the left back hip forward to equalize the right hip.

The body pliés with the proper alignment.

**FOURTH POSITION—
OPEN—DIAGONAL INTO
SPACE**

Fourth position traces the right leg out into a full diagonal step. This diagonal is equidistant between forward and sideward or backward and sideward for the backward diagonal.

Pliéing in open fourth position extends the body into six directions simultaneously. Forward (R. arm), sideward (L. arm), diagonal front (R. leg), diagonal back (L. leg), up head and down (seat). All of these radiate out of the center of the body. Arms and legs radiate the multidirectional graining equally in all six directions on the descent and then draw the grain back into the body for the vertical rise, with the head leading upward into place. With open fourth, the body is at its most extreme extension into space. Again, one can see the change of the motional path and distinction from lowering and reaching out to drawing in and going up.

TECHNICAL CHECK

On the descent the weight is equally distributed between both legs. The knees are directed over the toes; the arches are lifted against the pressure of the turned-out knees. The hip over the back leg adds the additional challenge of pressing forward to keep the hip from twisting against the turned-out knee. The flow of outward action is at its most expansive on the descent.

**FIFTH POSITION—
PREPARATION FOR
DEPTH DIMENSION—
CLOSED POSITION**

Right heel in place between big toe and ball of left foot. Arms forward in half circle at sternum, chest level.

Again, you should take all possible care for maintaining body alignment. In the plié, the torso grains down on the descent, reverses, and lifts without changing its alignment. The arms grain up and down, respectively, without changing their position in space.

In both closed positions, third and fifth, the back leg tends to twist the hip a little out of its forward alignment. You will constantly need additional pressure forward.

TECHNICAL CHECK

The arms surround a circular spatial volume. On the descent the space between them is lowered without changing the placement of arms. The arms do not change their position and move up and down but grain the enclosed space to do so.

SIXTH POSITION— DEPTH—OPEN POSITION

The right leg moves directly forward from the fifth position placement to four or six inches' distance so that the back hip can maintain an equal pressure forward. Weight centers between both legs. Arms are parallel and over the head; the energy is released in them so that they rotate slightly in and do not face outward. The torso and arms grain down on the plié and grain up through the arms on the rise. You should use the pliancy of the abdomen here to fulfill the motional fullness of up and down. Place the arms up so that they are just visible to the sideward vision of the eyes.

Fourth to sixth positions include a separation of legs (depending on turnout ability), which challenges the forward hip placement. The back hip works to maintain its forward placement. The torso helps expand and stretch and condense to fulfill both height and depth.

I. PLIÉ—RELEVÉ SERIES

Plié to low level.

Insteps press through—forced arch—torso lowers a bit more as arches press through and over.

Relevé to straight knees.

Use heels to pull the body down to straight (feel the back of the knee stretch).

(Reversing series)—move up into stretched leg relevé.

Lower to flexed-knee second position keeping forced arch in plié.

Lower heels to floor.

Straighten knees to standing in place.

Repeat in all positions on both sides, with appropriate arm placements.

II. PLIÉS WITH QUARTER TURNS

(Faster tempo)—turn to right, pivoting on L. foot, R. leg steps in each position.

Facing forward—plié first position.

Rebound up to second with quarter-turn plié. Rebound up quarter-turn plié in third—rebound quarter-turn plié in fourth. Quarter-turn plié in fifth—facing forward again—plié sixth forward in place. Back to first position plié—repeat series in other direction and other footing, turning on lifted rebounds.

(Regulate jump tempo.)

Jumps in six positions—both sides—repeat with quarter turns.

III. WALK SERIES

Forward four steps—backward four steps—side right three steps—sideward left three steps—turning right three-step circle—turning left three-step circle. Catch step repeat on other side. Leading with the body weight in all directions and body arcs in turn-circles. Weight arrives over front of foot with each step.

Baggy Warm-Up Clothes

The body is the the dancer's instrument, and its eloquence becomes muffled if it is encased in baggy and shapeless clothes. When the studio is cold, as it generally is early in the day, it is understandable that warm-up clothes be used to keep the muscles warm. But once the dancers are standing up for pliés, the floor series, and across-the-floor action, it is important that the torso and legs be seen. Needless to say, during performance baggy clothes are not worn on stage, unless they are the costume for a dance. Wearing shapeless warm-up clothing also indicates a careless attitude about the class (and unfortunately the performance).

If the teacher has to struggle to see whether the knees are stretched or legs rotated or whether there is proper hip placement and the abdomen is lifted, he is not going to bother with correction and consequently the class could well be wasted for that student.

The dancer should present as professional an appearance as possible during class. Leotard and tights and hair that is contained help to create that appearance. When the muscles and limbs don't have anything to hide behind, they become that much more sensitive to movement and the motion within that movement.

ACROSS THE FLOOR

During the Bennington years of early modern dance, the Holm Technique was called a "space" technique because the dancer not only moved knowledgeably into space, but projected and lengthened outward as well. Nikolais continued this basic principle of outward projecting awareness.

Across the floor basically deals with moving a three-dimensional body through space within a time structure. The directional identification of the forward of the room is established from the onset. In addition, the dimensional directions of the body are made clear. There is the room's forward and the body's forward. The room forward is very moveable, whereas the body forward is stationary. The body forward is always the dancer's front, whereas the stage, the choreographer, or the teacher freely determines the room forward.

A GENERAL CLASS OUTLINE

With a group of diverse students working together, it becomes essential that you establish a basic organization or framework. This begins with the lineup for going across the floor.

Depending on the size of the class, two or three lines are set up. The dancers keep their place for the entire class and become familiar with their partners on either side. This awareness is also the beginning of ensemble training. Starting off together and working in unison allows both the teacher and dancer to have a common reference for accuracy and criticism.

MOTIVATION

Before he establishes a pattern of movement, the dancer needs to be motivated. There is no room here for the dead eye, the lethargic body, and the plodding leg. The live eye reflects the live mind. The weight is forward over the front of the foot, and the thigh is prepared to lift to introduce the first step. Without this self-motivation, there can be no motion, only movement.

DIMENSIONS

In basic dance, locomotion extends the three dimensions of the body into space. From these dimensions one can move into ten clear and discernable directions. In addition, there is shaping the body in preparation for turns.

1 and 2: depth—operating within the foreword and backward slot.

3 and 4: width—sideward going, right and left.

The range of attention and body types in a beginning class. Alwin Nikolais shows University of New Hampshire students how to carry a movement across the floor.
Photo by Vach Adams.

Points in Space

Geometrically there are 360 points in the space that surrounds the human body on a horizontal plane, but because of the thickness of the body, it can only define eight horizontal and two vertical points clearly. These points are backward, forward, sideward right and left, the four diagonals, and up and down. The legs step clearly into those directional points carrying the torso with them. The clarity of these points in space is in a sense the ABCs of spatial orientation. It is essential that the dancer articulate them clearly for basic spatial communication. However, one can pinpoint many additional points by tilting the body.

5 and 6: height—vertical, in-place action—up and down.

7 and 8: diagonal—a path evenly divided between a depth and width dimension, both forward and backward.

9 and 10: turning right and left, and going "around the corner"—these are two additional directions.

The dancer should place his feet accurately; otherwise the directions into space can become muddied and confused. In the backward walks, insist on authority while stepping into backward, with no change of level or insecurity. Unless variations are called for, backward walking should be as secure as forward walking.

There are also three body weight placements possible in the vertical dimension—centered, forward, and backward. These definitions are important, so that variations are clearly defined. A large spectrum of motional and spatial flavor rests in basic locomotion. The mix of the directional going offers constant spatial challenges.

Across the floor spatial developments eventually will include level changes, turns, stop, go, fast, slow, circles, air work, directional changes, changes of shape, space, leading with different

Five-Finger Exercise

Because most physical technique is gained by repetition, so too, in dance, exercises have been assembled to develop certain skills. I called such an exercise the five-finger exercise because it limbered and prepared the body in many ways, just as the piano five-finger exercises prepare the fingers of musicians.

The five-finger exercise I evolved is a very simple structure yet one that could be tailored to many points of view. It dealt with space, time, body parts, various locomotions, etc., in various combinations. It was a simple form that got the class moving without complications. It continued and maintained the energy flow between warm-ups and across-the-floor action with a familiar introduction to space and movement pattern.

The form consisted of four steps forward—half turn—four steps backward—half turn—three steps sideward—reverse—three steps other side. The body weight was always over the ball of the foot, in forward, back and sideward.

Students did the basic phrase across the floor in both directions to warm up to space and locomotion. Sometimes the whole class was developed on this basic pattern.

The form can be varied and developed with:

Specific change of facings

Specific leg and foot accuracy—moving leg passing the ankle of the standing leg

Accurate time arrivals and time variations

Torso variations—chest and hip shifts—leading with various body parts

Adding leg extensions and additional turns

Extending the 4-4-3-3 time phrase to create longer rhythmic phrases

body parts, and so on, all of which grow more challenging as the classes and premises develop.

As you add new skills, combine them, if possible, with earlier ones, which the dancer can now identify and adapt to quickly. Also, time interest in movement phrases and kinetic challenges should become apparent. Each locomotor phrase is built on the premise of the day. With this technique, you can construct and alter phrases almost daily as the various challenges occur.

BUILDING ACROSS-THE-FLOOR PATTERNS

Creating across-the-floor patterns becomes a major responsibility for the teacher. Not only does it call upon the teacher's creative skill, but it also challenges the dancer's versatility and adeptness at performing different movement phrases daily.

This may all seem more difficult than it really is. The vocabulary of movement is precise. You will add to the dance vocabulary daily, and the dancer's skills will grow accordingly.

Generally, the instructor begins class with a locomotor pattern including directions and turns at a pulse that can be doubled or slowed. A simple way to begin a class is with a basic floor pattern. Then add the premise of the day to this form.

The phrase develops as various body parts are added to this basic form, all of which lends further detail to the phrase. The teacher introduces spatial designs, volumes, peripherals, levels, and under- and overcurves, and through this locomotion variations follow. Time values and textural detail are further embellishments.

The complexity of movement patterns is not the object of technique classes; however, movement clarity and physical skill is. This generally takes repetition and careful correction. Often a correction can become part of the phrase. The contrast between an inaccurate arm gesture followed by an accurate one can be both interesting and challenging. What becomes essential in the devised movement phrase is that it serves as a means for both dancer and teacher to determine progress, accomplishment, and achievement.

The class should offer a progression of challenges: a series of turns, a jump turn, a metric intrusion, a spatial change, a balance, a held leg extension, a complicated footwork pattern, and/or sudden changes of direction. Very often the challenges suggest themselves. Doing the reverse or opposite of what preceded works well. These changes and developments lend dynamic interest.

Above all, we seek dexterity and quick response, so that the body and intent are clear, alive, and kinetic. The abilities to change and contrast movement bring the all-important spice to movement, since dynamics are created by change and contrast.

Throughout the class the dancer should be aware of the following principles:

Totality (the body and psyche similarly focused)

Presence (the immediacy of doing)

Decentralization (release of ego or self, so that the personality or attitude does not intrude and the interior of the form can be seen more clearly)

OTHER BASIC LOCOMOTION VARIATIONS

Walking: transferring weight evenly from leg to leg on a level path.

Hopping: locomotion on the same leg, transferring the weight in the air to the same leg.

Transferring the weight through an undercurve or overcurve.

Jumping: locomotion on two legs. Transferring weight to both legs. Full turns in the air, landing and pushing off from both legs.

Leaping: transferring the weight from leg to leg in the air. Creating a long, horizontally level path as opposed to an overcurve. The different leaps vary in their character of traveling through the air.

Skipping: as opposed to a 3/4 undercurve, skipping can be a duple or a 3/8 rhythm with the emphasis on the push off to upward instead of low transfer of weight.

BUILDING TO END OF CLASS

Begin with small one-count overcurves. Lengthen overcurves into leaps to accentuate the horizontal forward. This frontal lead can be the front of face, chest, or hip or can change to accent the up or vertical height of the leap with the top of the head. Two of each give a curious movement quality to the leap.

Across the floor with legs leading.
Photo by T. Mike Fletcher.

Leaping for low-level accuracy: by not going into the height of the leap but by stressing only the forward, these become low-level split leaps.

LOW-LEVEL AND OVERCURVE COMBINATIONS—RUN, RUN, LEAP

A detail of leaping: the leap is an overcurve and consequently with this curve in mind the dancer can use the legs to gain height to "sail" over the curved form. At the apex the back leg adds an additional lift, which suspends the lift of the figure in the air, giving the body a suspended "sailing over" look. This additional life often takes the dancer by surprise if he is not prepared for the suspension the back leg lift affords. At this moment the dancer has to have a suspended moment in his mind, as well as in his body, to "take to the air." Being able to ride the leap, as the back leg gives an additional lift, is an experience in fulfilling suspended air work.

RUNNING ACROSS THE FLOOR

Press into forward with the chest leading and running as fast as possible. The drum sound is a roll, no pulse. Each group sets out every four counts. Students can use their voice and shout as they rush forward. Physical and vocal release into space is the purpose here.

TO CENTER OF FLOOR FOR JUMPS

Four jumps in place.

Four jumps in second.

Four crossing legs—changing fifth position.

Four spectacle jumps of the dancer's choice, which includes turning with body and leg variations. Slow the pulse to accommodate the height.

Technique classes as a rule should end in air work and large spatially released patterns, so that there is a physical kinetic release. Also, on some occasions the class should do the reverse and wind down the energy.

GRAINING

Graining in locomotion lends a totality of action to coming across the floor. Graining is the ability to focus the attention of the body to a point in or outside of the body. It is an internal focus. The focus of the eye releases its dominance and the many internal eyes look to the point of reference. One lends oneself totally to the action. If the point is the elbow, the legs and hips look through the body to grain to that elbow. If the action is a descent, the entire body grains toward downward, and reversibly to upward. One can grain in all directions by releasing the locked eye focus and looking through the interior of the body.

WEEK 1: LOCOMOTION AND DIMENSIONS

INTRODUCTION

Basically, locomotion is the transference of the body in its entirety from one space to another. This also holds true for any of the body parts, but for now we are dealing with the entire body in locomotion, walking, and its variations.

PREPARATION FOR WALKING TECHNIQUE

What constitutes the distance of a step is the length of the dancer's leg and how far it reaches in a normal stride without flexing the standing leg. In a step, as the reaching leg touches the floor, the weight is transferred to that direction, and the body arrives at its new placement, quickly aligning itself. The spirit in the sternum pushes the torso forward to gain this instantaneous alignment action as the back leg lifts to take its next step.

There are three placements of weight when standing in vertical: back—center—forward.

In a basic dance walk, the weight is always forward, so that the dancer is not behind the beat in the transference of weight from the heels to the ball of the foot. This allows the dancer to be on the beat, rather than behind it or before it, and creates a physical immediacy. Where time or timing is important, such as in certain sport and dance actions, forward weight placement is essential. In pedestrian activities where timing is not essential, it is not important that one walks with the weight back and on the heels.

FORWARD WALKING

Before walking across the floor, have the class demonstrate this weight transference for themselves, feeling how much time is lost in shifting the weight from backward to foreword before a step can be taken and the difference of immediacy when the weight is forward. Make it clear that this is the reason for walking with one's

End-of-class runs in Troy, Alabama.
Photo courtesy of the Nikolais/Louis Foundation.

weight forward, not to walk "tippy-toe." In the stepping, the ball of the foot presses into the floor and receives the weight with a secure, tactile, cushioned, and wide base assurance.

Locomotion is achieved in any direction. When traveling in locomotion, it is necessary to motivate some point in the torso into the direction of going in order to keep the weight of the body over the ball of the foot. In locomotion the leg reaches and lengthens out of the hip. The lift of the thigh introduces the leg into space. The lift is only a breath in the thigh, which gives a breath to the walk. The dancer lifts the leg from the thigh to introduce it into locomotion. This is the same lift employed in *developé* action. The toe automatically stretches to reach for the ground while taking the step. This stretch action occurs very quickly. The foot should do this automatically.

The stepping foot passes closely to the standing foot. Any variation on this close stepping becomes a movement variation, such as a circular swinging out.

Weight arrives on the front of the wide based foot, keeping the body alive and continuously forward or directionally oriented.

With space a vibrant entity before us, we must make our presence equally vibrant as we move through it. The setup of the body will now displace itself. This displacement will call for motivation and willpower. Transferring the weight from foot to foot within these performing boundaries gives both the dancer and the teacher the same framework of reference for achievement and correction.

Some of the boundaries of forward walking are:

> The length of the step to maintain the even level of action across the floor
>
> Sustaining a degree of energy necessary from step to step
>
> Fulfilling the pulse and rhythmic values
>
> Maintaining the setup of the body so that all factors maintain the necessary orientation found in a basic walk
>
> Graining the entire body toward the direction
>
> Open and clearly focused eyes

About 60 percent of most choreography is comprised of some form of locomotion or moving through space, especially walking and its variations. The importance of simply walking on and off stage also makes a statement about the authority of the dancer. The basic walk in all directions will become the locomotor structure for many of the variations in the technique class.

To Instructor

Don't attempt to bring in too many details in the early classes. However, persist in daily review and achievement. The repetition will clarify and correct many things. Focus on those students who tend to lag and let their weight fall behind.

Walking backward is obviously a precarious practice, and the body knows it. Not being able to see where you are going demands a faith that your path is clear, that the potholes are filled, and that no clawing hands are reaching up from hell ready to grab you and take you under.

But after all the primary challenges have been dealt with there is always, especially with beginners, a basic fear of walking where they cannot see the way, and it manifests itself in a cautious bent knee walk. There is a natural conclusion that the closer you are to the ground the less you will fall and harm yourself, and so walking in a slight plié will lessen the distance between you and the ground.

Fear has its form. Putting on the brakes and walking backward cautiously with a bent knee are part of its form. The problem then becomes building confidence, and courage, and of course straightening the knees.

BACKWARD WALKING

Backward, like downward, carries with it some negative connotation. Retreat and fear are a few of the burdens backward bears. Simple as this may appear, have students look at the floor to be traversed. Assure them that no sudden gaping holes will appear. No unexpected hands will reach up and drag them below. With these fears erased, they are to treat backward with as much confidence as they do forward. They should walk with assurance and no approbation or hesitancy. Backward is a simple direction and should, in basic dance, be performed with that simplicity.

Graining the body to its backward going is a matter of reversing the forward going sensation. One does not lean back or lie back, but instead the whole body has the slightest fall into backward, as the body does when it goes forward or into any direction. The entire backward area leads the body into space, not just the upper portion by just leaning back. The leg steps back in time to receive and transfer the weight smoothly. A fear of backward going will manifest itself by a slight continuous plié. The dancer feels safer being closer to the ground should he fall or be taken by surprise. Focus on stretching the back of the knee during the walk.

When the class comes across the floor backward, have the first line stop when they have arrived and face the oncoming group. Stepping a few steps forward, they should reach forward with their hand to stop the oncoming line from colliding with the wall, and give assurance to the dancers so that they do not slow down too soon as they come close to the wall. Each line warns the following group. When they touch the oncoming dancers they should sensitively bring them to a stop. This, in a curious way, prepares them for later ensemble cooperation. You can begin to see those dancers who will have trouble working with each other.

SIDEWARD LOCOMOTION

The structure of the human body is not compatible with sideward walking: it is easier to turn the head and body and walk forward into the sideward path. However, sideward is part of the body's width dimension and can, with training, become a provocative addition to the locomotion vocabulary.

Just as the forward going transverses a forward slot determined by the width of the dancer's body, so too is the sideward path determined by the body's depth. This narrow body depth measures the sideward slot. This becomes the limitation of sideward walking. Any encroachment either forward or backward makes the sideward a diagonal path. This careful flat limitation is another challenge to the dancer's turnout and also challenges and develops the accuracy of his spatial orientation.

The leading arm and chest lean into the sideward slot and carry the body with it. The face loses its forward orientation and the appropriate side of the head grains and shifts into sideward without tilting.

The locomotion of side going is simple. As an example, the right leg steps open to the side, the left leg cross closely in front. The hips keep their pressure forward, which limits the crossing and keeps the step small and close. This moment is the challenge in sideward going, the crossing leg against the steady untwisting or tilting hip. Again, the steady forward hip pressure communicates the clarity of sideward locomotion. The right leg opens into sideward again to continue the sideward going. This time the left leg crosses in back.

The first crossing leg in front will tend to press the body backward a bit, but the second crossing leg closing from behind evens out the sideward dimension. When you give a dancer a directional path, you should make clear if it is in reference to the dancer's or the room's architecture. For the dancer, forward is very fluent. It moves to wherever the body is facing, whereas the stage or room architectural forward is stationary and not variable, unless deliberately changed, such as calling the side of the room or stage "downstage."

Sideward is relative to a forward. As an exercise, facing the left side of the room, dancers walk sideward R., making the room's left side forward. Three steps right side: half turn: three steps left. (The turn can go forward or backward for variation.) Continue across floor. Continue with various combinations of sideward going and half and quarter turns, always challenged by the accuracy of the body's flatness as it steps into second. Simple as the pattern may appear the challenge of accurate facing and footing are quick to appear. The achievement and correction of these challenges become the reason for across-the-floor phrases.

Turns in basic walk patterns are accomplished with the foot passing close and in the vertical. The dancer steps out of the turn center clearly into the direction being traversed.

DIAGONAL WALKING

To prepare for diagonal walking, the closed and open plié position of third and fourth should be practiced in place. Then a moment should be given to discuss the room or stage architecture. Room forward is more important now than ever.

The walking into forward diagonal paths calls for a very active and accurate chest orientation. I use as my four diagonal pointers the pectorals for forward diagonal and the shoulder blades for the back diagonals. These points press into space and lead the body into the forward or backward diagonal directions. Be careful of the prominence of these points or the chest will become a dominant leading factor.

The head grains into forward diagonals through the cheekbones, and the diagonal back leads with the diagonal back of the head into the backward diagonals.

The leg path has a diagonal orientation as well. From the right foot's placement in third it reaches out into a diagonal line to open fourth position. The left foot crosses in front, the heel pressing forward to continue the diagonal walk line. The body should be careful not to twist with the crossing leg.

CLASS PLAN

TECHNIQUE

Premise

Locomotion into dimensional directions.

Establish the technique of walking. Establish forward, backward, side right and side left, and in place as dimensions. Transfer weight from foot to foot through space.

Monday

Forward and back locomotion combinations.

Half turns—different forwards—develop patterns of forward and backward.

Time—quarter and eighth notes (double time).

Introduce walking technique. Weight shift. Leg technique. Repeat and insist on proper walk technique throughout course, especially this basic week. From the very beginning, introduce the relative time, shape, and space of the movement, sensing the even motional quality involved. For the dancer, this is the taste of the feedback they will savor from the movement, as well as the quality they will communicate to the onlooker. Avoid jerky, interrupted transfers of weight. Feel the space on the body, like a ship cutting through water. Sustain normal horizontal level. Do not intrude into other dimensions. Do not go up or down or side to side.

Runs—chest lead—arms reaching forward lead—contrast both.

Jumps—in place—second position—crossing, changing fifth position. Big released individual jumps turning in air.

Tuesday

Introduce side right and side left with forward and backward combinations.

Facing the room side, walk sideward into the room's forward. Practice sideward walk technique. Front and back crossing legs while maintaining the body flatness in sideward slot. R. leg three steps—half turn—L. leg three steps—half turn—and so on.

Develop this set of steps with forward and backward walks. Extend arms respectively forward and sideward. Do half turns. Include quarter and eighth notes.

Continue with jumps center of floor and in place. Four with legs together in place, four with legs in second, four changing fifth position from front to back, four as high and spectacular as they can make them. Aim for vertical height. Keep form in air. Do not buckle on landing. Land with weight forward. Emphasis should be on sideward accuracy. Stress sideward footwork.

FIVE-FINGER EXERCISE— A DAILY LOCOMOTOR EXERCISE

Introduce what will become a daily locomotor exercise to drill the dancer in spatial accuracy and prepare for more detailed legwork later. It also challenges the speed of the focal change and grain. Basic steps: four forward, half turn, four backward, half turn, three side right, and shift weight three side left, repeat.

Check leg passing through—flatness of sideward going—shifts of weight—accurate directional stepping and path.

A change in rhythm is added to the walks, so they go from 3/4 to 4/4. Feel the time, rather than counting the time.

Dancers should learn to visualize geometric floor patterns.

End classes with free, released runs with chest leading across the floor from now on.

Wednesday

Side right and left, forward and backward.

Tread in place and then release into locomotion.
Half and quarter turns. Time—quarter and eighth notes.

Step hops going (vertical) upward for height on hops, and then traveling forward with step for horizontal travel.

A hop is a one-footed walk. A jump is a two-footed walk landing on both feet. Do not lose body setup or orientation to space, especially in jumps. Head reaches up and feet stretch long and down. Remain vertical in air.

Thursday

Continue with different floor patterns and time values.

Persist in accurate action—treading in place.

Quick footwork for sideward speed, as in runs.

Step hops: accenting horizontal and vertical travel on the hops.

Runs—fall into direction and keep feet moving quickly to keep up.

Jumps.

Friday

Continue repeated challenge of more complicated floor patterns.

These should not be excessive or frustratingly difficult patterns.

Run, run, jump, jump—develop with jump turns in air.

TECHNICAL REMINDERS

Basic leg technique—a lifted breath in the thigh before stepping.

Sustain normal level—students should not introduce up and down or side-to-side dimensions when going forward. Teachers call attention to these personal mannerisms.

Maintain an even transference of weight. Steady treading.

Total body participation: face, open eyes, and steady hips.

Time values: accurate arrivals and starts.

In locomotion, the legs do not carry a lifeless "rest in place" torso, but a directionally grained and motivated body.

Hops—walking on the same foot, landing and pushing off the same leg.

Jumps—transferring weight from both feet to both feet, landing and pushing off.

Leaps—small for beginners, transferring weight in the air (run, run, leap, etc.) alternate legs. Be sensitive to the time variation between runs and leaps.

Turns—quarter, half, and whole turns, accurate spatial arrivals.

Stasis—stillness (alive and active)—in place.

Motivation and motor base: both made visible.

Release from in place into locomotion.

Consciousness of path through space.

Sensing the nature of the energy will identify the motional character of the movement.

Totality of psyche and physical orientation.

In vertical rest, the weight is evenly placed on both the front and back of the foot.

When the weight is shifted forward, the body is already in motion, in an active rest: stasis.

IMPROVISATION

Monday

The immediacy of response to sound.

The whole class is up and assumes an individual shape without looking at the teacher. The teacher will beat a single loud and unexpected note on the drum (unexpected is the key here.) The challenge is the speed of response by the dancer. The response is a complete change of shape and level. Make sure the dancer is not locked with the tension of expectancy. The psyche (mind and willpower) remains in sync with the change of shape. It is the speed of their unison that is evident here: coordinating and stimulating the entire body to a motivation and response.

Response to sound (drums): dancer hears but does not see the sound source. Begin with the whole class standing up and on floor.

Half the class sits to watch the other half.

Dancers change shape in a quick response to drum sound.

Quick response to voice command using action words: go, stop, drop, run, slow, fast, laugh, and so on. Half class up.

Dancers develop movement phrases, and new sounds immediately change their development.

Tuesday

The immediacy of response to touch.

In duets: the toucher and the dancer. The toucher lightly taps a part of the dancer's body, trying not to be seen by the dancer so that the touch is only felt. The dancer responds by graining toward the touch with movement emanating from that contact point. The movement plays itself out until another spot is touched, which interrupts and redirects the action. The toucher directs the action so that it flows, and the dancer grains from point to point; the toucher directs the dynamics through the pressure of the touch. The touch must be a sensitive one, not a karate chop. The toucher begins to style his/her own movement as well. Eventually as the skill develops, the duet looks almost choreographed. Change places and roles. You can dictate the other's movement by the way you touch them: push/pull, directional change, circular, speed, and so on. The toucher can lift the dancer in a shaped form and carry him to new positions on the stage.

Working in duets, have your partner touch six different points on you. Remember the sequence and improvise by changing the grain reaction. Reverse the process with your partner. Then work alone. Try them in different speeds. Fast and low and mixed. Repeat phrases several times.

RESPONSE TO TOUCH (WITH PARTNER)

Choose a partner. Have your partner touch you on various parts of the body. When he/she touches you on the shoulder, the shoulder moves toward touch. When she touches you on the hip, it moves. The part should move in the direction of the touch. Don't go away from the point; go toward the place where you were touched. Occasionally don't locomote for a moment, but just stay in place. Don't change touches so fast that your partner doesn't have a chance to correct himself. Never retreat from a gesture, but always go on to the next gesture.

Partner is always behind dancer and not seen. The dancer feels the touch but does not see it and moves toward touch. Toucher moves his hand away quickly, to next point. Toucher makes movement interesting, and eventually they create an integrated duet.

Toucher should not let a development to a touch go on too long. Interrupt the flow with a touch that will lead the movement into another direction. Play with interest of choreography.

Touchee, keep getting faster but allow for each reaction to be visible. Let the body be very free.

Change your point of contact to different parts of the body.

You might try responding without a partner as a solo improvisation, letting your body respond to imagined touches.

This requires the ability of making the audience see what you want them to see. Use all the minute graining particles of the body to call attention to what you want them to see.

Don't let your psyche, the inner attention of your mind, to be distracted or disinterested.

Let the dancer's movement phases be as long as the toucher chooses.

The toucher is choreographing the improvisation.

Wednesday

Leading the group.

Place a group of five in a star position so that as the movement turns the group's forward orientation changes and a different person is always in front. The group follows whoever arrives in front and leads. The movement should seem continuous as it develops from person to person. The leader must always consider that there are others behind following him and not move unreasonably fast. There should be a

CRITS ON TOUCH IMPROVISATION

The classes and crits are not written in a literary manner but as spoken directives. They will often be short and terse. This is not an antagonistic encounter; it is a cooperative thing. It shouldn't become a catfight. It should be an aesthetic inter-relationship rather than a dramatic confrontation.

Don't overmove. Stay still if you find that you are beginning to junk it up with over reactions, with a lot of stuff that is irrelevant.

Try to use a motional motivated response rather than an emotional gesture.

Be specific—we really want to see which point is being pressed into space. Also, it should not have a languid quality when slowness is called for. It can be slow without being languid. Languid is a condition of slowness. It implies that you are resting a little bit or a little bit lazy in the gesture.

Be careful—a big gesture might be distracting and become more important than the pinpoint itself.

Give yourself to the gesture, but don't keep pressing it constantly. It is the difference between a sustained energy and a percussive energy. Combine them. Try to develop the skill of percussive energies as well.

Don't react too slowly—see if there can be no time elapsed between the time of touching and the activity, so it really is almost electric fast.

The whole body must grain toward the particular point of interest.

Be sure not to stare hard at a focus. This makes the action dramatic and personal.

The grain of the body all directed to one direction will focus the viewer's attention to that going.

Several things to remember and correct: (1) quick reflex; (2) the grain of the body toward the point; (3) the vitality of the whole body in that grain, so that its generative power toward the act is high-spirited, not lethargic.

quick pickup whenever turns create new leaders. The unison and ensemble quality should be visible. The movement leader should keep their body graining visible, so that the group following him seems to see the direction the movement is going to take and anticipates it.

Thursday and Friday

Group walking chorales.

Aim to master dimensional locomotion (forward—backward; side left—side right).

In group walking chorales, the tide of dancers ebbs and flows in directions and counterdirections. The group should maintain its forward and sideward dimensional slots.

Regardless of how large the class is, split it into groups so that the sitting group can watch the dancing group. A great deal can be learned from watching, including how to see movement and when quality and success occur. This viewing will help the dancers crit themselves and should be continuously used as a self-crit device.

Teacher keeps a soft continuous drum beat pulse. Occasionally stopping so that the group maintains its own pulse. Warn students in advance that you might do this, otherwise they'll stop to see why the drums stopped. In small group, then in large (half the class) group choruses. Feed in quarter and half turns, double time, and pauses.

Work for a continuous flow of locomotor action.

Design the action for the performing space.

Focus on immediacy of response and quick directional changes when a dancer passes or comes close to another dancer. Often both dancers will pick up the same direction—encourage these unisons and keep the locomotor flow alive.

Point out effective sequences to viewers.

Avoid having too many people separate and move alone on stage without relationship to the group. These "loners," you will find, are the fiercely egotistical who refuse to relinquish their "personalities." Remind them that in this improvisation they are part of a group.

The psyche should be with the movement and not behind it.

When you move backward, don't retreat from something; go backward toward something.

Be very precise about being on the pulse. You may look very well trained stepping on the beat, but you have to have a sense of presence within time. Get that first, because being on the beat is not necessarily being present in time, on the beat; it is a psychical matter as well as a physical matter.

By now you should walk without thinking about it spatially. Every time you pass someone, going in any direction, you feel their passage as a motivation. It might turn you into a new direction or effect a change of some sort. Don't turn just to turn. You turn to change direction, not to do a little pirouette.

CONCLUDING IMPROVISATIONS

When the allotted time for an improvisation is over, give a warning, "Bring it to an end," and conclude the drumbeat. Let the dancer practice "endings." Let the dancer continue and end in silence if that is the case. But don't encourage it. Let the final group tableaux register in stillness before the group breaks its concentration. As the class progresses, you can substitute the improvisation period with a composition assignment.

REMINDERS

Locomotion involves creating and determining a structure to house dimensional locomotion. This will also include changes of:

Direction: forward and backward, side right, side left.

Time: slow, medium, fast, pause.

Turns: half and quarter turns.

Remember the three states of energy during stretches: tension, relax, and release, so that relax is not understood as a collapse. Theory, investigating the theoretical basis of movement, in our case is explored through improvisation—that is, instant choreography and instant performance. Keep pushing for length of organic development of material, sensing where the movement wants to go and going with it. Stop when nothing happens and start again. Establish forward in relationship to the room architecture: its orientation. Prepare class for stage and audience awareness.

Technique class as a rule should end in air work and large spatially released patterns. This usually satisfies the dancers' craving for kinetics and sweat, and builds stamina.

Sharpen imagery. The dancer should begin not only to know what they are doing, but also develop an internal objective picture of what they look like and what the audience is actually seeing.

Where a class premise is employed in the stretches, indicate it, so that it will have that point of view in future warm-ups; for example, rotary—peripheral, and so on. All of these points should be reiterated daily. Many of them are applicable to the movement vocabulary still to be presented.

Remember immediacy. Maintain general alertness and presence.

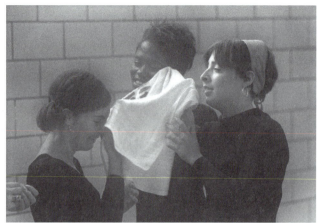

Sharing a towel. Artist-in-Schools, St. Louis, 1968.
Photo by T. Mike Fletcher.

A statement of physical availability to how a movement wants to develop: total going, total focus, and total participation.

In technique class stress the skill development and analysis of the premise; in improvisation, the richness of invention; in composition, sentient fulfillment of inventive structure. All effort should lead to identifying the nature of the movement, to make abstraction legible. There is dancing of the mind or the psyche as well as the body. It is the way the dancer handles the relationship between mind and body that will distinguish him as an artist. It also distinguishes the difference between a technique that concentrates solely on physical dexterity and technique, and one that integrates the union of body with the mind to develop the skill of poetic dance communication.

COMPOSITION

No composition assignment the first week.

Instructor Notes

When standing in place, work with the dimensional concepts. You stand there in place, in presence, in time, by virtue of the fact that you radiate vibrations in all directions. Try to introduce the concept for the day during stretches. Distinguish between straightening a limb and extending it into space. The turning out of the leg doesn't mean that the legs never turn in.

In coming across the floor, all sorts of variations are possible, especially with changes of space and time. Don't be too physically analytical. Try to get students to understand the simple principles of:

1. Consonance or presence within a desired form.

2. Willful disturbance of that presence and the resultant movement.

3. Total arrival in the desired new presence.

Dynamics occur from the juxtaposition of energies: with time, fast, slow and stop; with level, high and low; with change of shape and quality, going from soft to hard. Contrasts are part of dynamic excitement.

WEEK 2: ISOLATING BODY PARTS (ISOLATIONS)

INTRODUCTION

Because dance can serve to express so many various intentions, it is best to understand how the body is set up physically to more serviceably fulfill the variety of action demanded of it. Once the dancer has completed his warm-ups and stretch series, before the premise of the class is presented, the teacher should consider and address the setup or alignment of the body and the focus of the mind.

The human body is a three-dimensional form. It has height (up and down), width (sideward right and left) and depth (forward and backward). It is comprised of various body parts placed on a general framework of 206 bones. The torso, which is the largest part of the body, includes the chest and hips. Emanating from this central mechanism are the extremities and attachments, which are joined to the body:

The head is attached at the neck.

The arms are attached at the shoulders.

The legs fit into the hip socket.

The chest and hips are made separate and independent by the elasticity of the abdomen.

The head is comprised primarily of the face and its highly mobile and expressive features.

The arms include the upper arm, elbow, forearm, wrist, and fingers.

The legs include the thigh, knee, calf, ankle, foot, toes, arch, and heel.

Muscles and tendons bind these many parts together and make the body an instrument of motion. Although it would take *Grey's Anatomy* to describe the complexity of the human body, for the purpose of the dancer this can be greatly condensed to body parts, bones, muscles, tendons, and joint connections.

Aligning the body, in place or in verticality, is roughly a definition of first position. Alignment means exactly that: bringing the body into a line with a common forward. The head, chest, and hips are all given their front and back, sideward, up and down orientation. These facings are what is aligned. The directional placements of these parts are easy to recognize, but their mechanism is what should be stressed in class.

You can explore an extremity (arms and legs) in a more thorough manner than simply as a body part by discerning:

Where the part is attached to the torso (joint).

The part itself (arm, leg, etc.) as a unit.

The furthermost peripheral end (fingertip, toe, nose, etc.), which will enable it to design, in a linear manner, on the space around it.

The teacher should make the student aware of this delineation as soon as possible so he can practice it from the beginning of the dance training. This awareness is the beginning of defining and strengthening an abstract (nonverbal) vocabulary by clueing the dancer into what the nature of the movement is about. Unnecessary emotional overlays can be replaced by abstract sentient or sensed responses.

THE BACK

The dancer should conceive of the back as everything through which the spinal cord passes. This includes hips through head. When the body is rounded forward, the lower spine and the neck participate, as well as pliancy in the knees. The same is true with other directional back rounding, such as arcs. Using the torso fully creates the arc, which always accompanies circles. The body arc shapes the upper part of the circle, either forward, backward, or sideward.

THE LEGS

In basic technique, the leg is introduced into any of its actions, be it bending, extending, locomoting, or swinging, with a breath in the thigh. This breath lifts and rotates the leg, which turns the thigh in or out. This breath will feed life into the rest of the movement. The attached leg lengthens independently out of the hip, so that the hip does not involuntarily move with the leg.

THE FEET

When the dancer lifts the leg, the toe instinctively stretches and reaches vigorously for the floor, giving the foot a pointed look. The toes when stretched are always considered to be reaching for and pressing into the ground as well as completing the line of the leg. This is the explanation for the mechanical instruction "point your toe." The arch is raised as a result of the knee turnout. Practice the coordination that occurs by rolling the knees in and flattening the arches, then rolling the knees out and lifting the arches.

THE HIPS

The hips are treated as a unit, which in the front begins at the top of the pelvic bone and continues a few inches into the top of the thigh. In the back it begins at the lower spine and around the gluteus. The front of the hips has a forward, which is lifted, and open in a rotary action, not a tucked-under or tilted-up placement. The back is released downward and the lower spine has a slight backward pressure. In the back, deep under the gluteus, there are two points that work to start the rotary action of the thigh. These two points also press the hip forward and rotate out the front of the hip and thighs. Gripping the buttocks for "turning out" only locks the movement of the hips and upper thighs. The buttocks should be made firm but not gripped. This is achieved by finding the two deep points at the gluteus–thigh joining which press the buttocks forward, without gripping them.

110

THE ABDOMINAL REGION

This area is lifted upward toward the chest area, not pulled in and locked as it commonly is to flatten the stomach. This area allows for the stretching and lengthening action of the torso. It also separates the hips and chest and allows them to move, independently of each other.

THE CHEST

This houses the sternum, the pectorals, and the ribcage. The pectorals work wide and down to allow the sternum to come up and through. The ribcage is held in place, not allowed to fall out of alignment at the lower end.

THE SHOULDERS

The shoulders are an independent part of the body, which often gets confused with the arms and chest because they are very much employed by both, but only as an accessory force. Together with the arms, the shoulders press the shoulder blades down in the back; together with the chest, the shoulders press the pectorals wide in the front. The shoulders also have a complete range of action of their own, particularly circularly and in the high and depth dimension. Their movement range must be kept independent of the chest, unless deliberately used as such. They also clearly denote the shoulder suspension points.

THE ARMS

The arms operate from the back. The shoulders press down to cantilever the arms up. When extended into sideward action, the shoulders press down, the elbows lift slightly, the wrists have a slight downward pressure, and the fingers extend out to continue the arm direction into space. The muscles in the upper arm are often ignored during training. The oppositional force of the shoulder pressing down and the upward elbow rotation helps strengthen this area, as does graining within the three-dimensionality of the arm. You should think of the upper arm as having the same muscular complexity as the thigh, as well as a similar strength.

In addition, the arm can call attention to a larger range of movement than simply used as an arm. Add to this, the arm's ability to create densities (interior compactness or looseness, hard and soft), grain (interior directional flow.) The arm is no longer simply a body part, but an eloquent and versatile, three-dimensional moving component of the body, as are the other extremities.

THE HEAD

The head sits balanced on the neck. Great care must be taken to keep the chin from rising and tilting the head back. In this instance the chin tries to compensate for a lazy, nonlifted forehead and upper eyelid. Practice the chin lifting and the head falling back as the eye looks down the nose, and then while lowering the chin into place feel the eyelid lift to allow the eyelids to stretch open and look out and forward. The neck lengthens as part of the spine. For weak necks, there is a muscle spot in the back of the neck which when the neck is straightened can be pressed backward, which will help to strengthen the neck.

THE FACE

The face often directs the audience's eye, and it is important to use the open forehead, clear eyes, and relaxed mouth and jaw to focus attention on the movement itself rather than reflect technical struggles. Students of all ages tend to concentrate their efforts in their faces, so that it appears as if the initial joy in dancing has turned to straining effort. I often stop class and remind students of the pleasure they once had in dancing and to never lose it: "Open your faces, let your hips and thighs do the worrying. Don't show me your difficulties. Lift your cheeks. Open your eyes. I know it is killing you now but learn to sublimate these intense looks. Let me see that inner person shine through. Show me the you inside who enjoys moving, and share it with me."

Focus

The directional focus of the eye is as potent a gesture as is a pointing finger. Graining employs the many eyes of the dancer's body. The viewer is keenly alert to the dancer's many focuses, especially that of the eye. Should the dancer suddenly change his eye focus, the viewer will just as quickly draw his attention away from the dancer's body and look out into space at the dancer's interest.

The change of eye focus is probably the fastest movement the body can make. One can demonstrate this by looking at a fingertip and then to the moon. The speed to accomplish this simple shift is inconceivable. The dancer should always be accountable for where the eye is looking. The eye, like any other body part, has to "breathe" to avoid looking frozen or locked.

CLASS PLAN

TECHNIQUE

Premise

Engaging body parts.

Walking with a different body part leading. Feel the energy and thrust difference of each part. Chest—power of hips—head.

Introduce a simple locomotion pattern to carry the body part across the floor. Different body parts lead the torso, reshaping the body with each change.

Note

The body part will now combine with and alter the locomotion direction of the body. No longer will we see the simplicity of a dimensional walk, but instead we'll see how movements mix and influence each other, for example, moving the chest sideward while walking forward.

You will be stressing body parts constantly in every class this week.

Being able to isolate your major body parts will be the challenge.

ACROSS THE FLOOR

Monday

Introduction of body parts to lead locomotion: the chest.

Identify structure and flexibility of chest.

Chest leading in all directions.

Walking backward: chest leading—moving sideward L. and R. Control energy for these changes.

(Five-finger exercise) Floor pattern with different body parts.

Facing side of room. R. side chest three steps shift to L. side half turn—repeat walks across floor.

Lift arm slightly to allow side chest action to be visible.

Chest leading across the floor. Class at 18th Street, New York City.
Photo courtesy of the Nikolais/Louis Archives.

Students will get confused, but persist and develop their coordination. Don't stop or slow down while coming across floor. Let them practice coordinating while waiting to come across the floor again.

Chest leads in all directions when walking. Forward, back, side and side.

Identify and stress the elasticity of the abdominal region to stretch side to side and be able to isolate the action of the hip from the chest.

Use rhythmic pattern—start with twos, and then threes, and then combine with accents.

Start with a locomotion pattern, then add time values

Include chest directions in step hops, turns, runs and leaps.

Tuesday

Body parts: hip.

The forward pressure of the hip: this includes a forward and sideward graining. Do not let the hip tilt under as in a peripheral swing, but presses evenly forward as in locomotion.

Feel the strength and thrusting power of forward hips, as it differs from chest or head.

Press hips forward with forward pressure, then freely slide side to side in sideward slot.

Step hops: hip accents forward in the air. Runs and turns hip lead.

Wednesday

Combination chest and hip.

Do not introduce peripheral or rotary action.

Call attention to each body part's physical distinction and power. Don't overinvent too soon. Just clarify the body part and its mobility.

Shifting from one part to another in walks.

Now develops movement into turns. Hip leads turn R., chest leads turn L.

Changing and shifting body parts during forward turn.

Show motional transitions.

Thursday

Whole arm, elbows, and hands.

The across-the-floor pattern will become more detailed as the shift between these three parts indicates.

Add to locomotion: turns, runs and leaps.

Throughout the week the use of time as pulse, fast, slow, and pause, should be an important, conscious part of every class.

A body part has two ends and a middle. With body parts we want to see the whole unit with its three-dimensional ability.

Don't let the action of one body part linger and unintentionally influence other body parts.

Be aware of the flexibility of the spine, which links almost all of the parts.

Insist on flatness of the front of hips and chest.

Sense the various time differences with various parts. Some can move faster or slower than others. Some have considerably more power than others.

Isolate the body part so that it speaks clearly of itself.

Be aware of how a moving body part influences the body. For example, the chest going backward while walking forward will alter the forward intensity.

The clarity of the body part shares importance with locomotion.

The direction of the body part and the direction of the locomotion make for different compounds.

Decentralization within the body. Shifting the focus to the center of different body parts both quickly and clearly.

The rest of the body grains itself to this multifocused decentralization action.

Body parts are like various instruments in an orchestra—make them sound differently by thinking differently about each.

Sense and communicate the size, weight, and other characteristics of the body part as a unit.

In the early classes, always pass the transition from body part to body part through the body. Later the transitions can follow more inventive paths.

Friday
Legs, knees, and feet.

Again, the pattern reflects the change from one part to another.

Legs leading into space with breath and thigh lift.

Take advantage of energy changes in transitions.

IMPROVISATION

Monday
Chest (solo—alone, then in duets). Conversations between different chests.

Tuesday
Hip (solo—alone, then in duets). Conversations between different hips.

Wednesday
Chest and hip (in duets), each partner with a different part.

> *Notes*
>
> "Alone" always means solo, but in groups. When in duets, assign a single body part for each person, for example, conversation between a chest and legs, and so on.
>
> Once anything has been introduced in a previous class, continue to use it in all further classes.
>
> Introduce body part awareness during pliés.
>
> Be sure to stress fulfillment of invention, motivation, and total participation in all actions.
>
> What is improvised must relate to the current premise.
>
> This is not to be a new vocabulary to hide behind, but to develop the fluency necessary for effective decentralization.
>
> Float the chest, keeping it lifted as it is supported by the lifted abdomen.
>
> At an early point in locomotion, note how the use of the body part flavors the locomotion, for example, walking forward while the chest or hip moves in other directions.

Thursday	Arms, elbows, and hands (alone, then in duets). In duets, each partner with a different part. Vary these. Change places.

Friday	Legs, knees, and feet (alone, then in duets). In duets, each partner with a different part.

COMPOSITION

Call attention to two body parts separately.

Invention, phrased dynamically (change of energy and time).

Development—beginning, middle, and end.

Focus on structure.

Developing a movement phrase across the floor.
Photo by T. Mike Fletcher.

WEEK 3: BODY PARTS (CONTINUED)

CLASS PLAN

TECHNIQUE

Premise

Across the floor.

All across-the-floor developments are based on locomotion, isolated body parts, and time patterns. Develop new locomotion patterns every day. Don't make them complex, just enough to give the body part a different flavor by change of time, shape, space, and movement design.

Monday

Review of body parts.

On a forward walk in four counts each gesture.

Hips forward, back, side R., side L. Feel how the sharing of directions in space and body parts changes the quality of the movement.

Repeat phrase two steps each action.

Mix two counts and one count.

With a half turn—two counts walking toward each direction half turns walking backward two counts each direction. Repeat.

Mixing locomotion direction with body part shifting. Add half turns. Develop to class skill.

Combination of chest, hips, arms, and legs.

Employ the energy of transitional (connecting movements). Develop kinetic phrases using the distinctive energy of the individual body part, for example, the bulk thrust of the hips as opposed to the linear action of the arm or legs.

Rhythmic body part combinations.

Repeat and develop previous classes.

Get class to familiarize themselves with what seems like eccentricities of body part combinations.

Tuesday

Head and elbows or other relationships.

Wednesday

Combination of various body parts.

Thursday

Shoulders and arm distinction.

Friday

Combination of body parts.

In run, run, leap chest shift in the air. Watch out for surprise landings.

IMPROVISATION— DECENTRALIZATION

Fluently place your center at any point in or outside of the body.

Monday

Follow the front person. Repeat of first week improvisation, but emphasize body parts.

Quick recognition of who is leading and smooth continuation of movement.

Even as the groups' focus changes, the movement maintains a continuous flow.

Tuesday

Groups in circle facing inward. Movement starts and is passed to the next person without interruption. Inevitably, the movement receiver makes slight embellishments but never loses the time value or general form. Everyone sees the movement as it is passed.

Improvising with backs.
Photo by T. Mike Fletcher.

Turn around everyone with faces out. No one but the handler and receiver can see the movement. Dancers sense where the movement received is to "go," develop speed.

Groups in a straight line as simple movement is passed along. The speed increases. First person begins again when last person passes it off.

Wednesday

Free improvisation body parts, alone, in groups. Body parts change during locomotion in duets and group.

Thursday

Contact in duets.

A single point of physical contact between dancers, the point changes constantly changing the shape.

Both bodies are thought of as a single shape. Graining toward the point of contact.

Speed of contact change. No attitudes regarding contact.

The confidence of a single unit. Consciousness of combined shape.

As in all improvisations, invention is important.

Friday

Contact-locomotion.

Locomoting makes it difficult to maintain point of contact. Both dancers have to be both quick and alert, and not release contact point at the same time.

COMPOSITION

Body parts: distinguish characteristics of different body parts. Dancer chooses part.

Body Parts

The body is a creature of comfort. It hates to be disturbed. The head, the arms, the hips, and chest all seek the most unchallenging methods of operation and function. All of this pedestrian activity just hates to be challenged. However, the dancer's job is to adapt to any choreography, and as a result he has to extend his physical abilities to serve whatever he is performing.

One of the objectives in body parts and isolations is to experience the variety of movement combinations and the kinetic flavors these combinations can produce. They are often bizarre, amusing, difficult, and always compelling to watch.

Tasting the eccentricity of mixing body parts with different time and space begins to reveal the potential uniqueness of the dancer. A great deal of invention rests in the juxtaposing of body parts and time.

WEEK 4: LEVELS

INTRODUCTION

A level is created by any linear action that remains parallel to the ground. It can be created by a peripheral linear action, as long as it is parallel to the ground. A plane has a thickness, whereas linear implies the fineness of line. But when used as a level, planes and lines are both parallel to the ground. The flexation and extension of the standing legs help to create and keep accurate level changes.

To avoid complications, focus the class on the simple practice of three level changes:

High level (in relevé)

Horizontal level (legs straight—normal position)

Low level (in plié, not deep plié)

Any body part that can create a line or path of action that remains parallel to the ground can create levels, be it the head or toe. However should the ongoing movement cease, then the line ceases to be and the body shape or time (stopping) becomes visible instead. Level implies continuously drawing the line and continuously graining to the level line created.

LEVELS IN LOCOMOTION

Review leg flexation and locomotion.

Levels are compounds. They are combinations of the height or depth of linear action. The top of the head creates the level line. With low level the chest presses forward to arrive over the ball of the foot. In high (relevé) level the leg lifts from the thigh to accommodate the high level, or increase the pulse to sustain the high level.

To see how our bodies adjust their height and identify with degrees of level, use this example:

With the height at standing, normal level, extend the right foot. Where the toe touches the floor is the length of a step for that person in normal level. Each dancer has a different leg size, therefore his step will reflect his stepping length and not that of the taller or shorter person next to him.

From normal level, plié to low level (not deep plié), extend the right leg again and see it reach further away. This constitutes the length of the long, low step.

At the same time, as the leg reaches, press the chest forward so that it arrives over the toe to achieve a low-level step. Do not step with the weight back or on the heel. Low level has a forward thrust in the chest to achieve the longer step length.

Now go back to normal in place and relevé. This is high level.

Extend the leg forward and recognize the smallness of step. The grain upward is now shared with the forward going. The foot arch is now more prominently used, whereas in low level the knee seems to introduce the leg into forward. The lifted arch in relevé is pressed through, and the weight is placed on the ball of the weight receiving foot. The walking leg exaggerates the lift in the thigh as it steps to emphasize upwardness. This lift in the thigh can also take up the extra time value, which the smaller step accomplishes quickly. Do not exaggerate the knee. Maintain the level line the head is making.

As with all stepping, the line of the level should not waiver up or down. However with the body remaining parallel to the ground, the head can create an additional side-to-side level while moving forward. Level is a discernible parallel line to the ground. A dancer should become skilled at transition of levels through the vertical. In the practice of level changes, the body stops its locomotor progression and changes the height up or down, through the vertical, then continues again into the new space. It does not go from high to low while the body is moving. This creates a diagonal transition, which alters the level line. Raising and lowering the body in place through knee and ankle action creates a clean transition between levels, whereas falling from high to low or swooping from low to high introduce a curved action, thereby destroying the level line. The transitions of levels are sharp, angular, quick, and discernible. These

---

Instructor Notes

Work on the normal level first, pointing out that the level is maintained in part by controlling the step length. In common walking, if the step is overlong, then the body weight tends to fall on the next step, thereby causing a level disturbance at that time. Although one can take smaller steps in a normal level, it will have a tendency to give the walk a character or situational look.

Check the timing of the hip and chest coinciding with the arrival of the weight, which will give a sense of totality and presence at that moment.

Watch also for the lift of the leg out of the hip joint, so that the joint also senses and performs the feeling of the direction.

Remind the student that the body always leans slightly into the direction of the line of travel. The faster the pace, the greater the lean. Be careful that the lean does not tilt for its own sake.

Stay for a while in each direction and level. Criticize fine points. Go through all the directions in different levels.

Don't develop complex patterns too soon. Always demand the performance of the act. If you give complex patterns too soon, students will skip over the sensitivity of the act.

Don't let students use the same quality for every change of directional stepping.

The thigh lifts and introduces every leg step. However subtle and imperceptible the lift may be, it nevertheless breathes life into the step.

Point out the dimensional change in going to a different level. A high level shortens the step, thereby diminishing the horizontal space in both depth and width. It extends the height, however, and must be performed with the projection of that upwardness.

On the contrary, working in low level, the step length is lengthened. The height is diminished and the horizontal space extended. Keep the weight forward. Don't walk with weight back like a Groucho Marx walk.

In locomotion, the top of the head creates the level line, and consciousness of this line makes the head important in communicating level. Because maintenance of the parallel line of action is a challenge the dancer faces, the steadiness and grain of the head is important.

restrictions are not rules, but challenges, so that both teacher and student have a common goal of achievement. Gaining a facile knee and ankle joint action is important.

PLANES

Planes can be thought of as spatial levels, no longer linear but three-dimensional slots. Although only the horizontal plane is technically level to the floor, the width of the plane is the width of the body dimension, which can widen with the sideward extension of the arms.

High: vertical—the up-and-down slot.

Width: horizontal—side-to-side slot.

Depth: forward—back slot.

Four diagonal slots.

By tilting the body, one can tilt the planes. Geometrically, by placing the body in any position on the floor, upside down, and so on, one can create innumerable sets of planes. For our purpose, however, high, deep, wide, and diagonals offer sufficient variation to the horizontal plane. Introduce planes only after spatial volumes have been investigated.

CLASS PLAN

TECHNIQUE

Premise

Perform levels of different type (low—medium—high) and at varying speeds.

Levels can only be achieved through some form of locomotion. When the locomotion ceases, the eye is directed to the shape of the body or everything else visible. This holds true with any peripheral linear action. A level is a path of action that remains parallel to the ground. In a walk, the head reflects the level of the body.

Across the floor in low level—sustain level line.

Five-finger exercise in low level—later in high level—then mix high and low—normal levels.

Level changes occur in the vertical with sharp pliés and relevés, so as not to interrupt too much the visual path.

Monday

Normal and low level. Awareness of plié action.

In place—practice leg length of stepping to create three levels: Low—normal—high.

Low is considered the depth of the dancer's plié in first position.

Practice the difficult accuracy of backward levels. The line prescribed by backward reaching toe.

In low-level walk, realize that as the back leg lifts to come forward, it sets the level of the line as it passes the standing leg for the step forward. Practice leg reaching circularly out and around, careful to keep its level to the ground, making adjustments in the knee and hip joints.

Develop locomotor phrase across the floor.

Tuesday

High level.

Create a new but simple locomotion phrase.

In high-level walk, make sure the upwardness is not jerky with each step. Keep the line, the top of the head is making, steady.

Take up excess time value with the stepping thigh lifting into the height, but keep the head line steady.

High is relevé height and each step is with as high forced an arch as is possible.

Drawing level peripheral lines with arms and legs.

Use care with legs reaching into backward line.

Because there is less locomotion in high level, be sure to project the top of the head both forward and high, strongly, and evenly. Keep the psychical lift in the body alive, and maintain the presence of being in high level.

Wednesday

High and low levels.

Careful flexation technique of standing leg for change of level.

Turns—change of level through vertical while turning.

In step turns—step forward in chosen level R. leg—L. leg starts back and makes a half circle, low level. Step back on L. leg as R. leg reaches forward and continues low-level line—repeat twice—four low forward steps—repeat turns in high level, and so on.

Develop with continuous half turns on each leg.

Develop with drop and rise in vertical for each turn.

Thursday

Faster levels.

Arm flexing at elbow and leg flexing at knee create oppositional horizontal level.

Top of head creates level circle—shift to chest circles then hips, all parallel to floor.

Step hops—thrusting hop into space so that by speed the head creates a level line stronger than the up and down made by the up and down action of the hop. Maintain horizontal line across the floor. These levels demand a faster pulse.

Friday

Create interesting movement phrase.

Chest and hip sideward levels. Keeping arms steady and level.

Chest and hip circular levels. Keeping arms steady and level.

Combination example: step turns—with flat flexed foot three-count turn to R. then shift three-count L. (6/4). Followed by chest to R. and forward circular level, step turns (four counts), then arms reaching side right and swinging around in level to L. side while walking forward four steps (four counts—4/4). Regulate tempo. Phrase time 3/4—3/4—4/4—4/4. Shifting from legs to chest to arms.

IMPROVISATION

Follow daily premise of decentralization.

A point about decentralization can be made here, because the attention is entirely outside of the body.

The line or level is to be seen. The whole body is projected into and focused on the height or depth of the level line.

The quality inherent in each level—the thinness of high and the forward depth of low, as well as the balanced placement of normal—is projected.

COMPOSITION

Levels: low—medium—high.

Use body parts to create levels as well. Take great care with the accuracy of the feet and legs, especially as toe passes through to take a step from backward to forward.

Create an uninterrupted level action to achieve a lyricism, an uninterrupted flow shifting from body part to body part.

Notes

Transition through vertical, no curves or diagonals in transitions.

The linear action stops if there is any cessation of movement, then the visible attention will shift elsewhere.

Clarify a body part that is being carried along as "a rest in place," a nonparticipating area, as opposed to one that is actively pressing into space to create the linear action. Example: For the chest to locomote from side to side, it moves as a unit to create the locomotion. Do not let it tilt.

Locomotion involves the totality of the moving body part; level is a parallel to the floor along one trajectory.

Be careful to grain the body focus to the line.

Check length of leg step.

Maintain the linear accuracy with the top of the head and arms.

Weight is always forward, especially in low level. If arms are in second be sure not to forget them and let their level droop.

Levels can be exasperating because they require meticulous care. Stay with it. It will give the legs, particularly, a clear ability to articulate.

WEEK 5: THE JOINTS AND JOINT ACTION

INTRODUCTION

The joints lie between and connect the major body parts with the extremities. They account for considerable articulation and are easily located throughout the body.

Agents of kinesthesia are located in the muscles, tendons, and tissues. These agents inform us of our flexion, extensions, and twistings. Such actions occur throughout the axial construction of the body. We move mostly by means of the hinging and ball-and-socket actions of the joints.

One area of major technical benefit to the dancer is a precise definition of where a body part begins and ends. For example, the relationship between the arm and shoulders can be determined by separating the activity of one from the other.

It is essential that each dancer explore and experience his own body's wonderfully complex system of joint articulation. This study should be done with intense concentration on kinetic sensations. The organs of kinesthesia must converse constantly with the mind and its consequent kinetic memory to create an abstract language of motion out of which abstract intelligence can emerge. The great variety of joint-oriented motional experiences should be explored and the sentient findings stored in the brain for recall and control when the need arises for creative and performing use.

We go about this by feeding isolated experiences into the kinetic memory. Some of this will be basic, such as where the muscles, tendons, and joints begin (thus defining the length of the body part).

One of the most important set of joints is the hip sockets. The process of walking has, in most cases, become so automatic that reference to the hip joint in the walking process has become obscured. Yet it is an amazingly sensitive joint, and sentient knowledge and control here is essential to the dancer, particularly in the process of locomotion. I recall in my own study the day I discovered where my leg emerged from my hip. This gave me an entirely different sense of leg action. Peripheral and rotary motions became much better defined, and the kinetic sensation was much more specific.

The most easily comprehended motional exploration by the dancer is in the articulation of the joints. Isolated experience in moving the joints is a good way to begin sensory judgment, starting with the extremities, the head, arms, and legs.

The joints allow the body the facility to change its size: flexing and extending from in to out, from big to small, from low to high, from close to far, and so on.

The next step is to see how the attention of the rest of the body can amplify the experience. When this amplification is accomplished, it becomes quite visible. For example, if we isolate the right wrist joint in the area around the right hip, this point now becomes the center toward which the rest of the body will direct its focus. This involves the concept of graining. The attitudes of the entire body grain themselves to accommodate the pinpointed interest in the wrist. Because the wrist is at hip level, the rest of the body adjusts itself to that point. The upper body would incline downward toward that point. The strong focus of the eye would also concentrate its beam toward the point of concern.

The premise here is the full communication of the joint action, not only to one's self but meta-kinetically, which is the process of communicating motion to the onlooker. This, consequently, becomes an exercise in performance as well as in the dancer's technical control. Bear in mind that it is the other parts of the body that are usually derelict in giving their attention to the concerned articulation. This pliancy of the body to shape itself quickly as one goes from one joint to another testifies to the body's intelligence of purpose. It is also best to practice articulation by focusing on joints not in close proximity to each other.

A common problem is the tendency of some body parts to be unwilling to give up their loyalty to a previous focus, thereby muddying the clarity of articulation. When a new focal point is determined, the whole body structure must divorce itself from the previous center of interest and focus uninhibitedly toward the new point.

Improvisation with axial motion is necessary, especially with those joint actions that were particularly different from one's ordinary experiences. With concentration, as single joint experience, the senses become more acutely responsive to the aesthetic definition of a specific action. One will soon discover that wild, disorganized, and abandoned movement, however pleasurable, quickly leads to dead ends and that the student soon discovers the importance of sensed articulation. An intelligence then begins to arise, and the meaning of dance begins to be clarified.

All this can be explored in technique class as well as during improvisations and, finally, in composition, where the teacher can more carefully observe performance quality. Bear in mind that the purpose here is to intensify both focal and grain sensitivity so that the kinesthetic and relative sensory experience can relay to the brain the qualitative description of the motion in the joint.

When one considers that a great pianist controls extraordinary aesthetic results through his fingers, no moving part is too minute not to explore.

CLASS PLAN

TECHNIQUE

Premise

Awareness of joint, hinge and axial action.

Joints are the hinges that join body parts and that allow the body to alter its size in space. These points can also create a hinge action with the ground or with created points in the surrounding space.

The joints:

> Head to neck
>
> Arm to torso
>
> Waist—chest to hip
>
> Hip to leg
>
> Knee
>
> Ankle
>
> Toes
>
> Elbow
>
> Wrist
>
> Fingers

The important objective in joint action is to call attention to the flexing motion and its recovering straightening movement. It is the opening and closing and change of size that must be visible, not the body part making the gesture. When this clarity is mastered, then the fullness of the body as it goes in and out or up and down can lend itself to support the hinge action. For example, the arms open to create larger spatial references and the legs bend for the action of descent.

Demonstrate where the joints are located in the body and their flexing ability. Define the plié again, with its turned-out leg and its flexing action. Knee over ball of foot and lifted arch. Try in relevé to achieve as high a forced arch as possible while straightening the knee.

Notice the body hinges. A joint can also be created by any body part attaching itself to another body part or to a point in space, to the floor, or to another person. But for our purposes, flexing and extending, bending, and straightening the body to change its size are its most common uses. Straightening should be thought of as lengthening out into space without calling attention to the space. Flexing calls attention to the joint bending. Pliés are flexing and extending in vertical, making the change of size visible through the locomotion of up and down.

Be sure to include flexation with all joints when devising patterns of movement. Although the knee and arm actions are dominant ones, don't forget head, chest, and hips.

Monday	Triple knee flexation with opposite leg extension.
	Both legs flex and extend together. Stretched on extension, flexed when in. Stand in place, with weight on one leg, free leg flexed in. Reach forward and flex in. Reach side and flex in. Reach back and flex in. Four steps forward—other leg flexes in to prepare for next step and repeat triple action.
	Mix with level walks and vertical change of levels.
	Calling attention to the joint flexing and extending into straight.
	Vary locomotion direction, turns, and time variations.
	Add arms flex and extending in leg direction—or in opposition—or forward, high, wide.
	Change height of leg extensions.
	Set limit of repetitions across the floor because the patterns can be tiring.
	Using the flexing thigh to receive the step weight properly. Turned-out knee over toe so that arch lifts.
Tuesday	Add arms to leg flexations—forward—side—up.
	Motional quality: in to out—open and close change of focus and grain.
	Curious walking patterns—head bending at neck.
	Curious flexation shaping—torso bending at hips.
	Always calling attention to flexation, not to shape, although shape is obviously very visible.
Wednesday	Repeat and vary combinations.
	Turns—high—low.
	Directions change with standing leg plié relevé and free leg extensions.
	Time variations. Regular beat and double time.
	Arm variations.
	Create interesting rhythm and other time variations.
	Devise floor patterns from premise.
	Flex extensions in air.
Thursday	Vibrations (see "Vibrations" section).
	Double pliés.
	Keep vibration going through leg transitions.
	Add direction variations.
	Turns.
Friday	Motional qualities of flex-extension.
	Time variation—legato to pizzicato.
	Turns—air work—up on extend gestures.

Notes

End all classes with released runs and jump turn patterns.

Take care to make the arms fashion and flex-extend to shape to the movement.

Grain the arms to give additional insight to the body's flexed shaping.

Recall the pop style of "vogue-ing," which used extraordinary flexing designs of the arms around the head.

When the arms are in motion, move them basically within the flex-extension definition.

Using flex-extend to perform the motional qualities of:

In and out

Small and larger

High and low

Up and down

Close and open

VIBRATIONS

Vibrations involve a small double plié while stepping. The knee actions allow for this pliancy. The vibrations are continuous so that the forward walk never stops nor is the walk jagged appearing. The pliéd knee is placed carefully over ball of same foot. The up and down action soon becomes an unconscious automatic walk characteristic.

Double bend in the knee.

Take the whole body with you.

Soften the descent. No drop shocks in the torso.

Get weight over standing leg so you can be on top of yourself.

Not "step then plié," but plié and step occur simultaneously.

Instep of free moving leg passes standing ankle in walking transitions.

Straighten leg between pliés. Reach the full extension of the legs by straightening the knees fully for a moment between pliés.

Vibration

Hanya Holm, in an interview, described the origin of the vibration as a plié development. In the early 1920s, when inflation had driven up the price of food and fuel in Germany and the poor dancers were forever in unheated environments, she found herself sitting on a spring bed with some other dancers one day. They began to bounce to keep warm and created a vibration. They then developed this into a steady reverberation as they walked and moved. They showed this to Mary Wigman who developed it into the double plié loco-motion.

Today the vibration that resulted from the original bouncing is the continuous double plié, a movement involving a very flexible knee and Achilles' tendon. The vibration action can continue through walking and transitions. Technically the heel must remain on the ground and the flexations are limited to the knee and ankle. A very sustained quality of movement occurs and the dancer "rides" the smooth reverberation.

The time factor must be carefully considered, otherwise with too fast or slow a motion the body part will become dominant.

IMPROVISATION

Follow daily class premise.

Three up at a time in solo. Flex-extend.

Define joint action clearly.

Invention with all joints.

Throughout all week be strongly aware of arms (elbows and wrists).

Eloquence of hand and arm placement.

Constant consciousness of arm placement and action.

Create phrase with arms as dominant factor.

Evolve arm transitions.

Constantly grain to arm joint designs.

COMPOSITION

Call attention to joint action.

Axial Points on the Floor and in Space

Extending the idea of joint action we can now anchor the joint to the floor or to an imaginary point in space and by moving toward that point or away from it practice a flexing action.

WEEK 6: ROTARY ACTION

INTRODUCTION

Rotary action is the third movement range of body action. There are four possibilities:

Locomotion carries the body or a part of it as a complete unit from one space to another.

Peripheral action holds one body part anchored in place while the other end can move freely, prescribing a linear design.

Rotary action permits the body or body part to move within its own space, which can result in turns.

Flex-extension is a joint action that extends or condenses the body in space.

The basic rotary action is rotation: the individual body part turning within its own space, reaching its limitation and then turning back or rewinding. The sensation of rotation should be practiced to experience its unique flavor. This flavor should instill all turns, so that the addition of locomotion into turns and circles does not become too dominant.

Although turning is a rotary movement, it also involves locomotion. The dancer achieves the turn by stepping within the space his body occupies, giving the body its rotary definition or movement within its own space. This means he has to always keep in mind the limited space available in which to turn or move. Locomotion out of that space becomes a step turn; extending the locomotion further extends the form into a circle.

Turning in place to the right and left moves the dancer's central vertical line. The dancer arches the upper body slightly to the right or left. The arms and upper body and head all grain and adjust in the direction of the turn.

The leg action for turns involves both rotating out and rotating in. The leg is turned out on the first step in the direction of the turn; the other leg completes the turn by stepping turned in. When the turned-in leg completes the turn, a whipping, spinning action occurs. The turn should ride that action and continue it so that the turning has an even revolution. The chest part, which is farthest from the center of the turn, needs an additional thrust to get it around the corner. The center of the body shifts slightly to the side of the body toward which the turn is inclined.

The level of the turn should be maintained on a horizontal plane unless designed otherwise. The body should move as a single unit, avoiding the head-whipping jerkiness that "spotting" creates. Spotting is a variation of turning.

Rotary action combined with locomotion becomes step turns and circles. Rotation of a body part, particularly the legs, is essential to understanding and sensing rotary action. The complex techniques of walking and turning are achieved simultaneously. A step turn can be complicated because all of the actions involved are equally shared. The turn degree is carefully judged to balance with the locomotion timing. The stepping and turning are coordinated. Separating them constitutes a variation of stepping then turning.

LOCOMOTOR TURNS

Turning while traveling combines the technical criteria of both forms of action. Here, the sense of the locomotor direction traveling through space unites with the whirling action of the turn. The one major difference is that turning eliminates a standard facing of the body toward the directional line. Instead, one selects a coincidence of facings; for example, in turning to the right, one may control the action so that the front surfaces of the body will face the direction of travel with each step on the right foot. One may also select the sideward, backward, or diagonal surfaces as the relative point. The most common locomotor turns, and seemingly the easiest to control, are the front diagonal facings. Here, in turning to the right, the right diagonal edge of the body aligns in that direction when the weight lands on the right foot.

In the initial practice of travel turns, one should avoid the usual "spotting." This is the action in which the head jerks around ahead of the body to hold momentary facing of the path of action. Although it gives a sparkling brilliance to the action, spotting does so at the expense of the whirling, continuous quality of the turn. It also tends toward a motional habit of the head, which makes other variations difficult. One should be able to vary the direction of the turn at will, as well as to spot not only with the head but also with other parts of the body.

In travel turns, the leg follows two lines of action. The legs turn out and in as they do in "in-place" turns, as well as stepping in the direction of the line of travel as they do in locomotion. The alternate outward and inward rotation of the legs aids the rotary action. Stepping in space directs the body into the desired direction. The free leg in passing should trace the toe along the locomotor line of action. The usual tendency is to swing it out in space, causing an undue centrifugal force in the lower leg. This outward gesture is a variation of the basic step turn. There is also the tendency in locomotor stepping for the turned-in leg to step shorter than the turnout leg. It is best to equalize these steps so that the locomotor action is even rather than jerky. Later, variations and developments can be made more easily when this basic skill is achieved.

Because of the shape and structure of the body, there are necessary forces involved in executing turns and circles, which lessen the body's straight and vertical stance—for example, inclining right or left in the direction of the turn.

PIVOT TURN

Turning on one foot is the most challenging of all turns. These turns involve strong physical and psychical energy. Balancing requires a secure vertical concept and the assurance to maintain it. Concurrent with this, the psyche and willpower must provide sufficient thrust to complete a movement while in the precarious position of balance.

Riding the strong impulsion energy, the torso can change its suspension point from the head to the chest or back or a variation of these points, all while holding the relevé. To gain the necessary speed for double turns, the arms pull into the torso so that the vertical center is taut.

TURN IN PLACE

A pivot turn on one foot where the weight remains steadily in one spot can be executed in vertical. When the dancer shifts his weight from foot to foot, however, the turn is consequently distorted because of shifting from one center to another. Therefore, to execute a true turning while changing feet, the dancer must make adjustments. One foot assumes the responsibility of the center, while the other treads more lightly and paddles a small circle around the pivotal leg. The consequence is an actual small, circular locomotor action. One side of the body becomes center while the outer side sweeps around the center, forming the periphery.

A common failure in turning often results from misjudging the speed required of the outer side of the body. This is usually because the outer side fails to move quickly enough and therefore drags the body back and away from the intended action.

The arms, too, may contribute to the turn, assuming a round shape coincidental with the size of the periphery of the circle being executed. If the arm on the centrifugal side does not round itself sufficiently or move with necessary speed, it will hold back the action.

The character and feeling of turning is that of whirling with an unbroken linear continuity. Variations of orientation and centripetal and centrifugal control as well as level change allow for an infinite number of motional possibilities.

CLASS PLAN

TECHNIQUE

Premise

Rotary and rotation action turns.

Move within the space occupied by the body or body part. Demonstrate all body parts rotating in their own space.

Introduce rotary action during stretches, rolling or rotating body parts in or out.

Do basic turn patterns. Repeat those from warm-up standing series with the whole group before coming across the floor.

Turn left and right, with catch step to change feet and direction.

To ensure a whirling action, make sure the furthest chest part presses the torso weight quickly into the turning. Do not let the torso lag behind the stepping.

Review the four kinds of motion: peripheral, locomotion, flex-extend, and rotary.

Repeat a turning session every day to overcome dizziness and build compatibility with turning.

To overcome dizziness, hold a finger about 10 inches in front of the eyes. Slowly bring the finger closer to the head and let the eyes cross. This exercise lends stability. Also try it without the finger, so that you simply cross the eyes quickly.

Monday

Rotating body parts: head, arms, legs, hips, and chest.

Create a floor pattern and develop it with turns in place and step turns.

Start with rotation of body parts; for example, in a forward walk, rotate legs—in three steps, out three steps—across floor. Add arms rolled in and out.

Create variations.

Add locomotion into directions and turning in place.

Turn technique: rotate feet closely out and in to gain whirling sensation. Keep chest leading torso over directional foot.

Tuesday

Step turns and turn in place.

Build pattern combining turn and locomotor evenly sharing step and time value.

Turn the whole body in place. Then turn faster with outside leg lightly paddling around inner leg for the sensation of whirling.

Check for even coordination and sharing of the locomotion direction with the circular turn degree.

End phrases with pivot turns.

Wednesday

Body parts lead in turns.

Build pattern to include various body parts leading "around the corner."

Sense change of energy and quality for chest and hip. Turn chest alone, release hip to follow. Then turn hip alone with chest to follow.

Let lower spine lead in backward pivot whip turns. Change from lower spine backward to hip forward.

Change of level, sensing spiral. Move from high to low in turns and create spirals.

Thursday

Create and develop turn variations.

Turns into locomotion: try travel step turns and travel whirling across the floor.

Pull in and turn around a tight upward grained center. Then release to a wider center.

At the end of class, include some rotary action in the air. Full turns in the air, pulling center of body in and up.

Friday

Create turning phrase.

Use all areas: step turns, spinning, spirals, full turn in air.

Turn in place to taste the motional sensation of turning or whirling.

IMPROVISATION

Monday

Develop rotation of body parts into torso motivated turns.

Tuesday

Turns in place and step turns with change of level. Spiral up and down.

Wednesday

Combine in quartets.

Thursday

Combine in quartets.

Friday

Choreographed duets.

COMPOSITION

Use rotations and turns, high–low combinations, spirals, and pivots.

Include "around" action (directing the action around itself).

Watch for proper leg action in turns.

Turning and Spinning

Turning, whirling, and spinning—when all factors relative to the unimpaired turn are coordinated, a state of transcendence occurs. In the early Wigman–Holm training, turning was a major part of every class, and after all the side effects of dizziness and nausea were overcome, it became a way to achieve a wonderful sense of balancing the physical, psychical, and aesthetic senses. The instructors included turn dances in almost every program. Spotting and whipping were variants of turning and practiced as such. In spinning, the body is calm and the action is sustained.

WEEK 7: GRAIN AND DENSITY

INTRODUCTION

GRAIN

Graining describes the interior landscape of the body. Graining directs internal energy and charts the itinerary of mobility. Graining is a visible indicator of the body's aliveness and its participation in fulfilling movement. This, in turn, translates movement into motion. Internal participation is a major part of motion and should be introduced and practiced continuously, in every class and with every premise.

To create a strong pictorial image of the activity of graining, one should conceive of the body as being filled with molecules, each with an arrow pointing out of it. When the body is not directed toward a specific action but is in a state of repose, the arrows on these molecules point randomly. Once the body becomes motionally aware, be it to a moving point, a part of the body, or any focus of attention outside the body, all the arrows turn their attention toward that area of interest.

Graining therefore is a process in which the body fluidly calls the viewer's attention quickly to the interest of the dancer and the choreographer. The fastest moving part of the body is the eye muscle. Graining the body must keep up with this speed.

This graining process is part of every directional movement and also plays a role in specific isolated suspension points. It can radiate out of the body to points of outer interest as well as sensitize the surface of the skin from within.

Graining gives visibility to the body's awareness of motion. This visibility in turn qualifies motion. This inner molecular awareness will be called upon for participation in any movement. From the basic aligning of the body, to its dimensional extension outward, to the most complex movement, graining the body to its designed action places the dancer in a state of rich sentient participation with the action demanded of him.

This participation is not to be confused with willful indulgence in the performance. Understanding the body's interior performance as opposed to its emotional overlay is another distinction between decentralization and centralization. The ability to decentralize offers the dancer a major insight in understanding dance. This ability adds further definition to the distinction between motion and movement. The difference between generalization and specific qualification echoes the difference between centralization and decentralization.

DENSITY

If one thinks of the space within the body as equivalent to the space outside of it, then comparisons are easy. Thinking of the molecular action within the body as engaging both achieves two-dimensional space (movement along a plane) and three-dimensional space (filling up a volume). These are the interior depictions of space: grain works on planes and density suggests volume.

By compacting or dispersing the number of molecules within the body or body part one creates varying densities, such as hard or soft.

Similarly, by directing the internal attention of the body to a point inside or outside the body, one achieves grain. This internal awareness both enlivens and enriches the practice of dance and is essential to the teaching of dance as a performing art. Identifying the condition of inner space also lends clarity to the process of abstraction.

CLASS PLAN

TECHNIQUE

Premise

Understand grain and density.

Introduce this vocabulary:

> Decentralization
>
> Grain
>
> Density
>
> Interior space
>
> Interior mobility
>
> Molecular image

Graining shows the spatial dimensions of the body and peripheral designs.

Degrees of molecular compactness are used to qualify density, such as hard and soft, etc.

Decentralization involves shifting focus from a centralized core to a movement's intention and thereby creating a fluid and mobile center.

Monday

Graining with different body parts.

Experiment with walking patterns with different body parts leading as grains: nose, chest, shoulder, hips, and so on.

Notice distinction of the fluid, linear quality of grain as opposed to the thickness and bulk of a body part leading.

Chest graining into dimensions.

Graining into space: shifting and transitioning.

Releasing opposition grains: for example, release vertical to go into horizontal.

Graining body into directional patterns: forward, back, sides, up and down.

Decentralize by shifting the body center from self to outward and to specific points of interest.

Relate this back to earlier touching and response improvisation.

Tuesday

Combinations with pulse, rhythm, accents, and speeds.

Graining body parts into spatial directions, vertical and horizontal.

Varying densities from tight to loose, heavy to light. Try a walking pattern where body is heavy in three counts, releases density to light on fourth count, and so on. Taste the play of densities and the dynamics these contrasts create.

Wednesday	Graining toward distinct points in space and to points within the body.
	Design different distances as points of focus and grain to them.
	Vary intensity of graining.
	Transition through the body when graining from one body part to another or when going from inside to outside.
	Press energy outward to spatial destinations.
Thursday	Combining inner linear grain with three-dimensional density: heavy, light, soft, and hard.
	Vary states of body's compactness.
Friday	Combine grain and density with runs.
	Combine density (volumes) and grain (lines) from across the floor patterns into runs/air work.
	Interior spatial change happens according to intent.

To Instructor

In presenting densities, don't use two closely textured conditions as contrasts, such as soft and light. This will render making your point unnecessarily difficult.

Qualities of grain and density will begin to substitute for the dancer's need for "dramatic" fulfillment of movement. These qualities now become their "script."

With this, dancers begin the practice of understanding the motional qualification of movement.

IMPROVISATION

Use content of daily technique class in each day's improv.

Grain to points in body and space: linear sensation.

Bring density to qualities such as hard versus soft, loose versus jerky, and so on.

Grain is a clear directional structure. Tension is a counter energy that locks and interrupts that clarity.

Work on inner space: graining, inner dynamics, energy, intensity and direction.

If you're graining toward this joint, what happens with the rest of the body? What happens with the other parts? Don't let your interests stray. Very curiously, it's the other parts that are difficult to relate to the focus or intent.

In a forward leg extension, for example, although the leg reaches forward, the torso grains up to enliven the leg as the leg itself grains forward and out into space. This opposition graining creates a vibrancy of presence.

COMPOSITION

Contrast density and grain.

WEEK 8: GRAVITY AND UPWARD WILLPOWER

INTRODUCTION

Gravity and upward willpower are made visible through graining. Gravity is a basic law of physics. It is a strong physical presence—so strong, in fact, that man has had to develop an internal force to combat its downward pull. The force he uses is his willpower for upwardness.

Gravity bears within it a magnetic field that draws everything earth-related toward it. This has both positive and negative results: positive in that it keeps everything from flying off into space and negative in that it intrudes into all movement.

Gravity is a natural force that must be contended with in dance terms. Gravity contains many qualities within its description, such as: downward, heavyness, and weight. It is also part of swing, momentum, falls, suspension points, and so on.

Gravity is a continuous force, which one has to deal with and regulate in order to offset its downward pull. The human psyche generates a willpower or life force that is directed to combat the downward pull with a strong upward assertion and action.

To go downward, one needs to exert little effort; simply releasing into it is sufficient. The effort here is in the upward exertion. This balance of gravity and will is in a sense an encapsulated drama of life and death trying to claim the body.

When one practices gravity, one practices controlling its rate of downward pull. Controlling gravity utilizes the leg muscles to a considerable degree. The thigh muscles act as a brake to control the rate of descent. Every body part can demonstrate the pull of gravity. Through grain, the body can use gravity as a flavor to any body movement.

Equipment for Living

From David Kaufer, Professor of English, Carnegie Mellon University:

"In high school in 1967, I ran track and did intramural football and never questioned the masculinity of men who danced. As best as I can reckon, these were my major qualifications for participating in Mr. Louis' special studio class given at University City High School, in a suburb of St. Louis. After the first day of class, I felt anxious because I could not categorize what I was seeing and hearing. I ran home to the dictionary and found words like "lithe," "limber," and "pliant." These were not the words of a tenth-grader aspiring for a physique overbearingly rigid, tight, and inflexible. In football, I had learned to be a shield and projectile. From Mr. Louis, I learned how to be fluid in motion, a graceful pen drawing space into letters of motion. Mr. Louis taught with words—composed, thoughtful, eloquent, witty, and insightful words. He taught with motion. Words and body blended perfectly. I kept hoping against hope that if I learned to recite his words, my body could be tuned to listen as finely as his had. In the years following our encounter, I learned, happily, that Mr. Louis' teaching survived, even surpassed, dance. Finding words to link mind and movement became, for me, equipment for living."

The upward pull, willpower, is a basic indicator of the life force within the individual. The upward force is not so much a conscious resistance to gravity, but reflects one's desire and urgency for life. What motivates the will force is a complex matter. The dancer must eventually understand and encourage the self-motivating complexities, so that they can offer him positive guidance throughout his life. That long-range vision being stated, let us return to down and up, and take the immediate shortcut and say that willpower is necessary to resist the natural forces of gravity. The dancer makes this upwardness his simple motivation.

Recognizing these two forces is part of the ability to decentralize, and not let a strong centralized ego stand in the way of either direction. Upwardness is not a struggle or aggressiveness, but the ability to reach a balance and arrive at verticality. Achieving and maintaining a normal or vertical upright stance demands a congenial degree of willpower. Gaining this balance of "holding oneself up" is one of the future rewards of dance training.

This upward power is generated by the conscious, subconscious, and possibly superconscious. The dancer is suspended between two forces, one created out of his control of energy and the other energy existing outside of himself.

Physical weight in dance motion is in constant flux. Only stillness and total inanimateness of body and mind approaches a stability of weight. The mind can alter the weight condition of the body.

The attitude toward gravity is a major difference between ballet and modern dance. Ballet is fundamentally air-oriented. The physical denial of weight in ballet was one of the reasons for the evolution of modern dance. Modern dance is said to have "discovered the floor."

Notes

Contrast graining downward and heavy weight. Remember grain and density.
Gravity is a direction, down, not a negative statement.
The two forces man has to deal with are nature and himself: gravity and will.
The will is part of the psyche. It is generated in the mind. Beware of cloudy eye focus.

CLASS PLAN

TECHNIQUE

Premise

Balancing the upward and downward energies.

Be aware of the will upward, the gravity release down, and the balance of suspension between both (not a suspension point, which is a singular pinpoint and requires a concentrated upward pull).

Monday	Different body parts release to gravity.
	Locomotion with the weight gradually releasing downward and lifting upward.
	Interesting locomotion pattern involving time accents and meter.
	Releasing and lifting within a rhythm. Controlling descents with conscious plié use.
	Add turns on ups and downs (spirals).
Tuesday	Head, arms, and chest.
	Across the floor. Mix time values in movement phrase.
	Don't fall or lay on movement; instead, release energy to downward.
	The gravity pull downward must be seen.
	Graining is essential. Make it visually prominent.
	Controlled liftings and preparations for release to downwardness.
Wednesday	Inventive across-the-floor phrases.
	Emphasis on the dynamics resulting from sharp contrasts of downs and ups.
	Tilts in downward turns.
	Release from gravity into air bursts.
	Intense upward will motivates jumps.
Thursday	Make new locomotion phrase varying body parts: arms, chest, and head.
	Make visible the upward intent of will and the downward gravity pull.
	Time degrees of controlling descents.
	The willpower of upward made visible. Sustaining leaps and air work.
	Translate movement into combinations of down and up and turns to create spirals.
Friday	Combinations, locomotions, and spirals.
	Sudden releases to upward. Released airwork.
	From low turns to shooting up into vertical with full turn in the air.
IMPROVISATION	Free improvisation during the entire week with gravity and willpower as the premise.

Use variations from technique class. Follow daily class.

Keep gravity and will fluid and moving. Don't hold them or rest in place and carry them locked into locomotion.

Be sure to add normal, or a balance between up and down, as a center point for contrast.

Graining through the body is essential to keep flow up and down visible.

The body does not lock and block the flow of directional grain.

Compose gravity and will solos.

COMPOSITION

Contrast gravity and upward will.

WEEK 9: SWING, CENTRIPETAL, AND CENTRIFUGAL MOMENTUM

INTRODUCTION

A swing is a three-part action:

A beginning force that is released into space.

A path of going.

A suspension at arrival point.

There are swings that are released down into gravity and swings that are released outward into centripetal and centrifugal trajectories. Gravity is a natural force, as is one of its outcomes: momentum. Gravity is in constant operation. The dancer must practice restraint rather than effort when he deals with this principle. In swings he sends the effort downward by releasing it. Gravity creates the downward pull. The resulting energy is the momentum derived from the release. The total action is the basis for swings. One releases into gravity and one rides the momentum.

Gravity swings are the most common swings. These are accomplished by any body part that has a peripheral range of movement. As an example, let us take the leg in a sideward swing action. Facing down stage with the body in alignment:

Count 1:

The free leg starts lifted to the side. With a beginning upbeat lift, it is released to gravity. This also releases the leg from its hip connection so that only the leg prescribes the swing. The hip is contained. The downward force further lengthens the leg out of the hip.

Count 2:

The release of weight starts the momentum into the resultant swing across the standing leg (if that is its destination and hence its trajectory).

Count 3:

The leg arrives at its crossed leg destination after prescribing its downward circular path and is suspended.

During the second part, through the force of momentum, variations of the swing occur: turns, air work, and so on, which use the resultant force to operate. The dancer must determine the necessary force during the first step to allow the second, complexity of the outcome, to complete itself. He must accomplish the third, the suspension at the arrival stage, to start the upbeat of force for a new swing.

With centrifugal and centripetal swings, the force is now the body, which throws the attached body part into space like a weight attached to a string. This creates the momentum to the point of arrival. These torso-motivated swings offer a very different challenge and kinetic experience.

CLASS PLAN

TECHNIQUE

Premise

Swings and momentum.

Monday

Locomotion with swings in normal level. Swing free leg, forward-back-forward, step-step-step. Change legs.

Swings are in three-quarter time. Make the three parts of the swing visibly clear.

Raise leg.

Leg weight release and descent to gravity.

The circular path of going.

Lift and arrival at a specific destination in space.

Swings forward and back. Locomote forward and backward with half turns. Swing right leg forward-back-forward, step-step-step, half turn, repeat backward. Left leg back-forward-back, step-step-step, backward half turn, repeat.

Sideward are swings across the body and open to the side. Feel the difference between the cross and open swings. Facing sideward, start open-cross-open, side step-step-step. Repeat other leg.

Variation: face forward, R. leg swinging: forward-back-forward, quarter turn L., R. leg side step-cross-step-step. Quarter turn (facing back of room) L. leg swings back-forward-back, quarter turn L., open side—cross side—open side, quarter turn face forward. Step, step, step.

Be sure to gauge energy to degree of turn.

Tuesday

Leg swings.

Check steady hip during all swings.
Variations:

In place, swing forward-back-forward, step-step-step. Alternate leg.

R. side facing to room forward. R. leg sideward open-cross-open, side step-step-step, half turn and alternate leg.

Leg swing: forward-back-forward, half turn back-forward-back, reverse half turn. Forward step-step-step.

Develop into air work.

Pivot hips to new facings on leg lift. Front and back.

Wednesday
Arm, chest, and upper torso.

Body part leads swing in locomotion with turns and change of direction.

Variations with locomotion. Throwing arm and leg out into horizontal momentum. Centripetal turns.

Centripetal and centrifugal are a form of horizontal throw. The best way to demonstrate this is with turns (since the arm or other movement part is attached to the body and takes it along).

Contrast the out and in swing. Reverse turns.

The force of momentum and its outcomes.

Thursday
Elbows and knees.

Distinguish swings between small and large body parts for dynamic energy changes.

Example: elbow swings across, swing open, reach forward, walk, walk, walk. Repeat: swing across, swing open, turning as elbow swings across, turn again, and elbow swings with open arm, all in three-quarter time.

Notes

Gravity should not be treated as a downward, negative quality. Downward should have the same dignity as any direction.

Control force released with gravity.

Ride the momentum.

With leg swings, release the leg out of the hip socket.

Define points of arrival to clearly denote beginning of new swing.

Variations occur en route to points of arrival (in turns, etc.).

Swings into locomotion and into space.

Centripetal: inward throw. Centrifugal: outward throw.

Swings can be introduced in the post-plié series, as a forward and back, side and side series with arms or legs:

Releasing of weight to gravity.

The swing outcome.

Arrival.

In the air try turning at height of leg swing.

You can create momentum in any direction.

Elbow leads turns, arm extends turn as force increases.

Distort circle outcomes, extend swings to reach out to level, change destinations.

Elongate and reach variations.

Friday

Everything in interesting movement phrases.

Sense the tilt and breath of the swing.

Notice interesting outcomes of swing.

Try turning at height of leg swings.

Butterfly and barrel roll swings in the air. In butterfly turns, body is flat in the air facing down and parallel to floor. Legs are thrown up for flatness. Hips are pressed forward in air. Barrel rolls: back facing floor and prescribe over curve with body in air.

Practice preparations for butterfly turns and barrel rolls. Swing preparations for both.

IMPROVISATION

Monday, Tuesday, and Wednesday

Everyone stands and alone explore principles, then in limited groups, try the below.

Released swing and variations of momentum.

Spinning on the released throw of energy.

Thursday and Friday

Groups choreograph their own short inventive phrase.

Follow the technique in class material.

Gravity—momentum—swing. Ride the momentum and keep up to its speed and spatial range. Include air work.

COMPOSITION

Swings.

Release into gravity—going with momentum.

ADDITIONAL PHYSICAL ENERGIES

MOMENTUM

Momentum is the consequence of the force caused by the act of propulsion. It is the going, the movement itself. Therefore, it is the basic substance of dance because it defines the kinetic condition occurring between the beginning propulsion and the ending outcome.

The strength of propulsion together with the resulting speed of the action determines momentum. We can also refer to it as the outcome and nature of the propelling force. One of the fine points of aesthetic technical control that must be mastered is the judgment of how much energy is needed to bring the impulse to a point of termination.

In this aspect of momentum, the dancer's concentration is often directed toward the conclusion of the act rather than toward the nature of the ongoing path that occurs in between.

To experience momentum, my suggestion is to propel the body randomly, to get a better sense of momentum on its own terms, rather than using it as a device to achieve a specific end. From a standing position, propel the body percussively into random directions to feel what actually happens during momentum. In improvising, freely experiment with momentum and, gradually, by trying different variations of force, become aware of the many possibilities of outcomes and how best to control them.

Practice percussive propelling in different parts of the body so that you can realize the great variety of possibilities and feel the experience of being thrust from one body shape to another. Set some of these sequences so that you can repeat them and their repetition can solidify your knowledge of the process of momentum.

The sensitivity and control of momentum should occupy the dancer's technical exercises for as long as he continues to study dance.

In further study, you will realize that the velocity of momentum is not constant, that motion starts at a high speed and diminishes as it proceeds, either until it is brought to the destined outcome or until, en route, it is recharged by additional forces.

There are other causes of change in velocity; for example, the friction of the floor can slow momentum, whereas the slipperiness of a polished floor surface may increase its velocity. A wall or other surfaces might necessitate a sudden change. Aerodynamics of loose, flowing garments or scarves, or the weight of heavy trailing textured material, add other qualifying speeds to momentum.

A minute sentient examination of the diverse qualities of momentum under the most varied circumstances will fortify the dancer both technically and aesthetically. Always keep in mind that momentum is not only a basic property of motion; it also bears within itself the very substance of the aesthetics of dance. What distinguishes the artist from the commonplace dancer is his ability to choose from among the multiple possible variations the most effective sentient designs to control momentum.

In the practice of achieving an outcome of disturbances and momentum, there is a very brief moment when the energy expended gives rise to another quality: sustained motion.

CENTRIFUGAL AND CENTRIPETAL FORCES

The indulgent dancer delights in centrifugal and centripetal forces. It's the "Viennese Waltz Syndrome." Yet these are two of the most significant natural forces to be controlled and used with disciplined discretion. Both are by-products of momentum when it involves circular action and within them rests all forms of swings, turns, circles, and some elevations.

Both relate to a central point of anchorage and to the forces that pull both powers toward and away from this central point. The dancer can perhaps best understand this by analyzing and practicing swing action.

The simplest swings are made with the arms and legs because they are attached at one end, while the outer tip is released into peripheral action. High-to-low vertical swings are basic. The arm held in high suspension without any flexion can swing into gravity. If left completely free to do so, it will pass the gravity point, and its momentum will carry it to the end of its path of weight release and then return in the direction from which it came, repeating the swing until the energy is expended.

When we submit to the gravity force, the release to downward becomes a sort of percussive power, and the height of the resultant swing will be completed at the exhaustion of that power. Each successive one, however, becomes weaker because of the gravitational pull, finally arriving at a point of vertical stillness. If one desires to keep up the same swing and avoid the energy decrease, one must add additional percussive power at the beginning of the swing. Greater propulsion can cause a complete circular form.

Dancers often use additional thrusts to increase the height of elevation. The arms make a considerable number of peripheral paths of action possible.

When the dancer adds the motional abilities of the legs, movement variations are multiplied. Then, too, he can add torso peripheries. The weight of the torso swinging in the air can lift the body into extraordinary acrobatic feats. Barrel rolls (back parallel to the floor) and butterfly turns (front parallel to the floor) are some examples of exciting air turns. Other attached body units can add their force to the swinging part; for example, the hip can thrust the leg, the shoulder propel the arm. These can be powerful forces, and if one is inept or careless in complying with the natural laws of these centrifugal and centripetal powers, injuries can result.

In executing centrifugal and centripetal movements, one must take care to realize the location of the pivot point. The careful study of where the legs begin in the hip sockets and where the arms begin in the shoulder joints is basic and essential. We must control and study the tension and release in those areas and in all of the joints of the body.

Swings are not all in the vertical plane. They can be horizontally directed out or tilted to any diagonal degree. When the dancer is tilted, the centrifugal force can easily throw him off balance much more so than when he is in the vertical, and requires skill in turning and circular technique. Thus we see the virtuosities in acrobatic and ballet displays—leap turns in the air that seem to defy the body's weight while inter-balancing the centrifugal and centripetal forces.

WEEK 10: UNDERCURVES

INTRODUCTION

The undercurve is conceived as the lower half of a sphere. It is a continuous half circle. The locomotion of an undercurve involves a triple action of the leg: plié—transfer of weight—lift. The fluidity of the flexing knee is the technical basis of both the undercurve and overcurve forms.

BASIC MOVEMENT

The standing leg flexes to low level.

The weight is transferred to the other leg, which receives it in low level.

The body rises in vertical to either normal or relevé level and in the same vertical (1) descends to low level again, (2) transfers the weight to the other leg, which then (3) rises.

The movement involves a fluid triple action and creates a smooth circular form. During the low-level transfer a still lower point in the circular form is passed through which gives the undercurve its lower curved form. This triple action of the knee and leg must become automatic and smooth. The flexibility of the leg in the descent will help enormously in preparing for descending from air work.

Undercurves are the basis for the quicker skip action, which has a three-eighth time value. However, the three-quarter undercurve waltz time needs to be carefully controlled so that the movement does not linger and become sentimental. The dancer also should not confuse it with the step hop, duple time, which beginners will often substitute for the triple time undercurve skip. If we now extend our relevé or upward thrust, taking us into the air but landing on the same leg in readiness to plié and transfer, we will be in the act of skipping.

In the basic undercurve or skip, the leg free from weight should always be en route to its next function, and consequently in constant action. The tendency is to pose the free leg behind or to thrust it through quickly for a forward posing; these are all legitimate variations of the basic act, but before engaging in such variations practice the basic undercurve action.

Again, one must be wary of romantic indulgences like falling into the submissive feeling of the curve. The dancer senses and experiences the undercurve with the whole body.

The curve of the undercurve should be pronounced and experienced as a released form. To further sense the flow of the undercurve, repeat the undercurve with the arms in second. The arms should have the same degree of curve, grain, feeling, and visual design as does the torso.

Another guide for undercurve accuracy can be tested in locomotion across the floor. Join hands with the person on either side and experience the dynamics of the undercurve together, feeling the same curved descent and the upward path.

Although the curved path is a smooth one, an extra bit of release to gravity on the descent gives the undercurve a swing momentum.

CLASS PLAN

TECHNIQUE

Premise

Master triple leg action and undercurve combinations.

Define triple knee action before coming across the floor.

Do the five-finger exercise with undercurves.

Monday

Establish triple leg action.

Plié—down in vertical.

Transfer weight through undercurve. It is during this transfer of weight that the undercurve is defined.

Arrive up in place and plié same leg, and so on. Forward and backward and sideward with half turns. Develop into air skips. The careful vertical descents are important here.

Tuesday

Repeat and add free leg variations and sideward going. Leg makes its gesture on the third count, rise in vertical.

Free leg forward and back.

Half and whole turns in air. Rotation of gesture leg in hip socket on turns.

Be exact with facings and timed arrivals.

Wednesday

Add extended undercurves: directions and turns, and air work. (Uneven undercurves.)

Use two steps for the transfer of weight, maintaining the curve with its lowest point still evident. 4/4 time—down R.—step L.—step R.—lift R.—repeat down R. leg.

Thursday

Combine with low- and high-level walks.

Mix the undercurves semicircular action with level line in all directions. (Time example: 3/8 undercurve, 2/8 level.)

Friday

Variations.

Skips into the air with half turns at the high point. Sense and gain the height of the air vertical.

With free leg extended either forward or back, feel the totality of body and mind in defining the form of the undercurve. Release into downward. Arrive at high point in high.

Think of going under the lowest point of the circle to achieve the curve.

To Instructor

Insist on the circular undercurve transfer of weight action.

Stress proper vertical landing in skips and air work.

Knee placement should be over ball of the foot.

Hip placement should be steadily pressed forward.

Be careful the eye doesn't become fixed in forward, but also releases to gravity and lifts.

Judge speed to how long the class can sustain the air work.

IMPROVISATION

Monday and Tuesday

Use material from classes in groups of four.

Wednesday, Thursday, and Friday

Student choreography with class evaluation. One choreographer with two dancers.

Choreographers should be judged on teaching and designing movement, articulating movement phrases, and correcting movement performed.

Dancers should be judged on receiving and performing movement.

Class judges performance *primarily* for execution of the undercurve.

COMPOSITION

Create study using undercurves.

WEEK 11: OVERCURVES AND MIRROR ACTION

INTRODUCTION

The overcurve is the basis of the leap, just as the undercurve is the basis of the skip. Consideration is given to the upper curve of a circle. The action involves going up and stepping over. This quickly becomes air work: accommodate the tempo to suit the action. Sustaining the high stepping-over action can be difficult, so the time and speed allotted to this form should always be considered.

It is difficult to sustain the overcurve transfer of weight. The count becomes a duple so that a phrase of undercurve, undercurve, overcurve, overcurve, overcurve would count out as 1-2-3, 1-2-3, 1-2, 1-2, 1-2.

The overcurve leg action is also in three parts (not three counts):

Standing leg rises to high level.

The other leg lifts and steps over the curve of the circle.

It lowers into plié as the weight is transferred.

Repeat (1) the same leg rises to relevé, (2) transfers weight prescribing the overcurve to the other foot, (3) leg down to receive weight.

The dancer combines gestures 1 and 2, up and over, into a one count and the descent (gesture 3) takes two counts. The torso and top of head lengthen and go over to define the overcurve. In the air, the dancer should think of going up and over and take to the air without any fear or restraint.

Everything, in terms of treatment of energies as they were indicated in the undercurve, also applies here, but in reverse. Out of the relevé (1) one may extend the form into the air as a resultant leap, moving away from the floor, thrusting the body upward and forward or whatever the intended direction. The leading front leg lifts immediately to describe the overcurve form by stepping over, lengthening, and reaching downward and out of the hip for its next

Taking the air. 18th Street class, New York City.

Notes

You are combining three-quarter and two-quarter notes now. Clap out the rhythms before you start across the floor.

Check and practice the duple and triple action in the knee.

point of landing. Again, observe the treatment of the leading front leg after landing.

COMBINATIONS

Remember that in the undercurve, the transfer of weight is always in low level. In the overcurve, the transfer is always in high level. We may make a simple analogy here. In an undercurve one seems to take an elevator down to the main floor, cross the hall, go into another elevator, and ascend in it. The same elevator descends immediately to the main floor and, again, one crosses the hall to repeat the process. The overcurve is the reverse. One starts on the main floor, goes up, crosses, and descends in the opposite elevator. Repeat the rising and cross to the other side and descend, and keep repeating.

The technical difficulties that arise are due to improper transfer of weight in the same level. For example, in an undercurve there is often a failure to lower the weight on the same leg before transfer. This results in a falling downward action on the leg receiving the weight. The weight should be lowered and transferred to the receiving leg so that it can thrust the weight upward and not be burdened by the weight falling on it.

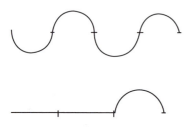

The combination under-over curve is a frequently used form. Here, out of undercurve relevé, instead of descending on that leg, the dancer makes a transfer in relevé to the other leg, thus creating the overcurve. The descent from this then passes to undercurve, which may again culminate in an overcurve form.

Another frequent form is the double low-level walk followed by an overcurve. This is the familiar "run, run, leap," the two runs forming a double preparation for the purpose of gaining leap height and distance.

The variation possibilities of the form and action of the legs while in the air are many and offer a wide technical challenge.

The danger in the execution of these forms rests mainly in the affectations and commonplace attitudes attached to them. All dance mannerisms, such as sentimentality and romantic attitudes, should be avoided in exploring their values.

"Taking the air," being confident in the air and conscious of the space and leap action, is the motional fulfillment of the leap movement. Lifting the straight back leg while in the air before the descent can sustain the air height longer.

ACROSS-THE-FLOOR COMBINATIONS

Combine levels, undercurves and overcurves, with half turns, turning on vertical transitions. The dancer can make many highly enjoyable and challenging combinations of these movements.

CLASS PLAN

TECHNIQUE

Premise

Overcurves.

Stress the action of the flexing and straightening of the standing knee as well as the articulation of the overcurve half circle line. The overcurve is performed as a two-quarter or two-eighth note count.

Monday

Overcurves.

Five-finger exercise with overcurves. Notice that these are sideward overcurves.

Forward stepping leg steps over the high point of curve and reaches for the floor.

Take care with exact placement of weight and legs.

Create small overcurves in the air across the floor. To be repeated often at the end of classes, stressing either forward or height, with the head or the chest.

Overcurve turning across floor: emphasize height and leg reaching out of hip.

Tuesday

Undercurves and overcurves.

Use exact leg action, knee and ankle, and willpower lift to describe form.

Levels distinction between straight and curved lines.

Vary time combinations. For example, one undercurve, three overcurves (1-2-3, 1-2, 1-2, 1-2), alternating legs.

Overcurve—overcurve—jump, jump. Jumps are in vertical.

Add jumps, full turns in the air, going up and landing in same spot.

Wednesday

Under-overcurve variations.

Practice breath in lifted leg and upward will action.

Add turns on high point.

Review undercurves with leg variations. (Gestures forward and back with free leg.)

Notes

From this point on, repeat overcurves forward with half turns at the end of every class.

Be sure not to let the pulse get too slow or the ebullience of the leap will get lost.

Under-overcurves combination is a three-fourth count: 1-2 under, 3 over. Always start on the same leg.

Work the overcurves in air for both height and forward thrust. Notice graining difference of the two, and use that difference for movement quality distinction.

Review overcurves in the air: vary tempo and directions.

Leap variations. Straight back leg lifts in air to sustain height.

Front leg leads to prescribe the overcurve at its height while back leg lifts higher to create the over sensation at the high point and completes the overcurve before landing. Be prepared for the extra energy at the high point when the back leg lifts. Ride the form and "take the air." Be present within form in the air.

Front leg should be reaching downward out of hip in landing.

Thursday

Under and over with leg variations.

Review all previous material.

Half turns, overcurves in air. Hip turns sharply in the air as leg swings through.

Friday

Undercurves, overcurves, and leg variations.

Leap variations. Split legs in air leaps.

Finale large leaps: run, run, and leap. Low, low, overcurve.

Air work: leaps. Emphasize height or length.

IMPROVISATION MIRROR ACTION

Mirror action is just that, mirroring each other's movements. Timing is instantaneous. No one leads, no one follows. Both dancers are alert and immediate in their reaction. This improvisation begins with two dancers, then two couples, and when it has become familiar as a premise and mastered to some degree any number of couples can participate simultaneously.

Be sure to draw a centerline in the room so that the dancer can judge distances as well as time and movement accuracy. The dancer symmetry from the centerline is evident for corrections. This is an excellent example of decentralization. The dancer's center is now projected into the opposite person.

Repeat all week with different size groups participating. Eventually opposite dancers should execute challenging phrases simultaneously.

Notes

You are going to face a dancer who is a mirror of yourself. No one will lead, no one will follow. You are both going to move in unison.

You can see the person move even when he doesn't think he is moving.

You can see the slightest nuance as you watch each other.

By watching the other's sternum, you can see the intention of his arm or torso and know what your partner is going to do and he will be able to see you and your intention.

You can quickly reflect this nuance when you watch each other.

Variation: en route, pick up another duo in the mirror and create duets within duets.

Mirror improvisation. Photo by T. Mike Fletcher.

As movement develops, add other dancers to stage, creating larger and more complex groupings.

COMPOSITION

Under- and overcurve phrases with variations, turns, air, and other locomotion.

MIRROR IMPROVISATION CRITIS

Too cautious. You're pussyfooting around. You played it very safe.

No signaling. Moving back to back? How can you possibly see each other? Be reasonable; align yourself to room architecture so that you can see each other.

Symmetry is essential here.

Maintain equal distances at all times.

Place yourself in a state of vibrancy, energy, control and immediacy.

Don't let the body go dead and break the connection.

Don't think about what or how you're moving. Put your center into your opposite image as soon as the movement begins. Challenge your body. See, think, and respond instantly. Don't let your response get slack and delayed in your mind.

Don't try to trick your partner with sudden and quick movements that you know are going to be impossible to relate to. Create a united flow.

Be sure to add body-part details with arms, head, and so on.

MAJOR PRINCIPLES OF DANCE (THE BIG FOUR)

Each of us is not only a unique individual, but also an idiosyncratic maze of complexities. Since these basic principles will be functioning within the judgments of the individual and not based on mass-produced instruments, we must call the interior psychical and sentient judgments—which vary to some degree with everyone's makeup—into play constantly.

Throughout this manual, we repeat definitions as well as areas to stress in class. Anyone who teaches realizes that teaching can be an arduous task of repetition. An experienced teacher knows how to persist and repeat without losing the class's interest or spirit. Imaginative articulation is essential for a career in teaching.

Before we undertake any of the body's technical responsibilities in locomotion, we must deal with some of the major principles of the dancer's art, namely space, time, shape, and motion. These principles will define and enrich everything the dancer does.

The big four dance principles are: space, time, shape, and motion. Nikolais called these major principles as such because of their importance in allowing his theory of decentralization to clarify itself. This does not lessen the importance of such principles as mobility, dynamics, motor base, energy, motivation, and so on, but allows one to focus on movement without any attached overlays, mannerisms, or attitudes. They became the fundamental ABCs in his analysis of dance. We constantly refer to them throughout this manual as their definitions are endlessly given new dimensions.

* * *

The space that surrounds us is a living canvas. To the eye it is invisible. The challenge to the dancer is to make this amorphous matter visible to the viewer.

In dealing with space, it is best not to think of it as an invisible void, but rather as an alive, vivid canvas, vibrant with sound, light waves, and bombardments of invisible particles. The way a swimmer might think of carving through water, a dancer thinks of pressing through space. Through his imagination the dancer makes this invisible matter of space a tangible material, which he can form, mold, and texturize.

Space is highly volatile. If we do not persist in our strong focus and concentration on it, it will quickly revert back to its formless invisible condition. To make the space that surrounds us serve us, we must project our energy, our metaphoric skills, into and on it to make the formless take form.

If, for example, we lose sight of the space within a volume or the line being drawn on the space, or the clarity of directions, we will be left with the body or the body part calling attention to itself as it moves aimlessly into and through space.

We can demonstrate the creation of "volumes" very simply by a gesture of the arms that can describe a form as being "so big." Here the arms define a space boundary or a suggestion or projection of a space boundary that indicates a three-dimensional size. The space so indicated is abstract_that is, the shape it forms does not represent a literal thing, but instead manifests a dynamic architectural value in terms of itself.

We can work with spaces in close proximity to the body or with projected outer ones. We might start with the perception of shape areas by using our physical parts to give them boundaries, thereby creating volumes. Here we may become more aware of the space shapes that can exist between the arms and the trunk, or between the head and the shoulders, or between the legs. We may then explore the values of expanding or diminishing their size, sensing the dynamic changes in the differing sizes. From here we may explore the treatment of actions of the arms and legs as they form or imply boundaries of space rather than as peripheral indicators of linear designs. Here, too, the body as a whole may act in such a manner as to project

a space shape, such as shaping to the round form by locomoting within a circular form. We may perform these actions with such persistence and concentration as to cause these spatial forms to remain alive and visible even after the action is terminated.

Our ability for decentralization is needed to effectively create these perceived forms. Let us consider these space shapes. Here, through the use of strong mind control, one can project the body's generative force into the center of the space form so that the torso itself is free to become a part of the boundary instead of remaining the center of the form. This new space form can now assume the role of furnishing the motional generative source. To further illustrate this principle, the dancer can create a spherically shaped volume, the size of a large beach ball placed at the front of the body at stomach height. Here the arm or arms may define part of the boundary while the stomach area, chest, and thighs define the rest. These body parts, like the arm, will reflect a tactile sense of their function as boundary and will shape themselves accordingly.

Challenging one's skill by inventing volumes of all varieties of architectural space patterns and imbuing them with performance life is an essential technical practice.

We can also visualize space as a blank canvas. With the most pinpoint peripheral end of our body parts, we can draw linear designs on this canvas. The awareness and concentration on what is making the mark and the mark itself needs the dancer's full performance concentration in order for it to be clearly visible. All the disciplines of decentralization, eye focus, and grain are necessary here to give the linear design a life of its own. Any weakness in these projections will seriously weaken the strength of peripheral design and call attention back to the body.

Through his strength of projection, the dancer organizes the space around him to conform to his own dimensional reference. Space gets directional signposts, which demand that the dancer garner the strength to press outward to reach these signposts in space.

Bear in mind that we have been spatially disciplined all our lives to a point of being afraid of spatial freedom. We have been confined to rooms, corridors, streets, and aisles, so that we need to overcome our fear of space. Our first attempts will be almost wholly in forward going, eventually involving turns, circles, and angles. Sideward, upward, and downward are not too frightening, but backward is downright hazardous. Ask children to run backward and there is suddenly a provocative, dangerous, and giggly thrill in the air.

Moving through space with any locomotion demands from the dancer openness of vision and destination. The body, in a sense, becomes anchorless. Here the dancer feels the tangibility of space as he cuts through it. It is as if one rides the air currents as the soaring eagle does—a heady experience indeed.

At the other end of this abandonment is the detail of grain to define volumes.

The power of grain and tactile sensation is deeply involved in relation to a form. For example, an arm extended forward for the purpose of forward linear projection is quite different in feeling than the same arm in position as a spatial boundary to the area above or below it. If the dancer uses the forward arm as a top boundary to the space between it and the floor, then the tactile surface of the whole under part and palm of the hand becomes hypersensitive to the space beneath it. The grain, instead of indicating forward direction, as it does in a gesture of forward linear projection extending out of the arm into a horizontal line, now spreads itself across the width of the arm and grains in a downward direction.

Space is common to all things that exist, things both animate and inanimate. It is not limited to the present, past, or future. It can become an area in which the artist can cause things to exist that can reveal and sustain knowledge not realized until now. One can address space in an instant and give it a boundary, etch it, form volumes that had not existed before. Just as easily, one can erase these volumes from our vision with equal speed.

159

WEEK 12: SPACE—VOLUME AND PERIPHERAL

INTRODUCTION

When it comes to the "big four" dance principles, you will find the same critiques generally hold for all of them, but obviously with different references. Space in its basic form is amorphic, without shape or form, texture or identity. Because of its constant presence and pervasiveness, it is taken for granted and often ignored and overlooked. But for the dancer it is an essential element in his craft.

Space is a canvas on which the dancers will make their mark, but before they can do so they must conceive of it as a tangible mass, alive with diverse energies. They do this primarily with focus and grain, and their other skills of decentralization. By redirecting their center from themselves and investing that vibrancy into the space around them, they can call the viewer's attention to space as a reality.

Once they have mastered this ability to project out into space, they can then qualify it with textural distinction, such as hot, prickly, oppressive, bouncy, and so on. They can use the space as an antagonist or protagonist. With strong focal projection they can look at the tip of their nose or out to the moon making the journeys from here to out there faster than the speed of light.

Because space is invisible, it is the task of the dancers to make the space they are dealing with visible; they do so by a strong projection of their imagination to both flavor and dimensionally clarify it.

Space as a reality is totally at the mercy of the dancer's recognition of it. Should the dancer ignore it, it can disappear instantly and revert back to its amorphic condition. Moving through space, feeling it against the body in fast walking and runs, is being able to recognize it. Being able to vary the density of the surrounding space, from thick and dense, to loose and open is another means of recognition. This mass can be textured as water or jello; it can be resistant, yielding, electrically charged, and so on, and identified as such.

SPACE AND DIRECTION

With pliés, one becomes involved with the body's dimensions as directional extensions into space: up, down, right, left, forward, back, diagonal forward right and left, diagonal backward right and left. Although there are 360 directional degrees surrounding us, the human body is so thick that it can only distinguish and clarify ten of these clearly. These ten points are the basic spatial directions on a horizontal plane for the dancer. These directions are practiced in pliés and are also extended into space throughout the rest of the training. In moving dimensionally, the entire body presents itself into its concerned direction. The clarity of these directions is essential in successful communication between the dancer, the teacher, the choreographer, and the audience.

Whenever you go into a point of interest in space, the body actually leads and presses in that direction. It doesn't go away from it. If I wanted to talk to you, I would lean in toward you slightly. The body responds much more completely when you give yourself fully to the action. In performance this accuracy becomes extraordinarily important.

SPACE AND VOLUME

We have already dealt with space very generally. Throughout this manual we'll be returning to areas of spatial concern with other references and points of interest. Space is a rich principle of dance and a vital part of every dance endeavor, from stretching to performing. The dancer exists in it and must acknowledge his presence in space at all times.

When we deal with volumes, we think of three-dimensional shapes of space. One thinks of volume as giving boundary to space. In solo work the maneuverability of the arms has a considerable range in which to devise volumes. Because the extremities, which are attached to the body, create the spatial volumes, they will of necessity include the body as part of their boundary marking. Therefore the dancer must enliven the body to its participation in shaping the volume.

In group work, there is a considerably larger scope for creating volumes. The use of many extremities can enlarge the shape of a volume to any size. Basically, creating volumes is to carve and give boundary to three-dimensional space. In order to gain these three-dimensional spatial forms, the dancers can employ various body parts at the same time.

Volumes are not necessarily round. Again, it is spatial volume that must become evident, not the body parts being used. Be careful that the shape of the body does not become primary. The shape of the space is the premise. The dancer calls graining and decentralization into play to achieve this focus. We are concerned here with giving a three-dimensional boundary to space. Volumes are spatial containers.

FOCUS THROUGH SPACE

To pinpoint or trace in space a point or path with the eye takes enormous projecting conviction and concentration, not dramatic tension. Your focal point is specific, not something vaguely "out there." Try not to let your focus become diffused before you reach your imagined point in space. Try not to go beyond your objective as well.

SPACE AS ILLUSION

Texture space so that it has an identity and flavor of its own: smooth, prickly, yielding, resistant, and so on. You can texture the space around you, or in turn be influenced by the existing texture of the space around you.

PLANES

In dance, planes have a certain thickness usually relative to the dancer's size. This should be presented as a flat surface, not necessarily level or parallel to the ground, but flat. Planes can be level (horizontal), tilted (diagonal), or vertical (up/down).

PERIPHERAL ACTION

Two factors are involved in creating a peripheral design on the surrounding space in a linear manner. The first is the body part, which is drawing the line, and the second is the space on which it is being drawn. Above all it is the line itself that must be seen, not the

Volumes: sculpting with space.
Dancers: Bob Small, Richard Haisma, Michael Balard, and Helen Kent. University of Delaware, 1976.
Photo courtesy of the Nikolais/Louis Archives.

pencil or the paper. The eye helps this clarity by tracing the peripheral line.

The line can continue out into space and return to be picked up again by other peripheral points of the body. The transition can also travel through the body. The body grains into an interior linear path connecting the two outer lines. These outer and inner transitions must be projected as a clear, uninterrupted continuation of the peripheral line. There cannot be any cessation of peripheral action because once the line of action ceases, attention is called to the body or time or whatever else is prominent.

The point drawing the line should be a small point which can be pressed outward into the surrounding space: toe, knee, the back of the hip joint, finger, elbow, shoulder, nose, head, and so on. The body part must press itself outward about an inch or two into space so that it literally etches the line into the space around it. There should be no question of what is the marking point, what is the peripheral mark it makes, and what is the space that is being drawn upon.

The word *peripheral* here means a line made by a furthermost point of the body or extremity. Linear peripheral action is two-dimensional. Peripherals also define a specific path of circular action created by parts of the body. Attached at one point the other end of the body can swing like a pendulum. The body part is anchored at a joint, and the free part can swing from there; however, it is the peripheral line, not the swing action, that is to be seen. The swing usually involves momentum and gravity.

Because the body parts are attached to the body at some point, peripheral action can tend to become circular in nature. This is not necessarily the case of linear action. Any design or pattern can be drawn on the space. When the arm is straight, the peripheral line will tend to be circular, but with the flexation of elbow and wrist the circular pattern can be broken and the linear design can lead anywhere out into space. The body is made alert to keep up to where the line leads. The body locomotes itself to accommodate the peripheral line.

Since decentralization is essential with peripheral action, it is best to make the dancer keep his eye on the line being drawn, thus forcing the focus away from himself and directing the audience to the peripheral design he wants seen, not to how the body is shaping itself, although he himself is conscious of how the body shapes itself.

CLASS PLAN

TECHNIQUE

Premise

Space.

Volume: three-dimensional forms, defining and giving boundary to spatial shapes in space.

Peripheral: linear patterns etched on surrounding space.

A major principle in creating decentralization is developed by placing the dancer's center out into the concerned surrounding space.

Monday

Volumes.

Create a simple arm pattern relevant to volumes.

Define volumes and locomote them. Moving volumes side to side. Up and down.

Keep torso involved as part of the boundary of the volume.

The body focus and grain change fluidly with volume changes.

Make sure volume stays alive. Don't carry dead volumes about.

Vitalize the volumes from the body's central generative source. Decentralization.

Volumes are not always round. Devise different shapes with three-dimensional feeling.

Tuesday

Peripherals.

Begin in place with writing a name on the space.

Go back and dot "i's" and cross "t's" accurately.

Etch the action vividly so that it remains in space.

Use different body points to draw with: nose, finger, knee, elbow, and so on.

Create a floor pattern relevant to peripherals.

Peripheral two-dimensional linear action.

Press out into space to etch the linear design on the space.

Peripheral is a fine line, not a swath or mass, although the back of the hip (lower spine) can convey a linear effect.

Once the line stops, the viewer's eye will shift to the dancer's body or whatever else is of interest.

Project an intensity that will keep the designs and forms alive once the dancer leaves them.

Changing peripheral markers:

Fingertips

Elbow

Shoulder

Top of head

Knee

Toes

Wednesday

Create an across-the-floor pattern.

Volume and peripheral space: contrasting two- and three-dimensional space.

R. arm reaches forward and out to sideward in a peripheral line, three counts. Then from sideward it curves in to create a volume with R. hip, as the hip grains to complete circular form, three counts. Repeat. (Peripheral reaches out, volume grains in.) Add turns and directional changes.

Thursday

Create an across-the-floor pattern where space becomes a textured atmosphere.

Devise a simple movement phrase and then perform it as if going through dense or resisting matter, walking through an unyielding environment then moving through unresisting matter such as smoke.

Do not make the action dramatic. Do not give the body an "attitude."

Use the body surfaces to sense the conditions of the space.

Friday

Combine, but clearly define.

Volume and peripheral action and textured mass.

The torso becomes part of the boundary to volume.

Peripheral lines diffuse quickly; the depth of etching sustains the designs.

Dancer's eye focus follows path of line.

Explain again the amorphic nature of space and how the dancer, by projection, gives it an identity.

The dancer imbues the space with his own living intensity.

REMINDER

It is the dancer's task to imbue space with life and an intensity that will reverberate with his action. The space around us, although it appears empty and void, is in reality alive with highly charged particles. Light waves emanate from various light sources, bounce off objects, and carry their image to our eyes. Sound waves carry voices, radio, and telephonic sounds from their source to our ears. Humidity is carried in the air. Aromas abound and are constantly assailing our noses. This seemingly calm spatial world around us is in reality charged and active with waves and molecules bouncing off everything. Space is a volatile mass.

The dancer must deal with space as if it had the density of water: cutting through it, shaping it, respecting it, and always conscious of it. The dancer must also be able to make this invisible matter both real and visible to an audience. This will only be successful if the dancer can conceptualize space, seeing it as a tangible thing. The dancer's ability for decentralization (transferring a life-giving focus from himself to things around him) is vital in his employment of space. He is now dealing with factors outside of himself. Dealing with the space inside the body will be called into play with graining, textural changes, illusions, density, and motional transitions. Through the power of conceptualization (the process of transferring the abstract image to a reality, and vice versa), the space can take many forms and also, on occasion, act as a protagonist and an antagonist creating spatial dramas. When we get to improvisational materials, we will find that space is a mother lode of creative riches.

IMPROVISATION

Monday

Space volumes.

In duets: one dancer (A) creates volumes in which the other (B) moves. (A) need not wait until (B) completely finishes his movement within the space. (B) moves away walking a path that allows (A) to create a new volume. They both keep their actions, continuously changing the time and energy. (A) moves closely in reaction to (B) and the result becomes a duet.

With a group of 6–10: designate half of the group as movers (A) and half as boundary makers (B). (B)s lean together and join and make spaces (arches, holes) for (A)s to pass through. (A)s note the shape of the space. They pass through and shape themselves to the space without touching or changing the boundaries, although on occasion (B)s can deliberately reshape the volume (A) makes, even to the extent of lifting an (A) to a new position. Increase speed. (A)s and (B)s reverse roles.

In solo: carving the space closest to the body. Use different combinations of body parts to prescribe volumes. The volume is carried as a live and vital "rest in space" shape into locomotion. Show the mobility of the volume breathing through space and clearly change its boundaries as it is moved. Don't let the volume go dead and carry a lifeless shape about. Focus on the volume and keep it alive. Let it lead you.

Combinations.

Moving a volume through space to define a larger volume; for example, a long tunnel of space created by rounded arms is carved into the larger volume.

Defining the boundary with various parts of the body.

Shaping oneself to magnify and intensify the volume.

Define a large spatial volume, step away from it, perceive it, and then move within its invisible boundaries. This can also be done with a peripherally drawn boundary as well.

Tuesday

Peripheral.

As an introductory preparation, have the student write his name on the space before him, making tangible and visible both the space used and the name written. The strength and vividness of both are essential in dealing with space. The conceptualization of space will become essential in creating abstractions.

Indicators of a weak spatial reference include writing the letters of a name over each other or not accounting for proper distance between letters.

Have two people correspond with each other. Write, with back to class, so class can also read messages. An introductory exercise is to have the student write his name on the space before him, being careful not to write over what has already been written and making sure the words are legible, and so on. See if everyone else can read it. Use different body parts as peripheral markers. Decentralization and projected strength of imagery are especially important here, as are clarity of articulation and transitions between body pointers.

Peripheral action includes all linear action created by a single point located at some extreme end of the body or its parts. Emphasize transition of this end point to another end point, either through the body or through the surrounding space, as it picks up the line and continues it.

Stand in lines of five or six; pass the line from one to another when it reaches the end, pass it back. Increase speed. Vary the linear design but always pass it on clearly. Don't stop movement.

Wednesday

Space as surrounding mass improvisation.

Instead of space being an individual illusion, now I want it to be a group illusion of an atmospheric thing. Let's start with something simple, like being underwater, with everyone up as a whole group, in one giant aquarium. Don't treat it as a foreign environment, or a hostile one. It is simply a different one than the one you're used to operate in, so it will affect your body in a different way. It is that illusion that we're trying to capture the pressure of the water on the body. The textural sensitivity of the skin comes strongly into play.

Don't solve it by thinking about how you usually act in water. That doesn't solve the problem. It has to be more from the idea that you are creating the illusion that this atmosphere is different from the one you normally operate in. That will affect you in your choices of shapes, spaces, time, and motion.

Let us change to an atmosphere now in which electrical charges are constantly shooting off. How will that affect how you go through the space? How will the time be affected? What are the motional qualities involved? Don't be an actor, don't be looking for those charges: wondering "when's the next one going to hit me?" No. Assume that it's not going to kill you, it's not going to hurt you. It is simply an electrical charge that goes through the air. It is not a painful thing. It is not a bad thing, nor is it necessarily a good thing—you are neutral about it. When you were doing all those other situations, you accepted the premise that you could be obese, or skinny, or brittle. Now simply accept the fact that there are electrical charges going through the atmosphere, and they will affect how the body responds. It's not how you react or how you feel about these charges that are going through the air; it's the simple fact that they are there. How will they texture the movement?

Thursday	Free improvisation with space. Volumes—peripherals—space texture.
Friday	Defining assignments.
	Free improvisation with space. Volumes—peripherals—space texture.
	Space study, delineate between linear and three-dimensional space, peripheral or volume.
	Define space by relating to it, not through pantomime.
	Make it visible through kinetics (motional excitement).
	Do not add additional qualities to it. I want only to see the concerned space. Use shape and time, but we should not see them dominate in any way.
	Space is simply relative until something is there to define it, such as volume or texture.
	The whole body is involved with the luminosity of space.
	Don't assume an attitude about the space.
	Don't interpret the content of the space.
	Check speed; is it right for the gesture or the space?
	Do not confuse space volume with line, when you create a boundary for space.
	Make your volumes abstract form, not literally suggestive of an object.
COMPOSITION	Volume plus peripheral plus textured mass. Don't make it mystical or "spacey." Don't let tension in another body part create unconscious lines. Don't get too clever and go outside the problem. Don't make it inconvenient for viewing. Keep it pure.
	Decentralization: focusing on line or volume outside of the body.
	Strength of imagery to denote strength of linear design.
	The body must be supple and yielding to follow the line created. Be sure to stress flexibility and pliancy in the knees and lower spine for all down and lower actions.
	Don't overdesign. Your body should be totally sensitive and grained toward the line. The whole body should be involved to some degree.

Volume study in Troy, Alabama.

Space Volume

On a tour of the Deep South, there was a week's engagement in Troy, Alabama. These classes were composed of ten-year-olds, and the premise for this day was space. Specifically, one dancer was to give boundary to and define a space volume, while the other dancer dealt with the enclosed space in some way.

The two boys involved asked me not to look while they prepared. I covered my eyes. "OK," they said. When I looked up, there was Bill (or Beal *as everyone else pronounced it) attached to the wall. I could not tell what he hung from.*

The other boy walked slowly onto the stage area, stopped, and looked at Bill's shape. He walked to the space beneath Bill's legs and stepped into the volume created. He then lifted his arms to take Bill's hands. Bill sat on his head and placed his feet on his partner's shoulders. With Bill secured, the second boy walked a half circle and stopped in profile downstage. The second boy lowered both himself and Bill to the ground. Both boys did a low somersault and jumped up facing downstage. They executed a formal boy's bow (one arm bent across the waist and the other across the back). They straightened up and marched off behind each other. It brought the house down.

The invention, the execution, the performing flavor was so seriously undertaken that, thanks to the photographer, this class remained indelibly in my mind.

The story had an additional happy ending. The Artist in School Program had a challenge attached to it. Only if the community contributed half the cost of the program would it be continued. Of the five schools engaged during that round, two continued the sponsorship for the following year, Los Angeles and Troy, Alabama. Bill's father was on the town council and favored the continuance of the program because, as he said, "I'd never seen these kids before. They showed themselves in a new light. They surprised me."

CRITICISMS

Follow the peripheral movement with the eyes and face within convenient range. When the line is behind you, grain through the back of the head.

Bring all attention to the peripheral motion and path.

Change body grain with each change of gesturing point.

Don't project out into the space beyond the line. We will then see the distance of space and not the line.

Each new point of focus requires an entire grain shift of the whole body.

Vary intensity so everything does not look or feel alike.

This is a line made by the furthest point of your body. The tip of the elbow, not the whole forearm.

Be careful of thickness of line. It should not be the width of the palm of the hand, which is like a Rembrandt painting made with a house paintbrush. There is no detail.

If the stare is fixed, and there is tension in the neck, the action becomes centered as opposed to peripheral and decentralized.

Swing is not peripheral, but the line it makes is. Determine whether it is swing or peripheral you want seen.

We are looking for nuances of the body to help us look at and see this line.

For this assignment, draw with one body part at a time; don't draw with two. It will be easier for you to do and easier for us to see.

Let go of the line in one body part when you start a line with another body part. Don't hang on to preceding movements.

Be aware and get rid of stylistic gestures. Don't have an "attitude" about the line.

For now, don't push or scoop space. Make the line dominant, not how you make the line.

The line is easy. Getting the whole body to go with it is hard.

Don't let the other body parts look surprised. The whole body is in this together.

If you are using your nose, beware of outward space eye focus. Bring your eyes to follow where the line is leading you, however strange it may feel.

Don't let the legs and feet be clumsy as you run—they detract from the line.

Don't be so careful and cautious in drawing. These hesitant characteristics become more interesting than the line.

With arms, for example, don't get too limp or too stiff. Wet noodles make ineffectual lines.

A student said: "But I like the other way better." Nikolais: "You have to learn not to fall in love with things you have no business falling in love with, for now. What you did was nice, but it was not in the problem. Stick to the premise so that we both know what's going on, and we can both work to improve it. Later when the premise is your choice, you can do as you wish."

If the head is too far in advance, it is aggressive. If it is too far behind, it is weak. Lines don't know aggression or weakness, lucky lines.

WEEK 13: TIME

ON TIME

The dancer's instrument is his body, which is wholly individual and idiosyncratic. In music, the musician's instruments are fixed, tuned, and calibrated. There is a great deal of difference between a musical instrument's response to time and that of a dancer's body. Although time is invisible, like space, the dancer can make it exist as a tangible and visible component of his materials. Time is a sensed activity as well as a regulator for our heartbeat and pulse. It ranges from the most obvious foot tapping to the subtleties that exist within stasis or stillness. In dance, the most common experience one has with time is musical time: pulse, rhythm, syncopation, rest in place, diminuendo, accelerando, and so on. Employing these variations in technique class is essential. Time lends more dynamic variations to movement than any other quality. These variations are the musical definitions of time. But there is also the dancer's time, and this includes the judgment of duration. How fast, how slow, when to do the next movement, how long to wait, how long to continue. All of these sensed decisions, plus their combination with musical time, give performance and composition a compelling range of play.

In addition, there is the curious situation of deliberately stepping out of time awareness, which creates an unconcerned "out of time" sensitivity. This is not being out of time as we know it, or being off the beat, but instead means ignoring time deliberately.

When you are young, time passes. When you are old, it just hangs around. Time can change its character.

Going from everyday unconcern to a sensed awareness of time calls the two into contrast, and presents time in a different way. Timing brings another necessary element of change and concern into the creative vocabulary.

Murray Louis accompanying on drums.
Columbia College, Chicago, 1974.
Photo courtesy of the Nikolais/Louis Archives.

Skill in handling the factor of time, among other skills, is the delicate ability to create the difference in performing monotony as opposed to being monotonous.

INTRODUCTION

Generally the time that is taught and used in class is musical time, with all the strict disciplines of music such as beats and their organization in twos and threes, fast and slow. This is the major use of time in dance, and as a result should be mastered first. Most choreography is set to this organization of time.

But in recent years dance has asserted its own claim on time organization, which we will deal with as "dancer's time." Musical time deals with instruments of prescribed size and nature, whereas dancer's time involves a single instrument, the individual body, which is wildly eccentric. With musical time there are two separate units involved: the musician and the instrument. With dancer's time the dancer is both the player and the instrument. This is the fundamental difference that has to be considered. In music the instrument does not think for itself; in dance the instrument does.

This dancer's ability for self-determination lends a vibrant unexpectedness to movement. Regardless of how strict the time factor may be, the dancer has the ability to play within the prescribed structures. The dancer develops this element of unpredictability in improvisation, and it is part of the vitality, aliveness, and invention of dance.

Although time is inevitable, don't make it predictable. Also, remember, stillness (stasis), when used effectively, can be very potent.

CLASS PLAN

TECHNIQUE

Premise

Musical time for dance.

Pulse: fast, slow, rhythmic.

Stop and go.

Syncopation.

Sensing duration (how long).

Monday

Create a phrase using pulse, fast, and slow (eight-count phrase).

Double time, half time.

Stop (active pause), then go immediately from held into locomotion. Weight always forward, for quick presence and immediacy.

Create an interesting combination: part of body goes fast, another slow, simultaneously.

Tuesday

Create a phrase using sustained time (eight-count phrase).

Lyrical, without interruption.

Even or sustained time, never faster or slower.

Fill the movements involved with changes of all sorts (directions, body parts) but always at a sustained time value.

Control the pulse; keep an even speed.

Wednesday

Create a phrase using duration (ten-count phrase).

Devise a sequence of movements to be done across the floor with a set pulse.

The dancer has the freedom to mix speeds and pause length.

The pauses between the movements and the movements themselves are not set—the time is variable—however, they remain within an eight-count duration.

Musical accompaniment (if any) should be a steady, unaccented pulse.

Thursday

Create a phrase using an established pulse (eight-count phrase).

Accent off beats, syncopation, and accurate rhythms.

Friday

Create a phrase that can change with time, speed, and quality (eight-count phrase).

Accelerando, decelerando: the sense of increased and decreased speed.

Technique in time quality: staccato and legato.

RHYTHM—SENSING TIME

Sense accented beats in repeated pattern. Play with rhythm and add occasional surprises to break established pattern. Be careful not to destroy repetition, which constitutes rhythm.

Time awareness is the ability to let the movement state its own time need and allow it that duration. Time and movement work very closely with each other. Generally, one knows time in musical terms. Beats and combination of beats. Pulse and measurements of tempo. Two-fours and three-fours and combinations of them. Fast and slow.

In and Out of Time

Without a clock or some equivalent timepiece, time can also be determined by attention. One senses or feels the presence of time—moving fast, slow, or standing still.

In dance, this awareness is abetted by musical pulse and rhythm. In addition to this awareness, the dancer can also step out of time consciousness and into a pedestrian state of unawareness. He can step out of time. This does not mean being off beat, but totally disregarding time boundaries and time consciousness.

One can see this demonstrated by watching people move on the streets or in their daily activities, where they are often unconcerned with time. This deliberate stepping out of time consciousness borrows from the pedestrian vocabulary and can, when used in choreography, yield startling or subtle statements.

These measurements are usually used after a movement is set. But in dancer's time, time organization has a far less restrictive definition. It is immediate and unpredictable. The duration or length of time can be measured in many ways. In creating and performing time knowing how long to hold a movement or pause, when to do the next movement, and how to use variable speeds are all part of the dancer's skill. In improvisation particularly speeds are sensed, not set.

IMPROVISATION

In groups and small units all week. Solos within a group, four or five at a time.

Monday

Stop and go. Sensing when to move and how long to hold a pause.

Tuesday

Monotony, repetition. Monotony follows an awkward period of boredom or dullness, then the monotony "experience" occurs.

Wednesday

Duration: how long to move and how long to pause.

Thursday and Friday

Free time improvisation: partners and group with "dancer's time" awareness.

Notes

Time is much more abstract than shape or motion.

Time in its essence is invisible until it is related to something. Examples: one speed against another, repetition against sudden pauses, slow motion against fast, pendulum action in time versus out of time.

Time can be absurd, surreal, and rhythmic; it can accelerate and decelerate.

It can be in a state of motion, but we shouldn't be aware of the quality of motion; all we should be impressed with is the factor of time. We want to be struck by the fact that the action you devise made the time element more important than any other element.

If you were a pedestrian waiting on a street corner, an onlooker would see your impatient gestures as your use of time.

Time studies are not always slow—there are good fast ones. Don't think of time solely as rhythm. Focus on a sense of the passage of time, and move accordingly.

We are too conditioned to musical time, which can be a danger.

Sense the essence of time, not its mathematical divisions.

Avoid literalism and get to the abstract impact of time: its speed and duration.

Have an awareness of the passage of time as you do it. Let your nervous system dictate the passage of time, judging how long you pause, when you do the next gesture, what that gesture is.

Have a sense of pause. How long can one stay within a pause before something should happen, before the movement loses its relevance and we look at other things?

Realize the time each movement needs and allow it that time.

Search into new dimensions of time that go beyond strict on the beat measurements.

The trick is to move inside the sensation of time. This involves a shift of mental gears. You have to concentrate enormously.

You may not be able to see time, but you can hear it if you learn to listen for it in silence.

Let the movement or phrase dictate its own time duration. Improvise with the amount of time necessary to complete a gesture. Give a time value to space, starting by running and sudden stopping in groups. Don't make a gesture until it is time provoked. Set up an environmental tension until you must break it and change. Let someone else's movement influence your time. Let decisions be intuitive rather than cerebral. Don't overdance. Don't destroy the grain of the group unless it adds something to the whole. Be simple and relevant.

Time is closely related to space (but we don't know how); time is like space in that it doesn't exist until you put boundaries on it.

There's more to time than fast and slow. Make it flavorful.

Don't let motion, space, shape, and so on, intrude on the time.

Don't think of pulse or rhythm, or time gets too square.

Just hold time as the most vivacious thing in your mind.

Create abstract challenges on the idea of the illusion of slow and fast. Transcend yourself; appear to go beyond normal physical limitations.

COMPOSITION

Use whatever you wish to make the viewer conscious of time and its passage. Keep study under two minutes. The interesting thing here is that you must not let shape destroy the interests of time. You must not let motion destroy the interests of time. Your shape and your space and your motion must support and enhance time, not distract from it. In that sense, it is best that they support time so well that we do not see them. We do not see space, do not see shape, do not see motion. We see the time awareness they are creating instead.

CRITICISM

Don't stand and make like a clock. "Clock" isn't "time"; it's a measurer of time.

Don't be a person going slow or fast; show fast or slow.

It needs a performance dimension; stand out of it a bit and watch it.

Be casual, don't act, don't make the body so important. We're looking at time.

We most often see slow motion as repetition and long pauses. Let me see how much more eloquent it can be.

Strong physical skills are important.

Stick to pure kinetics, not pantomime.

Have a singing quality of slowness, not a lugubrious weight.

Vibrations can work for fast but they must be sharp enough to be visible.

Don't make fast time tense. Don't lock the body.

Design the fast and slow interestingly.

When the whole body runs in space, it is too large to give the illusion of speed.

Slow down your slide into gravity. It will work better than resisting it.

Don't make it so slow that the motional energy stops.

Time is duration and speed. Know what time is in its essence as opposed to space, motion, shape, and so on. How you employ it is your business. Time is a matter of how long the duration between two events takes to achieve itself. How long are the gestures? And in between the gestures? Sense muscularly, "This is taking this long." Know time in your body. Later you can step out of time, into pedestrian, unconscious use of it. But that's for later.

Timing is essential to employ. Don't ignore it. Learn to recognize it.

His sense of time could have been more elastic instead of metronomic. Let it do what it wants to do. Give each movement all the time it needs. This is how motion identifies itself.

It was so controlled it became slow motion, with same control throughout.

Nature's time is constant, pure, and unhurried, and as a result sometimes boring. We're too impatient to allow that evenness; we keep intruding. Of course, those intrusions make for more interest to us.

Time is intangible, only sensory; we set up artificial mechanisms to compute it so that we're not late for work, or class. Overcome all these stereotypical definitions and limitations when they are not necessary.

You almost always use time in the employment of the dynamics of contrast. A "time" dance alone risks being dull.

By changing speeds, and by changing from one body part to the other in different ways, you sustain our interest. And, of course, one thing is if you interest yourself by this wonderful little excitement about tasting the different speeds and the different linear things that you can do in space, it's rather likely that you'll interest us too!

Slow dances take the most exhausting control. A slow dance is the test of the artist. This is not time in the rhythmic sense, you know. This is time as length, as duration, the judgment of speed. Don't let it fall into the dullness and trivia of expected rhythm.

By moving the head very fast we see speed, but by moving the head slowly the head becomes visible. You decide what you want us to see by the time you use.

Doing a study in "fast" time is going to give you some problems because you'll run and equate that with "fast." Very curiously, it won't be fast. Someone can stand still and be much faster than you, who ran through the space. The accomplishment of speed will be nowhere near as impressive as when someone does much smaller movements with great speed, standing in one spot. Timing is a key to illusion.

Schmutz

I must relate an occasion of how a class and I witnessed two pungent examples of time.

One day in class as I was fussing, getting comfortable, a quarter dropped from my pocket and rolled out onto the dance floor. The people in class focused on it and wondered who would retrieve it for me. But first the coin had to stop moving, and we all waited and watched. Much to our amazement, it continued to move. The coin began to make a circle. We all began to wonder how long this coin was going to move on its own volition. Suddenly it stopped and veered into a tight circle. Then it lost its circular path and fell over. It then began to rock from accelerando to decelerando. Finally, after a slow, deadly last rock, the movement came to an end. The coin had been in action for more than a minute as we all watched it play with time. I don't remember if we gave it a hand, but it certainly was a compelling study in time. The pure time of physics.

The other event was literally a dance performance. In our school in NYC on 36th Street, we had a school cat named Schmutz. Schmutz would come regularly to the third floor to visit me. This day, however, was a fortunate day for her to visit because the class was dealing with time and how to make an audience conscious of it. Schmutz entered and sat down in the middle of the room, in the center of a spotlight of sun, naturally. Well, what can I say? We all stopped and gave her our attention.

First she turned her head away from us and waited. Suddenly her tail lashed. We waited: What next? She lifted her hind leg and stopped moving it in midair. We waited: What stopped her? Then, very slowly, she began to clean herself, pausing occasionally and looking at us. She stopped, walked three steps toward us, then ran suddenly across the room, stopped, sat down and cleaned herself again, lifted her head, and listened. Her leg came down slowly. Her back rippled. No one knew what would follow. She continued this way with her own time logic for about three minutes. Three minutes. Imagine holding an audience for three minutes. Finally she began to leisurely leave the room. We gave Schmutz a big hand and she tore out of the room. We all felt exhilarated and a little embarrassed that without any formal training the cat could turn out such a sophisticated dance.

After we stopped buzzing, I said, "There is your definition of time consciousness. Use Schmutz as your standard. Now take the rest of the class to work on a study as good, as sensitive, and sensed as that." I really miss that cat. She turned in the best study that semester.

When we had to leave that wonderful studio we had to leave Schmutz because the superintendent of the building had become so attached to her, he begged to keep her, so we all hugged Schmutz goodbye, and we parted.

TIME

Permeating the entire scheme of motional dynamics are time and space.

There is no precise definition of time. We understand time mainly through a recurrent pattern of happenings. Natural and artificial structures exist for its measurement. In artifice, we have the clock and yardstick. In nature, we have the rising and the setting of the sun. We have our own recurrent breath and heartbeat and the live presence of the body experiencing its existence.

A bird can migrate and arrive at its destination with an amazingly accurate schedule. We know that other animals and insects also have acute time perceptions. Perhaps in the process of man's evolution, this sense has become obscured.

We cannot attach time exclusively to sound or motion or space; rather, it is an integral component of all of them. Its presence cannot be eliminated. Time flows continuously, and because it has no substance we cannot alter its speed or presence.

Time is relentless. It cannot be stopped. The only way to deal with time is to go with it.

Long ago, musical tradition and the use of musical notation set a system of time analysis and writing, on which dance relied heavily. This became firmly embedded in dance because of the interrelationship between the two arts. Dance has long been dependent on the musical time system, which was actually devised for the ear rather than the eye.

Dance is commonly defined in dictionaries as rhythmic movement, implying that rhythm is an essential ingredient. This is the usual "quicky" definition; however, its implication is incorrect and misleading.

In musical terms, rhythm implies the regular recurrence of an emphasis during a succession of pulses or beats. A pulse is simply a real or implied division of time of any duration, just as an inch, a foot, or a yard designates linear measurement. In sound, an emphasis on every second pulse implies a two rhythm; one on every third implies a three rhythm. We may seriously question whether such dynamic recurrence is essential to the definition of dance.

Contemporary music has been trying to relieve itself of this historical limitation, as has dance. Both dance and music are reevaluating their concept of time and experimenting in new areas that cannot be described, notated, or conceived in terms of the traditional sense of musical rhythm. We were so accustomed to measuring time in terms of seconds or pulsations that we forget that this is only a measurement of time, and not a definition.

I do not mean that in dance training the musical treatment of time should be ignored. On the contrary, it is essential. But we must carefully consider and experience pulse as a framework of time. Within the structure of musical measures, there should be a sense of time boundaries as qualities. The student should sense the reason for the choice of 3/4 time, or 5/4, 6/8, or 2/4—and the musicality each represents. As there is musical musicality, so too there is motional musicality.

Time has no pulse; it has flow. That which we attribute to pulse actually has no strict regularity of occurrence in time. Currently, as dance reevaluates its concepts of time, the construction of choreography becomes based on a sense and perception of time rather than on a mechanical beat and rhythm.

In choreographing and performing, the dancer can allow his movement to dictate the necessary time it needs to identify and fulfill itself. Pulse should not coerce choreography; time will accommodate it.

I spent the entire period between 1957 and 1958 exploring time: What constituted fast? What was the sensation of slow? I sought the "how" of how long in a stop, and the "when" of when did one begin again. All were practiced in class and sensed for sentient identity.

I worked twenty years only on time problems. I did some interesting things, such as taking a large group of about twenty-four people on stage and moving them so slowly that you couldn't see motion at all. All you were aware of was that they were changing. All you saw was the stage change; you didn't see the motion.

Time, for the artist, is basically a sense and perception of change. When there are no sensations or realizations of change, there is a sense of monotony and the feeling that time is passing too slowly. At the opposite pole, perception of quick change can also alter our sensation of time.

Mathematical computations of all the various relationships of time are far too vast and subtle to practice within the confines of a beat or rhythm. So dancers must depend on their ability to sense time. We operate on faith, for little is known scientifically about our manner of sensing time. We do not know whether or not there are actual organs or a coordination of organs that allow us this perception. We know only that we do perceive the progress of time, some of us more acutely than others.

A dancer can expect more artistry from a sense of time than from a perceived rhythm because, although it may seem paradoxical, a sense of time can lend itself to specific detail better than can the confines of rhythm.

Time, to the human mind, is one of the aspects of change and evolution. As such, it is a sensation. Although we speak of a "sense" of time, we are as yet unable to explain, except in general terms, precisely what sensory organs contribute to this perception.

There is a difference between movement and motion; there is also a difference between pulse and time. The practice of accurate metronomic pulse does not necessarily create sensitivity to time itself. Time is not a pulse, meter, or rhythm. These are designations of measurement, but the substance of what is measured is not necessarily revealed by the measurement itself. A distance of two miles does not describe the journey. An inch of string is not the same as an inch of wire or wood or copper. "I've got rhythm" may mean that quality and that alone is insufficient for the artist.

Reality forces us to face the challenge of immediacy from the very beginning, to place ourselves wholly and sentiently within the unfolding of the immediate happening. We tune in to the passing flow of time.

In order to be still—to return to an enlivened stillness—we place ourselves within the ongoingness of time, like a thing floating in the current of a stream. Here there is no time segmentation, pulse, meter, or rhythm. There is only the horizontal unfolding of time. This is the essence of dance: a sustained lyricism without the interruption of dynamic emphasis. To perform lyricism in stillness is to achieve the purest sense of change, continuity, and evolution.

In sensing time, we become aware that there are many different "clocks" operating within us. We slow the clock of the ear to intensify the clock of the eye. We reverse speeds to equalize action. Perhaps there is never a moment when all of our clocks are in agreement, but according to our needs our perceptions of time can be intensified by the sensory organs allied to those needs.

The manipulation of time is the essence of change, not time in the traditional metrical or clock sense, but in its relentless, uninterrupted, lyrical, monotone flow. Our dreams and imagination can shape time beyond the capacity of the body.

Time is one of the most elusive and abstract concepts, and how one studies it from the point of view of sharpening one's perception of it is not a matter of precise knowledge. We know that the talented artist has an acute sense of timing, which often gives him the liberty to ignore mathematical precision in favor of a richer expression of time in his performance.

In the study of time, if one sets a boundary— a time limitation or a kind of time to be tasted—the practice of repeatedly facing the same segment can sharpen one's impression of that experience.

The artist is concerned with a reality that he, in turn, must recreate into a vision or illusion. Out of the reality of time, the dancer must recreate it as illusion to give dimensional substance to his subject.

For example, in my own creative work, when I presented *Prism* I had a remarkable experience. I had set three black panels across the center of the stage. In front of each I had focused a spotlight with a filter that eliminated the usual afterglow when switched off. Each light was individually controlled within a rigid time structure in which the choreography also occurred. After the curtain rose, a single figure (male dancer) was illuminated in the center panel. The light was shut off. It went on again, illuminating the same figure in the same attitude. Again a blackout. Then, in the dark, the figure dashed to one of the end panels where that light revealed it again in the same attitude. Again, blackout, and within three seconds another figure (male dancer) was revealed in the same posture as the first but in a different-colored unitard. There continued an appearing and disappearing game using these same devices, replacing dancers in the same dance attitude but in different colors and ultimately in changing attitudes. Finally, I added motional motifs to their appearance and disappearance.

Interestingly one critic remarked that, in the ballet consisting of eight pieces, this one was the only segment in which kinetics were especially apparent. What she did not realize was that in this particular segment the dancers were rarely seen in motion. The piece succeeded in destroying the common concept of time. Here I created a false illusion of time, which suited my choreographic intent. It was as if a time barrier had been broken.

Later, while I was conversing with the Gestalt psychologist Rudolf Arnheim, he mentioned one of his experiments. In a completely darkened room, he placed three people, each with a shielded light. They turned on their lights at different times. Onlookers were invited to share their reactions. Their unanimous reaction was that there was only one light, which darted around with great speed. The timing of the lights going on and off created the illusion of movement.

Time, as both reality and illusion, structured or free, slowed down or speeded up, is a major element of dance. Time is constantly evolving, and what is now, as I speak, is already in the past. A performer can alter the existing time of now. He can create or recreate any time conceivable and necessary to illuminate the material with which he is dealing.

Only through time can we compute action.

WEEK 14: SHAPE

INTRODUCTION

Of all the principles of dance, shape is the easiest and most rewarding to explore. First, it is the most visible principle, and second, the body need not transform itself physically into something other than what it is, unless we extend it with other properties. Shaping varies considerably from amusing to disturbing and most of the time the principle of shape is rewarding in its creative presentation. Although it may appear simple, we must deal with it imaginatively and clearly because it has the dancer's physical and pedestrian habits and mannerisms to contend with and overcome.

Shape is specific. What you see is what you get, therefore the dancer needs a keen inner eye to recognize what the viewer is seeing. This is where the dancer's skill in conceptualizing what he looks like comes into play, when the ability to deal with the many parts of the body at the same time becomes important. Designing where a toe and the shoulders might relate or how the placement of the head and the left knee are to look is intrinsic to sensing the totality of a shape.

In designing and performing shape, the ability to focus and to adjust a shape demands an internal eye to pull the entire body into focus, like a camera lens. This focus is achieved by the body's sense of consonance: the desire to seek a totality or balance of design. When the dancer achieves this shape, he achieves this consonance and the shape will speak for itself. Once a shape is determined, then the ability to determine its mobility into another shape or into locomotion becomes its next challenge.

Shape awareness is an aesthetic skill. Designing three-dimensional forms with the body is another sensitivity. Developing the mobility of shapes is still another achievement.

Creating spatial volumes.
Dancers: Richard Haisma, Jerry Pearson, and Sara Pearson.
Photo by Robert Shankar.

CLASS PLAN

TECHNIQUE

Premise

Learn to shape and sculpt the body inventively. Move shapes effectively.

Imbue the center of the shape with an energy that radiates outward, enlivening the entire form. This involves using principles of decentralization.

Shape the entire body. Use total body consciousness. Grain the body to its totality.

Monday

Start with a simple locomotor floor pattern.

Set a shape (dancers can set their own) and carry it across the floor. Let the shape influence the nature of the locomotion.

Start with just arm variations to determine the shape. Then add chest and hips. Combine them.

Change shapes every four counts.

Change the shape from slow to fast as you move across the floor.

Generate energy out from center to enliven the shape.

Develop shape phrase with under- and overcurves, and other locomotions.

Tuesday

Develop shape phrases with levels, hops, turns, and so on. Shape is a totality, not a singular isolation of a body part. Shape speaks of itself.

Shape is total body involvement. Let shape influence the locomotion.

A close tight shape won't have a large loose walk, change shape during patterns like run, run, leap. Let the shape dictate the time and space and motional quality necessary for it to achieve itself.

Wednesday

Constant shape awareness during a lyric nonstop phrase. Check for smooth transitions.

The speed should be slow enough that you can see the shapes evolve. Dancers create their own phrases across the floor. Dancers begin after every twelve counts.

Thursday

Contrasts: shape the space around you with volumes, then change to concentration on sculptural body shapes. Go from outside around the body to the total body itself.

Call attention to a single body part, then change to the attention of the whole body.

Let locomotion vary with every body change.

Friday

Create a shape phrase using everything but always calling attention to the total body's shape.

Don't move too fast or we shall see the movement.

Small-based precariously balanced shapes have a more kinetic sensation than wide-based shapes.

Relevés and balances for kinetics.

Stabiles have a large and secure base on the floor, like sitting or lying on the floor.

Motional illumination of the form from the inside radiating out.

Shape is torso-generated and three-dimensional. Design is peripheral.

IMPROVISATION

Select the week's improvisations from this list of suggestions.
Get rid of baggy and torso-obscuring clothing.

Divide the class in halves. Create four shapes. Evolve a transition between the shapes. Evolve a locomotion as transition, clearly arriving at each of the four shapes. Repeat the whole phrase three times, changing the time values of each variation.

Half of class at a time: group moves to general drumbeat. Drum slows when the dancers begin to arrive in a finale shape. Teacher directs: "Adjust the shape and bring it into focus and now enliven it from the inside." Counts 1 - 2 - 3 - 4 - Hold. The rest of class watches this process to see the subtleties of correction. Like through a camera lens, the shape becomes clearer and focused. Repeat process and adjust new shape.

Students pair off; one of each pair physically forms the other one into a series of shapes.

Create three different shape transitions. I want you now to go from shape to shape, without any pausing at all. So in effect you are going through millions of shapes.

Get in threes. The first person assumes a shape; the second tries to duplicate it exactly; the third makes corrections, trade roles.

Get in twos. Improvise moving in relation to each other sculpturally; keep the sense of shape and don't let it get motional. Think, one body shape plus one body shape equals three, a new body shape. The dancers should sense the third shape they are making all the time.

Walking: In groups, walk first with awareness and change of shape, then walk plainly. Alternate.

Walk four counts, hit shape on fourth count. Repeat.

Walk four counts with four different shapes. Repeat, changing shape order.

Walk with a partner, sculpturally relating to each other.

Walk four counts; add four shapes turning.

Free improvising in groups of four to six. Sense how to sculpturally relate to create an aesthetic totality. It seems this ability of sensing consonance is inherent in humans. Give this improvisation four or five minutes for each group. End it with, "Bring it to an end," and let the group sense the ending without sound accompaniment. This improvisation has almost never failed to produce some of the most memorable and successful studies of the term.

CRITIQUES

Devise a manner and path of going that makes the shape juxtaposition interesting.

The body grain is evenly directed into all areas of the shape.

You say, "This is the shape." The whole figure has the same energy, and shines equally.

Fulfill the shapes with their inherent elegance and interest.

Shape is three-dimensional, although you can imply a flat two-dimensionality.

Call attention to the sculpting of the shape. Your body not only has to design the shape, but also has to call attention to the shape itself.

Don't let space, time, and motion become too prominent and interfere with our seeing the shape.

Don't make casual or banal shapes. It takes an artist of great skill to let us see a simple shape with wonder. Design your shapes interestingly. Remember you have literally all of the body parts to put together: head, arms, legs, and so on.

Challenge yourself to move quickly; however, arriving at a shape doesn't necessarily mean slow motion to get there.

Every shape has a specific time to sink into the eye of the viewer. Try to feel that time and let the shape find its own time.

A sculptor starts with an armature of bones, then builds the rest on it. Sense your skeleton as an armature.

Let the shape movement evolve as it goes through transitions.

Let shapes evolve motion-wise in a way determined by the shape.

Your strong projection of arms outward gives an impression of space, and also drama.

Some of these are too casual or ordinary, so we are not captivated by a fresh design.

Be more daring.

We can see how ravishing you are; now divorce yourself from yourself and show us how ravishing the shapes you produce are.

Leaning against the wall was sort of out of left field as far as shape is concerned.

Be possessed by the idea of the form, of the shape, of the sculpture. Be involved with it; make it a pungent tasty thing.

Duet: learn to pause at these handsome places. Give me a chance to see them. See if you can find the way to arrive at that shape in such a way that all parts of the body move and arrive simultaneously. At the completion of the shape, be aware when one body part arrives early and rests, while the rest of the body catches up to it. Your whole body is the shape. You should be looking at the body as a totality. Don't focus on a part of your body, otherwise you will call attention to that part.

Move out of the shape with enough energy to carry through the whole development of the new shape.

There's nothing more disturbing than expecting something new and then seeing a familiar movement.

Sense what wants to move. This determines the first movement from the beginning shape. Grasp the inherent motional drive that rests within the newly created entity. Go with it. Follow it, let it lead. Get precarious, hurt, fall, be ravishing!

Don't be eager to rush out of a thing if you know your partner is moving. Stay still, and let your partner continue shaping it. Remember the two of you are part of the total.

Don't make your point of contact too thick, too gross.

Sculpt the body: shape the limbs and the torso to incite images and by their continual juxtapositioning create a poetic continuity. A sculpture with its one single potent statement seems almost primitive compared to the continuous flexible complexities the human body can achieve.

The body is a three-dimensional form. It is a malleable form. It is primarily axial in character. It can bend itself into so many different positions that as a sculptor you can do thousands of different shapes with the body. This is not at all strange to dance, nor strange to form, nor is it strange to life in general. You form your body to do certain things. I am sitting down, and I have to form my body sculpturally into a sitting shape in order to be comfortable here.

Make shapes now that are abstract rather than literal in their connotation. Even though you may not be thinking literally, the shapes will look it.

Style (the manner of doing) qualifies the shape, and directs its meaning.

Shape should look at itself, not beyond.

Beware of shapes that have cultural or symbolic connotations.

Watch out for movement becoming important; don't set up a motional flavor. We're looking at shape, and shape is only a part of motion.

The dynamics of contrasts can emphasize shapes.

Define the shape. They don't all have to be angular.

Don't be someone doing shapes, be the shapes.

You have invented it, but you are not experiencing it. Unless you experience it, you don't really know quite how to treat it.

[To a particular student] Yours was close, except that there were times when your face looking outward had a very devotional intent. Look, when you have your hands up in the air and your face turns up, what does that look like? The shape becomes incidental to something else, perhaps in this case a reverential feeling, devotion toward something upward. Be aware of unintended communications.

She choreographed her shapes well, but unfortunately she allowed her strong design of the motion and her time to diminish the value of the sculptural quality.

It had a throwaway, glib quality. That doesn't mean that you can't move quickly, but if you do move quickly it must be for the purpose of this particular problem.

COMPOSITION

A shape dance. Let us see the vividness of your shapes and the manner of their evolution and locomotion. Concentrate on calling attention to the entire physical form. You can either move evolving sculpturally or dart from shape to shape. This change of speed will contribute to the kinetic effect.

Play a two-way role: there is a shape-taker you, and a choreographer you. The first performs and the second watches. Develop in your mind's eye the skill to see what people will be looking at in your shapes. Make sure the vitality goes through all the extremities.

You can shape space, you can shape time, you can shape motion. But we're shaping the body's shape, which means we're shaping bulk. When you use what you feel is a distorted or ugly shape, don't think of it as distasteful, but fulfill it as you would any shape. Bring it to life as a total. By doing so, it will find its consonance and reveal the intrinsic beauty of whatever form it takes.

Sense how you look and pause when you've arrived at an interesting shape. When something handsome happens, pause. It takes time for shape to register, and it also helps you to know what wants to develop from it. You are not dealing with what the shape represents, but enlivening the shape itself. You're performers! Be concerned with shape. The message exists in the shape, so dig into that shape! Release its potency.

Shape duet.
Dancers: Sara Shelton and Raymond Johnson.
Photo courtesy of the Nikolais/Louis Archives.

Shape improvisation.
Dancers: Sara Shelton and Raymond Johnson.
Photo courtesy of the Nikolais/Louis Archives.

SCULPTED FORMS—SHAPE

Motion involves four major control factors: shape, time, space, and motion itself. Inadequate perception or control in any of these areas will reflect in a major way on one's skill as a dance artist. There are a myriad of other control factors a dancer must acquire, but these are the "big four."

Shape is a term that may be applied to the abstract as well as the concrete. We may make or imply shapes in space, or we may speak of the shape of time or even the shape of motion. In this chapter, however, our reference is to the actual physical shape of the body—the sculptural form. We are concerned with our sense and perception of the size, contours, and placement of the various body parts into sculptural design.

To achieve such a strict focus, we must control our perceptions in such a manner as to eliminate any extraneous awareness that interferes with or distracts from those sensations that inform us of the physical forms the body has assumed. The perception of ourselves as always being in our one, recognizable, predominant body shape must now be denied. Now we are focusing our full powers of concentration on the newly created shapes we will design with our bodies.

We have basic names for geometrical shapes, such as *cube*, *triangle*, *sphere*, and *icosahedron* (the geometric form Laban used to organize the space surrounding the body). On the other hand, there are much more complex shapes that identify recognizable forms. A chair, for example, is a piece of furniture, but it is also a shape. A table is similarly identifiable. There are shapes in nature that are formed from understandable germination such as flowers, vegetables and fruits. We distinguish a lily from a rose mostly by shape, although they may share the same color. So, too, an apple differs visually from a pear by virtue of its shape.

From nature we get our greatest variety of sculptural forms. Our response to their beauty is certainly not governed by narrative exposition or erotic desire, but by our aesthetic response to them mainly as a structure. A form that was spawned by a single germinal force, no matter how complex the structure is.

Geometric forms are also dynamic entities that relate to specific forms of energy; for example, spherical forms relate to a vortex of power and the balance of centrifugal and centripetal forces of energy within them. There are suggestions of momentum within elliptical forms and, perhaps, even suggestion of lyrical sensations because of a lack of any angular boundary. Spherical forms can also suggest balance of pressure on both the intrados, the living inside, and the extrados, the outside. One can easily suppose that some shapes are tactile (relating to the sense of touch), and others kinetic (relating to the energies associated with motion). But what specifically causes the feeling of an artfulness of an art form as opposed to the indefinite lumpiness of a rock is still a mystery. One can only suggest that one has order or comprehensible structure, and the other does not. Yet this says nothing. We have many works of sculptural art that are as lumpy and complex as the most disorganized assemblages of garbage.

The human body is a complex shape to begin with. It is capable of infinite variations. Besides the major differences that distinguish male from female, we have all varieties of large and small, fat and thin, big-boned, small-boned, long-legged, and short-legged, various ethnic traits, and all combinations thereof. Some bodies bend and twist easily. Others carry out only the ordinary shaping activities necessary for common acts.

But the flexibility a dancer achieves allows for thousands of sculptural attitudes. His body can arrange itself in many ways to convey specific feelings, although in many instances these feelings can be misinterpreted. For example, lowering the head, bending the body, and allowing the shoulders to hang inevitably connotes sadness. Charlie Chaplin used a classical example of misinterpretation, however, in a film where his wife dies, and one sees his back in a seemingly dejected attitude, which is further qualified by a small, upward and downward shaking of the body. This was immediately interpreted by the audience as sobbing. But Chaplin had the camera swing around to front view, revealing that he is really shaking a cocktail shaker. The comedic effect based on the anticipated misinterpretation of the implied meaning of the sculptural position was a potent example of Chaplin's genius.

When we come to dance, we are indeed in a quandary. The dancer is a humanoid form and recognized as such. Within this form there are many varieties, as mentioned earlier.

Then there are the viewer's judgmental criteria, which recognize some physical human shapes as being more beautiful than others.

From the point of view of dance artistry, the design of the sculptural use of the human body is exceptionally wide-ranging. We are not concerned here with the common shapes of human beauty in their more obvious aspects, but rather with concepts of sculptural design of the body for aesthetic purposes.

Here the dance artist arranges his body to cause a transcendence, which will temporarily suspend his immediate psycho-biological presence. Even if there is no extraordinary change, when he merely assumes the attitude of himself as a dancer, he needs the skill of shaping a sculptural image in relation to a particular dance image.

Forms of dance—ethnic, folk, entertainment, or art—have vast differences in sculptural and transcendent demands. Consider the Balinese *legong*, with its peculiar postural and angular design, compared to the square and weighty stance of the Hopi Indian antelope or snake dance, in contrast to the attitudes in *Swan Lake*. In many instances, costumes help the transcendence and shaping, particularly in East Indian and African dances. We can recognize many kinds of dance from their sculptural design alone. The dancer's skill lies in shaping his body to the needs of the stylistic distinctions of any particular dance.

Aside from such skills, which are relatively obvious, there is the direct aesthetic study of the use of the body in terms of sculptural design. Here we are concerned with the exploration of the three-dimensional design of the body—not for human representations, but so it can communicate as vitally as possible on its own sculptural terms.

Dance's kinetic impact has always been recognized. Yet it is a visual art as well and, as such, can entice the eye and mind to experience and react to its sculptural possibilities. Sculpting the body for its own value rather than as a supportive factor is not using it to represent a dog or cat by getting down on all fours to depict a dog or cat. We can sculpt a body shape that entices interest in the beauty of the shape as a thing in and of itself. We form the shape in such a way that the onlooker is not led to expect a character sketch, mood, or situation but is instead compelled to react to the aesthetics of the devised shape, on its own terms.

A sculptural form exists—good or bad—in any comprehensible chunk of matter; however, the art of sculpture, the accomplishment of a three-dimensional structure, is to arouse interest by the particularly compelling quality of the shape itself. If the shape in any way assumes a literal suggestion rather than remains primarily within the experience of the shape itself, it does not meet the purist's definition of shape. For example, if one creates a form that begins to suggest a cat, then it is likely that the onlooker will begin to relate to his experiences of that animal. He is, consequently, distracted, at least partially, from the purer sculptural reaction. This certainly does not imply that representational sculpture is bad art. When a representational aspect dominates a sculpture, however, there is a danger that the person looking at it will miss the impact and vitality of its pure form. One must sense the vitality underlying the basic form. That vitality also enlivens the realistic creation if realism is the desired end.

For anyone dealing with abstractly shaping material, the question of at what point the final shape identifies itself as a completed, finished, whole gestalt, or res, is the heart of the matter.

The German word *Gestalt* was made popular in the English language by its association with Jungian psychology. I use it to identify the nature of an abstract or nonverbal entity. Like DNA, all the materials of the composition, such as the time, space, shape, and motion, contain its flavor, identity, and its intent. It is easy to see when an aspect of the composition strays from its intent, unless of course the choreographer's purpose is to be irrational or absurd.

Through the explorative ranges of improvisation, the dancer can gain skill in identifying the gestalt or identity of his creative work.

For many contemporary artists, abstraction is a matter of continuous concern. Since the artist has freed himself from the representational, in that he is no longer obliged to create a likeness of a known thing such as a statue, a hand, an animal, he now faces an endless choice of designed shapes.

In dance, when we wish to enhance the power of a shape, we should bring all attention to that shape. There can be all sorts of distractions; for example, certain sculptural designs—even though nonliteral—might involve or suggest projections into space, inviting the eye to look away from the actual form of the body. There is nothing aesthetically wrong with this, but in a class dealing with shape, the experiencing of the shape will be weakened.

Another distraction that sometimes occurs is that of accidental symbolism. One might, for example, design a shape involving hands covering the eyes and the upper body rounded over. Even though the creator had no intention of conveying dejection, the position itself is such a strong symbol of dejection that it will court the onlooker's eye to that dramatic possibility.

One might wonder how a dancer, equipped with the human body, which is so powerful in its literal suggestion, can hope to achieve an abstract sculptural design. It is because of the metaphoric facilities of the body that this can actually happen. Again, it is a matter of performance power. When the performer creates the sculptural design, he must willfully illuminate the shape. He does this by strongly concentrating on the design, which, in turn, causes the onlooker to focus with him meta-kinetically. If the performer grains his entire interest toward that structure, then the shape will be clearly apparent.

The dancer injects the entire shape with a radiating grain emanating from the center of the shape, which magnifies and energizes the shape as a total, extending it into its close aura capacity, but not projected beyond its physical boundaries. This center of the shape is a fluid physical center. It changes according to the design of each shape. It is simply a point around which the body balances itself. Thus, as the shape changes, this point will relocate to its new center. This is decentralization at its best.

In designing sculptural forms, the facility of the body is truly wondrous. Here, the dancer's creative imagination can make his choreography distinctive.

A NOTE ON SHAPE

Shape is the skill of sculpting the body. When one considers that the sculptor has only one form with which to make his statement, his art, one shape to represent weeks or months of work, the importance of a single sculptural shape becomes evident.

The dancer, however, because of his extraordinary mobility, can change his shape every second, like a strobe light. The turn of a head, an elbow lift, a twist of the chest, a lift of a leg, the whole facile ability of the body to shape and reshape itself is a sculptor's dream, or an overwhelming nightmare, as the case may be.

But because of his facility for rapid change, the dancer takes this malleable gift for granted. The simplest positions begin to lose their flavor in favor of distortion and extreme design. The task here is to deal with the idea of bringing a shape, no matter how simple or complicated, into focus so that no attention is brought to any one part of the shape, but to the shape as a whole. This is a good way to practice **totality**, one shape at a time. Like a photographic lens, the smallest adjustment can bring the picture into a sharper focus. In improvisation, while half the class is watching and the other half is performing, both have a chance to see and correct shape inconsistencies by making simple adjustments. The dancer searches his body for tensions that intrude and alter the balance and identity of intended shapes.

In moving across the floor, maintaining a shape of the body or changing shapes en route lends variations to the nature of the locomotion, and also gives motional value to the locomotion.

While carrying the shape into mobility, the presence of shape consciousness remains. The dancer always maintains sculptural emphasis.

Shape is basically torso-generated, whereas in design the extremities and peripheral interests are emphasized. Shape is three-dimensional and gutsy. It radiates out from the center of the torso. It feeds the rest of the body and the space that surrounds its form. It has weight and depth and speaks with richness.

Once the shape is arrived at, then the body performs or fulfills it by evenly projecting into it from within. A projecting energy presses the shape out into the surrounding space, which both vitalizes itself and the surrounding space or aura.

A statue is multifronted. One can walk around it and see it from any angle. It generally doesn't favor one direction over another because of its three-dimensionality. Favoring one point of viewing has to be a deliberate choice. In class or on stage the dancer should consider the viewer. Presenting the most interesting vantage of a shape upstage away from the viewer doesn't seem reasonable.

We must also consider the awareness of kinetics in this otherwise stationary principle. As with the sculptor Alexander Calder's "Mobiles" and "Stabiles," the smaller and more precarious contact the shape has to the floor will increase the kinetic excitement of the shape, whereas the grounded and more securely based shape will have less kinetic excitement.

Bring a sculptor's eye to the shaping of the body, account for the entire body and awareness of the entire shape. In basic work, we emphasize the entire shape, and every part of the body has equal emphasis. Once the dancer has mastered this skill, he can begin to practice imbalance, distortion, or selective emphasis.

MOTION

Motion, as Nikolais distinguished it from movement, had to do with the dancer's sensory skills. Granted, there had to be movement in order to experience motion because motion was an inherent part of movement. Simply put, motion was sensing the doing. Sensing in the case of dance included sensing the shape, time, and space involved, along with the interior sensibilities of grain and gravity—the whole raft of principles of physics and the physical composite of the human body. All of these factors defined motion.

The dancer had to understand arriving at motional fulfillment because only he could achieve it. It was because of this responsibility borne by the dancer that Nikolais was so concerned with motion being the basis of a dance training. But before the dancer could achieve the totality of motion, he had to master the many parts that comprised the art of dance, at least understand them to some degree.

We therefore undertook the parts separately in class. They were defined and identified. In technique class we practiced them further, then experienced and explored them still further in improvisation. Motion then became the most complex action possible. It not only included all of the principles of the art, but it also included all of the facilities of the individual's physical and psychic makeup.

The word *motion* is an ambiguous one to begin with. *Motion*, when applied to the displacement of inanimate matter, is an important word in physics. In regard to the animate human form, it has another complex definition, especially in dance. It was important to know when Nik was using the word interchangeably, from physics to the aesthetics of dance. Everything in this book is part of his definition of motion. Everything he taught in class was directed toward the totality and inclusiveness he sought.

To reveal the motion that exists in movement was to reveal the life force and gift of change that distinguishes the animate from the inanimate.

* * *

Motion, as the medium of dance, is the basis of its technique and artistry. Motion includes within its definition all the dimensions related to time and space, as well as the additional companion dynamics involved in the physical laws of motion. One can explore separately all of the components involved. One can taste the nature of gravity or momentum, the mathematics and sensations of time, the volume or length of space, and all of their known values or mystical implications. But for now our concern is with the sense of the motion itself.

If we could reduce the motional capacities of the human instrument and relate them to the most elemental control of the psychical stimuli that cause us to move, we would probably experience a wonderfully direct and primal meaning of the nature of action.

We have traced the human body as a predominantly axial instrument. Bones, tied joint to joint, are pulled into action by muscles, which receive their power from the nerves, which in turn receive their power from message impulses from the brain.

We cannot relieve ourselves of all motional censorship, nor would it be safe to. We have learned to stand upright and to walk by means of the self-censorship that experience brings. The child, after learning about the disasters of falling, finally learns what not to do as well as what to do. On the other hand, many motional inhibitions stem from fear. These are not kinetic restrictions; they are mental and physical restrictions. Many of these must be unlearned by the dancer.

In this exploration, however, we are concerned simply with mobility and the basic feelings of mobility— devoid of the literal drama of "mad, sad, or glad." Mobility is by no means a simple act. The propulsion of the body through space is a fulsome endeavor.

Because dance as the art of motion is subject to the same physical laws of action as all moving objects, it cannot place itself above these physical laws. While man enjoys the unique privilege of motivation because of his physio-psychological energies, his physical action itself is as liable to gravity, momentum, centrifugal force, centripetal force, aerodynamics, and friction as any other body of physical matter.

From the cradle, the baby learns subconsciously as well as consciously to cope with these laws of motion. His first walking steps are precarious adventures in which he strives to control and direct his body into harmony with external forces.

He learns to lose his balance into the direction of his interest, and automatically plies his feet in that direction in time to prevent disaster. He learns to lift his feet high enough to overstep obstacles. He begins to compute his actions in relation to his limited space and time. He refines his motional skill until he achieves control within the normal range of maneuvering required in his society. His learning process involves the energies of his mind as they direct the energies of the body.

In dance, the skill of motion is challenged to the highest degree. It goes beyond the special skills of sports and the manipulation of objects outside of the body. It deals with the skill of handling the body itself in action. Ultimately, the dancer must make the motional forces serve him—not dominate him.

Motion is the result of various laws of physics. It occurs when energy displaces a body of matter. It is the law of motion that governs change. Because varieties of motion are infinite, motion as the medium of dance offers a limitless range of kinetic possibilities.

The motion of a body of matter involves three elemental phases: passivity, disturbance, and outcome. These stages apply to dance as well.

Passivity for the dancer refers to the state of stillness, pause, or stasis. Stillness, or the passive phase, is predetermined by a state of mind and therefore varies considerably in its qualities and in the shape that the body assumes.

All physical bodies in the passive stage have certain properties, which condition the manner of their potential motion. The properties of a rubber ball make its reaction to the impact of a blow different from the reaction of a wooden ball or a balloon. Size, shape, weight, and the nature of the physical properties predetermine, to some extent, the nature of the object's action.

The physical, psychological, and biological characters of the human body are different and perceive differently. These complex characteristics are transmitted through the muscles and affect the ability to change the body's texture. Muscles can be hardened or softened. Through axial facility, the body can change its shape. That the animate thing can furnish its own impetus in the disturbance phase marks the difference between the animate and the inanimate physical thing. Man can move at will; a rock cannot.

Action follows the path of stasis, disturbance, and outcome. *Disturbance* implies a degree of unexpected shock. The human body is as subject to shock as any other piece of matter. The body can, however, furnish its own energy or motivation to move out of stasis.

Because the state of stasis must receive some form of energy that causes it to move, the dancer usually furnishes his own impetus: when he is not pushed, or pulled into action by an external energy. His power to move stems from his own will, his psyche.

Disturbance also includes the direction into which the force has activated him. Direction is a progression from point to point, and refers to the path from impetus to the logical consequence of that impetus. With the animated object—the dancer in this case—disturbance is further qualified by the time factor as well as the quality of the force, be it either percussive, push, pull, sustained, held, or released, depending on whether it is expended immediately or extended in its release.

In another form of "action out of stillness," a position is held and then simply released into gravity. No energy is expended to cause action, but rather the reverse occurs; energy is removed. Falling, dropping, and swing actions result from this nature of doing. In this instance, it is gravity that supplies the driving power. The release is the *disturbance*. It is in disturbance that motion particularly defines itself as dance.

The human instrument, for the most part, offers its own disturbance, delivers its own impulsion, by way of a wide range of motivation.

192

Propel is another word used to describe this disturbance phase of motion in dance. It can be devised, imagined, or concocted, but in any case it deliberately causes action. Even if we wish to perform that propelling as a surprise, it is nevertheless concocted. The choices of which manner or propulsion should be used are considerable.

It is in the vitality and control of this explosive motivation that we can distinguish a fine technical performer. He has the ability to suddenly fire up the exact impulse necessary to propel his muscles to act; in addition, he has the swift ability to control the expulsion of the energy in the muscles. There must be a swift release of energy after the disturbance action, or the body unit will appear sluggish in fulfilling the desired destination enabled by the disturbance.

Every action enacted by the body (that is, from a self-motivated source) is initially a percussive action. (Gravity can be considered a percussive source by a sudden release into its downward power.)

The human body, especially if one is emotionally disturbed, can explode in almost all directions and usually does so in fits of emotional outbursts. Percussive action is explosive and consequently sprays its forces in all directions, unless, of course, it is blocked and channeled by some barrier. In dance, we can choose the barrier so that the percussive-force results are directed into a spatial definition of our choice.

When we first practice this principle, our main concern is the control of simple focal destinations. We need to determine the architectural design of the body so that we can agree on what constitutes a forward, backward, sideward, diagonal, or upward and downward direction when the body is propelled into motion. Although simple, these architectural directions define the aim of the body toward specifically understood destinations. Architectural skills are therefore necessary for the technical as well as for the aesthetic accomplishments of the dancer.

The third stage, *outcome*, brings into greater play the laws of motion: gravity, momentum, and centrifugal and centripetal forces. In the inanimate object the nature of this stage is predetermined by the properties of the object plus the direction and degree of the disturbance source. Thus a rubber ball will respond to the friction and degree of force according to its properties of resilience, its size, weight and shape; and the laws of motion governing such an object.

But with the complexity of the human mechanism, the *outcome* can be completely unpredictable. The human instrument, with its psycho-physiological endowment, makes this stage infinitely variable. The body may change its shape or textural properties while en route according to the particularities of the motivation. These variants can effect actions within the body, which, in turn, can affect the outcome as a whole.

The outcome for an inanimate object is generally predictable, but the human being is such a multidimensional instrument that he can metaphorically assume any kind of form. Therefore one's first decision should be to determine what form the dancer has assumed and what is the nature of that form. The design of the body and its characteristics will now refer to their identifying gestalt. That gestalt, that new identity, will determine whatever action the dancer assumes.

In the still or stasis state, the characteristics the dancer sets up in his body do not necessarily relate to a human mood. Instead, he can devise action that relates metaphorically to whatever his subject might be. If one were to dance an abstract state of space or time, or anything nonconcrete, the poetic state would alter the outcome of action.

To review: in the passivity or stasis stage the dancer, now a metaphoric figure, need not necessarily represent mankind either specifically or generally. Both his physical and psychical attitudes are free to design themselves as he chooses.

Proceeding to the second motional phase, that of disturbance, the impulsion to move relates to the identity the dancer has established in the state of stasis. The metaphoric nature of the body will dictate the nature of the disturbance.

The third motional phase, that of adjustment or outcome, is now determined by the nature of the gestalt. Tensions of emotional derivation are likely to destroy a delicate metaphor; their chance of obliterating an illusional subject is great. Tensional manifestations of emotion are very powerful and visible, and the slightest appearance of any of them will cause all other action qualities to be relatively subservient to them.

Going further, other realms of motional language now become possible. Instead of being a human being in a particular space, the metaphoric dancer may become the nature of that space instead. In this case, instead of designing himself as a human creature in space, he must create the means whereby his literal state of being human is subdued. His body becomes, instead, an instrument that directly reveals the quality of his space idea. It's as if we don't see the piano being played, yet we hear its sound.

In dance the figure may transcend its being human and, like music, become anything. The dancer may be abstract or concrete. He may be the essence of a character without being the character itself. He may be a sound or a color. He may be an emotion without being the one who emotes. He may be the quality of a time or a space. He may be a thing of nature or an invention of the mind. In the act of transcending himself, he uses the most powerful and valuable aspect of being human—that is, his power of change, of becoming, of full transcendence. He can reduce himself to the microcosmos or expand himself to macrocosmos. Instead of only the world, he can now encompass the universe.

SUSTAINED MOTION

Dance is kept alive and is propelled by explosive energies caused to take place within the body. Percussive motion, explosive motion and/or disturbance are not the only means of propelling motion, however. In describing sustained motion, we go off on a different method of action.

By sustained motion, we mean a continuum of undisturbed action: a process where the velocity is never altered by minute impulses but gives the illusion of sustained lyrical ongoing action.

In the performance of sustained action, the dancer treats both momentum and gravity as if they did not exist. The challenge and test of skill is sustaining a swing action while avoiding its tendency to capitulate to gravity.

Gravity is the hardest part of the swing to control in this instance. The inclination to succumb to gravity is most prevalent in all downward peripheral actions. This downward release accent results in swings, rather than a sustained circular peripheral action.

After one achieves control and masters the quality of sustained action, then one can introduce changes in speed while still maintaining the same sustained quality.

One of the most beautiful accomplishments in sustained motion is achieved by placing the whole body in the fluid state of mobile continuity. Here, the coordination and pliancy of the spine is essential to avoid the disruptive action that tends to occur when the quality from one body part is passed abruptly onto another. Achieving these changes without interrupting the ongoing sustained sensation is a challenge the dancer must overcome.

In the study of sustained motion, there is a strong, necessary space-time control factor, which calls for an even allocation of the motion according to its allotted time. For example, in the simple lifting of an arm from low to high within the time span of four beats, one might see erratic control. Although the dancer may not sense them, the instructor can easily see variations of speed. Often, I see a too-fast start and a consequent slowing to reach the destination at the correct moment. Any inaccuracy mars the sustained quality.

To maintain an uninterrupted flow of motion in a change of direction, a small circular action in the transition is necessary to absorb any abruptness and prevent a loss of continuity, so there is no loss of sustained continuity. Achieving success also requires our purposely eliminating any emotional attitudes or exhibitions of extraneous actions and sensations that will distract from the basic quality of our intent. In all sustained action, gravity, shape, time, space, and so on still exist. But, through the performer's aesthetic and technical skill and the magic of his performance, their existence can be subdued by the illusion of sustained motion.

In its initial investigation there is the tendency to associate sustained with slow motion (which it can be), but it can be maintained at high speeds as well.

After achieving the quality of sustained action comes the practice of controlling various velocities without sacrificing the quality of sustained action. We can then proceed to the excitement of accelerandos and decelerandos.

194

SUSPENSION

Gravity is an ever-present force. It is in constant operation and in readiness to pull down any physical object that has exhausted itself and is left without further energy to sustain its outcome.

The force that acts as an antidote to gravity, enabling the body or body part to rest in the outcome position, is called suspension.

We speak of suspension here as a quality of motion, not as hanging from suspension points of the body (which is another premise), but rather as suspended motion. It requires the skill of maintaining an outcome or arrival position with the minimum of muscular effort.

Suspension ignores gravity because its use of energy balances both the upward and downward of verticality. Neither dominates.

In achieving a point of suspension, one of the greatest difficulties is the simultaneous arrival of all body parts to the conclusion of the action. This is most difficult to accomplish when the body is designed in one sculptural position and the action to follow must bring it to another entirely different position. Here there is apt to be a race. Usually, certain body parts will arrive at suspension while others follow along as late arrivals. Some body parts may be further away from the destination than others, so control of varying speeds is required. Consequently, the percussive push must be greater on the more remote parts than on those that are closer so that momentum causes their simultaneous arrival.

Moments of suspension can serve as points of rest or pause, just as in music there are frequent moments of desired silence to allow the previous sounds to complete their resonance. The dancer must diligently practice rest or arrival because its contribution to the aesthetics of timing and phrasing is essential to the art of dancing.

Achieving the quality of suspension requires sensing exactly how much energy to use. If the dancer exerts too much effort, certain parts of his body will tense and give the appearance and kinetic feeling of "overcontrol." One will also, most likely, have a tense dramatic look. Too little effort, however, will cause an opposite appearance of weakness and insufficient vitality. Actually, what is achieved when the correct balance of energies is arrived at is a new state of stasis or stillness, a new beginning point.

These time-length judgments of suspension are the commas, colons and semicolons of dance. These moments allow the gesture to register to both the dancer and onlooker. If the gesture is simple, then perhaps only a very brief moment of suspension is required to highlight it. But no matter how brief the outcome of a gesture may be, it should show its full breadth and suspended arrival.

THE PATH OF MOTION

Determining the path of motion is a function of design. For example, if the right hand rests on the left shoulder and its next action is to bring the palm of the hand to the right hip, it would seem that, geometrically, a straight diagonal line to that position would be the correct motion. This is not so, however. The straight path is one that dynamically shoots past the hip. Because the body is three-dimensional, the more expedient path is a curve; the action makes an arc so that its terminal point is on the hip. This would be true at all speeds. By doing the straight line path quickly, one can readily see that the directional momentum brings the hand past the hip or causes the arm to tense or "put on its brakes" so that it does not go beyond its desired conclusion.

The judicious path of action of any movement should not be overlooked—however unintended or brief it might be, it is sure to be visible and seen.

A NOTE ON MOTION

Motion includes so many factors that it is best to keep its definition simple. Basically, it is the quality and nature that exist within and identify a movement. It is not something imposed on a movement but rather the revelation of the inner nature of that movement.

To obtain the richness necessary to imbue life and identity into movement, the dancer must draw from all of his aesthetic sensibilities and references. To do this and gain fluidity, richness, and skill, he must practice this process as diligently as he does his mastery of movement. Eventually, even in his pedestrian movement he becomes sentiently aware of motion. How one walks, or lifts an arm, or turns or bends—every movement is to be savored. He becomes conscious of every movement: how the chest breathes, the movement of time passing, how the space swims around his head. He lives daily in a passion of awareness. For the dancer, motion is everything.

All motion bears within it the emotion of that motion. Motion bespeaks the emotion of abstraction: a nonliterally defined emotion, of which there are many. In the Asian-Indian musical lexicon, there are hundreds of *rasas*, qualities that are felt but not necessarily verbal: delicate emotions. These *rasas* are musical poems composed about times of day, qualities of light, softness of the air, scents of flowers, feelings, many sensations which abound and indicate aspects of life. They are not limited to the strong emotions favored in the West, such as pity, fear, greed, hate, love, and so on. Beauty is a composite of all emotions, from elation to the most crippling despair, and since "beauty rests in the eye of the beholder," its definition can be either individual, singular, and unique, or general and shared. *Motion* is an all-inclusive descriptive word, which Nikolais makes important by giving special attention to the inherent motional intent that exists within a movement and qualifying that movement as dance. Motion can best be seen when the vitality and flavor of a movement is revealed. These fine tunings are essential to achieve, for they reveal dance as an art. Without these tunings, movement becomes a pedestrian function. It is essential, then, that one establish a finely tuned vocabulary, particularly between student and the teacher.

The training should begin from the onset, with an understanding of the capacity of the dancer's instrument, and his ability to achieve this sensitive aesthetic condition through his body. The body becomes the generative source of the motional life force, which not only enlivens the space around him but the space in the body as well. The time value both in action and in stillness relates to the nature of the motion.

The vividness of the sculptural shapes the body assumes and the distinction and flavor of the choreographed movement all carry the presence of motional identity. This inclusive statement is what this technique is about. It is not about patterns of movement, but about the nature of movement, all movement. Motional participation begins with the first stretches, the first dance involvement, and it lasts until the stage curtain falls.

Motion separates dance from being a mere pedestrian activity; however, if a pedestrian activity is the intent of the choreography, then the motion of that activity becomes the art intent as well. Without the qualifying nature of motion, we simply have movement. Motion contains the flavor of the life that courses through all the principles and aspect of dance. It becomes evident when the dance becomes alive and identifies itself.

Motion makes the motor base visible and flavors it with its distinguishing intent and nature. It qualifies movement, the gross act, and its definition is the basis of the dance art. It creates the art's pungency and vividness.

Motion offers the performer an internal "script" to follow when performing abstraction. It is a substitute for the personal narrative a dancer might be using when performing abstract movement. It allows an audience a chance to savor the richness of movement without extraneous dramatic overlays. In dance it carries the message of abstraction.

MOTOR BASE

Motor base is the physical energy that motion uses to imbue its flavor and quality into a movement or space or shape. The motor base primarily uses the power of the physical body, whereas motion also employs the internal factors of the imagination, the senses, the intuition, the willpower, presence, immediacy, grain, and so on.

Motor base is the basic generative energy, which fuels and energizes the entire action. The motor is "kicked over" by the dancer's desire to move. The motor base sustains the kinetic vitality, and can also be projected into space. Often in the simplest action, such as walking across the floor, the motor base will give out and, like an automobile whose engine stops or slows down, the car or body has to then be pushed to its destination. One can see clearly those dancers who do not have the energy to sustain a level of movement, whose motivations and will cannot rise to energize the body.

It is not necessary—indeed, it is almost impossible—to use all of these principles mentioned in every dance. However, it is necessary to be conscious of what you are deliberately not using as well as what you are using.

Movement and Motion

Here's a simple example of movement and motion:

If I asked you to raise your hand to scratch your head, and you did so, and if I then asked you what you were doing, you could say, "I'm scratching my head." Your head itched and your fingers went directly, instinctually, and purposefully to scratch the itch. That was your movement.

Now I ask you to lift your arm, and you do so, and while doing so to sense the roughly 15-lb. weight of the arm suspended before you.

Now I ask you to lift that 15-lb. weight up without looking at it to a point over your head, and to sense this weight hovering over your head.

Now I ask you to sense lowering that weight until the fingers make contact with the head and sense that one moment of contact.

Then while maintaining contact with the scalp, flex and stretch the fingers; and if I now asked you what you were doing, you could say you were dancing, because you were sensing the nature of the body parts being used, the space, the time, the energy, and all of the motional factors that were involved in the gesture.

Sensing all of the factors that occur within a movement is sensing the motion of that movement, which includes its timing, shape, and spatial use.

WEEK 15: MOTION

TECHNIQUE

Premise

Motion.

Tasting, experiencing, and performing the qualities that rest within movement and, by doing so, identifying the nature of the movement.

Motion and movement should be experienced separately, otherwise they become confused. Movement is the choreography; motion is the responsibility of the dancer's performance.

The dancer uses all of the elements of dance to define motion. Motion is a composite of both the physical and the psychical, calling for the ultimate ability. It qualifies movement, and these qualifications define dance. The technical challenge this week will be devising movement phrases that employ many of the basic principles of abstraction: space, time, shape, dynamics, motor base, and others.

Motion is an enriching composite. This totality identifies itself as the nature of the movement: the purpose of the performance. The result is often greater than the performer. The performer becomes secondary to what is being performed by his focusing on the motion rather than on himself. By decentralizing his ego concerns, he brings a current of illumination that enlivens the movement.

Motion is the flavor or nature that exists within a phrase of movement; all of the dancer's facilities contribute to it: grain, sentient awareness, the appropriate space and time, the imagination, and technical skill. Motion, briefly, is the ability to bring a dance to life, and to reveal its identity.

The challenge in choreography is to invent interesting movement phrases that can house various motional qualities as a preparation for whatever choreography the dancer may be called upon to perform.

Monday

Qualities of motion.

Develop a floor pattern and slowly add details of body parts, spatial relationships, time values, and motional qualities. Persist in revealing the quality or motion of the movement phrases.

Be specific about all details. Use all of the skills and references from preceding weeks: density, grain, time, body parts, and so on.

Teachers should create and perform phrases from these qualities:

Heavy	Itchy	Slow	Hard
Light	Smooth	Erratic	Fast
Soft	Languid	Jerky	etc.

Dancers: your teacher will call on you to select one of your own, but be sure to make it clear. Don't translate the quality to literal terms. Don't tell a story.

Motion is very often sensed and not specific. Enrich the sensation as a performing artist would, so that viewers can also experience it.

Tuesday	Performing phrases of contrasting time qualities.
	Performing phrases of movement to reveal abstract identities (as listed above).
Wednesday	Performing phrases with the qualities of the various body parts (e.g., the many jointed actions of the arm).
	Performing phrases with the qualities of directions in space and rotary action.
Thursday	Changing motional identity. Experience the moving flow of motional action as it changes from one focus and flow, to another from spatial to body part, from shapes to various speeds.
Friday	Revealing motional qualities through technical challenge choose contrasting motional of qualities. Develop class into challenging concluding air work.

IMPROVISATION
GESTALT

The totality of movement is reflected in its parts.

Gestalt is the recognizable and sensed nature of a totality, the identification of an entity that cannot be divided. This new identity is sensed and imparted into every part of the body so that everything speaks of it. The feelers of all the nerve endings and the taste buds of all the sentient equipment in the body work concurrently to imbue the muscles and the motion toward the revelation of the new life.

Once established, this flavor will serve as a creative and compositional guide in extending the seed to its fruition. In contemporary terms, one can think of the recognizable gestalt of an abstraction as its DNA, a commonness that links all the parts of an entity. This involves both the outer physical and the inner psychical participation of the performer.

When choreographing for groups during improvisation, the time should be divided into: (1) choreographic time, forty minutes; (2) showing, twenty minutes. The teacher gives ten- and five-minute warnings of when "time is up."

Monday	Working alone, devise a structure emanating from a seed or starting identity. These are short studies. Divide time to include choreography, showing, and crits.
	Everyone shows.
Tuesday	Working alone, concentrate on and develop specific shapes that reveal a specific identity. Emphasize shape as a major vehicle for the gestalt.

Wednesday	Stay with whatever successful gestalt you've created in previous classes and extend or improve structure. Having seen other studies, work now for invention. Try to enrich motional interest.
	Everyone shows.
Thursday	Create a new solo gestalt.
	Motion includes all the major principles: space, shape, time, and the dynamics of the elements as they contrast and support each other. Work for invention.
	Everyone shows.
Friday	Create another gestalt solo and develop it fully.
	Keep this gestalt to develop into composition assignment.

CRITS ON MOTION

Don't confuse motion with motor base. Motor base is part of motion; it's a moving energy that propels the body. Motion is a qualifier of movement. It's what the movement is about. It includes everything that gives insight to the choreography. It demands dedicated performance to be seen. It reveals the intent.

Motion bares the message. Your performance is essential to make the motion clear.

Don't be casual in performance. Design it. Qualify the motion. You qualify it by giving it an identity.

Avoid any excessive or distracting movement.

Don't dramatize. Motion is what you want. Don't overtense and unbalance the energy.

Study your form and make it come out without excessive hardness.

You seem to swat at it and show anger. Anger has nothing to do with it.

Whenever you use more energy than is necessary for a form, it is going to look dramatic.

Define the sensation—let it show the quality of the motion. Is it hard, soft, hesitant, sharp? What?

Call attention to the skittering you did. It had a quality. What I saw was retreat from a point. Combine them. Show me skittering as a means of moving away.

Motion lies in the itinerary between two points. The less defined it is, the less qualified it is, the less it works. The more defined and qualified, the more chance for gestalt.

Find the right time, dynamics, and form to define the motion. The more you feel there is only one way to do the motion, the more concentrated and pungent it will be. To the extent it is unclear in your mind—to that extent it doesn't work. It is usually true that there is only one best way to do a thing. Try to find that way. That unique gesture.

It is hard here because your motivation is too vague.

Make motion happen innocently by itself. Don't force it.

Dance is the art of motion.

Motion qualifies the nature of the process between the beginning and the end of the movement.

Mobility is a current. It is the life of your action. Kick it over, keep it running. Feed it with the right gas and see that it's lubricated in the right areas so that it doesn't stop.

The more your body says, "don't look at me, look at the motion," the more visible you are! It's a magical thing.

You took the wrong road. Go back and find where you lost the motional thread and pick it up from there.

Some dancers move brilliantly but their motional ignition often is never turned on.

Motion is like the current that electrifies a lightbulb. In the case of dance, it illuminates the moving body.

Motion housed in movement has recognizable identity. When one speaks of motion, one speaks of its recognizable nature, which is released with performance.

Since motion deals with the nature of movement, it stands to reason there should first be movement.

To show motion, you may show fast motion and slow motion, which seems like time. But the quality of the motion will distinguish it from time.

It is your attitude toward it, your attitude of tasting, whether you taste the motion or whether you taste the time structure of the motion.

For the first time, it started to be a thing that wasn't you! The value of the motion was so great, it just took over. Just as painters revere color, the dancer reveres motion. I was talking with a young painter who told me, "I bought a new primary red today! It was so beautiful I had to paint with it all day." This is your primary color: motion.

COMPOSITION

A dance with rich gestalt identity.

A gestalt should say, "It wants to do this," instead of "I want to do this." It should exist in the quality and in the attitude toward it. Find a gestalt that states itself to you; find something identifiable, self-explanatory.

Three dance potentials can be:

A shape gestalt.

A movement gestalt.

Gestalt with a dominant implication of time and space.

Find two contrasting kinetic gestalts. Develop them, but don't add things that aren't inherent in them. Make sure they're something you can develop. They should have a motor source that evokes continuity. Make them specific, not vague.

GESTALT CRITS

Gestalt. Going deeper into sensed experience and sensation of action. Begin and develop the "seed" to its identification. Discover its nature or gestalt or raison d'être.

What you have done is only to identify the beginning, where you start. Now identify what you're doing and stay with it, within it. But in terms of structuring a composition be selective in your use of space, shape, time, and motion.

It should be the beginning of a poetic essay.

It must take hold of your mind and imagination.

Be true to the gestalt—don't overthrow it and go on to something else.

Don't repeat just because it's easy.

If it's a motional gestalt, it had better be juicy. You should be able to sink your teeth into it.

Don't mug; people usually mug because they can't get enough passion into the body.

Don't be afraid to let one thing develop for a while. You're switching too often before you establish or even have something to develop.

The nature of the dance begins to dictate what it's about. Once it begins to grow, you have to grow and go with it. Treat a starting shape as an entity, a seed. In the beginning you don't know how that seed will grow. You don't know what you're going to create.

All of you, because of your size and shape, are of different materials. If you have length, use it. If you have a large head, place it, and so on. Make it eloquent. Stand up to it. An artist tells; he doesn't ask.

This was a good example of how you have to work. You just keep working with the material until you discover where the thing begins, where it begins to assume its character. Suddenly it defines itself. You suddenly see an entity happen here, and it soon takes over.

This is truly the art of creating: when from nothing you create an entity, a gestalt, whose fruit you have no knowledge of in advance. You are, in a sense, a hothouse. This thing has just incubated in you. You are going to let it take its form, its own course. It has no identity, yet. This is creating something that never existed before.

The seed comes to life without any motivation. Once it finds its identity, your motivation is to recognize it and develop it, otherwise you are "just moving." There is a difference between nature and art: wiggling around as nature would have you, or taking the idea of "wiggling" and pulling it apart and investigating the elements of "wiggling" and then composing with them.

WEEK 16: ABSTRACTION

Generally in dance, abstraction deals with the nonspecific, nonreal, and nonverbal. It is an essence. It is illusional. With the gift and ability for decentralization, the dancer can now use his body to manifest new realities comprised of space, shape, time, and motion. This ability to transform requires an additional range of sensibilities and takes communication to another level.

CLASS PLAN

TECHNIQUE

Premise

Abstraction and decentralization.

At this point the dancers have been exposed to a large vocabulary of movement. They should be urged to use this material constantly in improvisation and composition.

We discussed and dealt with the principles of space, time, shape, and motion in the preceding chapters. Now we integrate abstraction.

Read ahead to crits on improvisation of abstraction first.

Density of molecules, degrees of molecular compactness achieve heavy and light textures, hard and soft, etc.

Find the means to create and identify new movement.

Abstraction employs the use of the abstract vocabulary of space, shape, time, and motion. All of these principles will help identify and give credence to the sensed image. To further sense the quality of a movement, use breath sounds which are equivalent to what you're doing. Not expressive sounds. Remember that the earliest accompaniment to dance probably consisted of grunts, vocal clicks, and hand clapping.

Monday

Change densities and experience how movement can derive from the force released by the changes.

Tuesday

Contrast shoulders and hips as light and hard. Reverse qualities.

Wednesday

Contrast arms and legs with staccato time and sustained time.

Thursday

Contrast torso, spine, and back with loose and staccato quality. Chest with percussive action.

Friday

Contrast hand touching body parts and percussive feet.

In dealing with abstraction, don't present it as an investigation in sterility. The passion of the doing must always be evident, be it in qualities such as hard or soft, or thick or thin, or energy intensities. As the qualities change, they motivate dynamics and new movement. For example, going forward with hard arms, when the density is released there is a release of energy. As a result, the form might take a downward or backward circular going, before hardness might repeat itself. Play with creating unfamiliar resultant movement patterns.

IMPROVISATION

Monday   Heavy and light—use inventive movement phrases. Solo—duet—group.

Tuesday   Thick and thin—use inventive movement phrases. Solo—duet—group.

Wednesday   Boneless and brittle—use inventive movement phrases. Solo—duet—group.

Thursday   Free. Dancer decides. Solo—duet—group.

Friday   Free. Dancer decides. Solo—duet—group.

ABSTRACTIONS—ILLUSIONS—TRANSCENDENCE

We will work now for specific qualities of action, which are communicated as sensed experiences. For example: weight—choreograph shape, time, space, and motion in such a way that the resultant illusion is alternatively heavy and light. Create illusion of heavier and lighter than self.

We are not concerned with sticking to the obvious uses of time, shape, space, and motion. You might achieve lightness through motion and heavy by way of shape. The way you use time is going to be important. It is not important that you use all the principles for creating, as long as you know what you are using or not using, that concentrating on a principle is a deliberate decision you have made. Not using can be as effective as using. It clears the way to see what you are using.

Avoid translating your premise to other examples—for example, a rock is heavy; therefore,

I will be a rock. What we see now is a rock, not heavy. Go directly to an intent, and concentrate on it. Don't use visions like "I'm a floating leaf," if floating is your intent.

You are dealing strongly with transcendence. Restructure your body to form other things.

Abstracting is a process of selecting; it's part of idealization. Find the taste of the thing.

There are many kinds of abstractions. Even the most literal art resorts to some form of abstraction.

The reception of the eye tends to be less abstract than the ear. Seeing is believing.

Possibilities for abstraction studies using contrasts:

Uptight/Loose	Thick/Thin	Heavy/Light
Brittle/Pliable	Fast/Slow	Soft/Rigid
Transparent/Opaque		

Know the feeling of the subject so well that it becomes its own thing. If you force it into an alien form, it dies.

The narrative or progression cannot be shown in illogical sequence (unless as in paintings by Picasso, cubistically, with several views of a head at once). At first we will work for the sense of the thing. Later when you work in absurd or pop ideas, its illogic becomes its logic.

HEAVY AND LIGHT

Dense versus sparse—hard and soft—heavy and light.

Imagine compacting and lessening the molecular content in your body. Here the ability to control the molecular density of the body is called into play. The number of molecules create the density of your body, be they packed hard or loosely. The fewer there are the greater the sense of weightlessness.

ABSTRACTION

Abstraction is not a particularly favored word. People fear it, mostly because it suggests the nonconcrete, the nonverbal, and consequently the mystical, the coldly mathematical, or nuclear age sterility. And yet, it is impossible for the artist to avoid it. It is a major communicative force essential to all the arts.

The most common meaning of the word *abstract* is to select or take out. Thus if one abstracts something in this sense, one isolates one component from an entity comprised of many parts.

The painter engages in abstraction in this sense when he eliminates details that are irrelevant, ineffectual, or that obscure the particular aspects of the landscape he wishes to expose. Again, he makes further abstraction by continuing to select and refine. Thus, he may abstract within abstraction again and again until it seems that nothing representational remains. This may go as far as to arrive at what seems to be a single essence. Consequently, in the process of abstraction he also engages in idealization: the search for perfection, for essence.

Another facet of abstraction rests within the process of learned symbol. The Christian cross, the Star of David, and the swastika are examples of this. They are meaningless unless one has learned what they represent. Mathematics is the highest form of this kind of abstraction. Here communication is accomplished by virtue of learned, spoken, or written symbols. We learn that two and two are four and we can communicate this verbally or in symbolic writing; however, this remains entirely abstract until it is applied to specific things. Two apples and two apples are four apples is no longer an abstraction—it is now concrete. This form of abstraction communicates by virtue of a learned rather than a sensed process.

In dance, another meaning of abstraction applies to that which is nonconcrete, although distinguishable through the senses. Thus color, sound, and motion are abstract, but their basic values rest in sensed perception rather than in learned symbols.

Colors, for example, communicate in abstract form, even when specifically green, blue, red, and so on. No matter how kaleidoscopic they may be, colors remain abstract until the moment when their assembly becomes or suggests the representational—a red apple, for example. At that moment, the communicative process changes. Instead of abstract sentient response a visual representation of a recognized thing is introduced, which then suggests the concrete. The concrete thing causes an associative process in the viewer's mind that is stronger than the color values themselves.

Teachers can now augment their descriptions of movement with both scientific and aesthetic imagery for richer performance qualities. More than the inviolate atom has been cracked and explored in depth—the language of abstraction has as well. There was a time when abstraction belonged to the world of theology, the world of the unexplainable. Now science offers insights, too.

Abstraction does battle with the dancer. Abstraction is its own identity and cannot share itself with the dancer's ego, the dancer's imposing "self." A simple example would be the depiction of a blue sky and not how one feels about it; that feeling is left for the viewer to experience.

Abstraction demands the sensibilities of the viewer to fully define itself.

Abstraction is a language that needs both the art and the viewer to complete and determine its meaning.

ILLUSION—TRANSCENDENCE

For a dancer, illusion plays a very strong role even in the face of the most scientific evidence—for example, bones don't stretch and yet a dancer works toward lengthening his limbs. The heartbeat is regular, yet a dancer works toward deregulating it for various artistic purposes. These may be stretched fingers I hold up, but shaken quickly, one behind the other before my face, they can give the illusion of the panic of a stricken deer.

We may think of illusion as the impression of a thing being something other than what it actually is. Illusion, as is most art, is the ability to create a reality in an inventive new form in spite of the facts.

The idea of illusion is basically one of abstraction. Abstraction and illusion. We use the word *abstraction* here because we're talking about transcendence. We're talking about transcendence in the sense that with the skills given to you to experience time, space, shape, and motion, you can work toward the reality of essence. You can now forget specific sensing and instead use these principles very cleverly to give the illusion of being what you are not.

Illusion is as essential as the actual doing. It is impossible to make the body actually thin; you must create an illusion. It is the sustaining of the illusion, so there aren't constant little breaks in vision to jar us back into the fact of flesh, that is difficult. We want to create illusions that are so wonderful that they illuminate themselves.

We may have exhausted every possible position of the human body, particularly in the last fifty years. But we haven't by any means discovered all the textural possibilities the body is sensitive to and can awaken in viewers.

Illusion is the basis of art. This is not the illusion of the entertaining magician, but rather the transformation or transcendence of materials to create meaning beyond their physical fact.

Dance as an art is an art of illusion. Illusion is the selection process by which the artist shows the audience what he wants them to see, not what it actually takes to do it or what it costs. For example, when we come down from a jump, we try not to land heavily and show the difficulty involved with our feet, knees, and hips. When we try to hold the stomach in, we don't grip and grimace. Part of the illusion is simply to draw the attention to something else so that the viewer doesn't see how something is accomplished.

As an example, I draw a peripheral 7 on the space before me. There, I've drawn it again and once more. What did you see? The students will say "a number 7." The number 7? No, I made a diamond shape. Did you see the line my hand made to begin the 7? You didn't because I didn't want you to see it. I created this illusion by my use of grain and focus. I can also make lines in space invisible by focusing elsewhere.

That is what we will try to do now. We will try to take space, shape, time, and motion and, through cunning maneuvering of these four elements, choreograph a form that enables us to create the illusions of the performing artist.

CRITS ON HEAVY AND LIGHT

If the study is only partly successful, look to each of the principles to see what area may be lacking. Is the time right? The space, shape, motion?

Do we have a gestalt? Is it specific? Assemble all your materials that qualify heavy and then apply your performing contribution to the choreography to make the statement of heavy.

Avoid emotion. Don't show us sadness as heavy. When it's performed, emotion of some sort might enter into the picture. Have you ever seen heavy joy? Try it—it sounds interesting.

Soft and hard design must be contemporary (what was soft for Victorians won't work now.)

You have not selected the right materials for lightness. When you worked in the vertical dimension you were the most successful.

You held too long. I saw "stiffness." Shorten it; chop it up. When you make a good salad you mash the garlic or rub it in the bowl. Don't just throw a lump of it in. Employ it so that the flavor you want is there. Break it down. Give it to us in appropriate ways.

It was cutesy. Not even cute. Cutesy. She translated it into what she thought looked cute. Cute can have lightness in it but it doesn't work the other way around. Lightness is not necessarily cute.

Reverberation can be important in depicting weight. Making the ground quake.

You must lose yourself to gain yourself. The more you can divorce yourself from it and let the artist shine through, the more you will gain.

Heavy is a qualification of energy toward gravity.

In the study let nothing contradict heaviness.

Here is where your skill of transcendence starts. You weigh x amount, but in the study you will deny your real weight to create the illusion of more weight.

You imply heavier than heavy. Use your skill to create illusion—art is not reality.

You went in and out of it. Lightness is not so much a shape problem as a quality problem. Heaviness has more of a shape element. Thinking "light" helps, but it is not being light.

Nothing was resisting, which allowed you to give the illusion of lightness. This was the first successful shape study of lightness. It was a judicious use of the material.

Translate yourself into a metaphoric condition. Create a state of lightness, weightlessness. Translate into the shape, motion, space, and time of light. It is not an intellectual thing, not "I'm going to be a fly" (to be a fly is to be small, quick, etc.). Go directly to your materials, not anything else. If you put all of them together in such a manner, I will see an illusion created. Keep out of the pitfalls of natural and kitsch (overpopular, corny.) Don't translate it through what you think we will think. Find the "light of lightness."

Don't interpret it. Don't say, "Light—oh yes, dancey." Don't draw our conclusions. Let us as viewers do it from your abstraction and our imagination.

Dancer's time is not necessarily metric; musical time is. Dancer's time can be breathy, erratic, and as illusional as the subject can be.

The space of lightness doesn't necessarily have to be up, see if you can use downward. Sometimes contradictory things work. See Disney's dancing hippos in *Fantasia*. Those ladies don't think of their size as a weight problem.

Think of buoyancy.

You have to choreograph it, because you are choreographers. You can't just stand there like a lump and say, "I'm heavy, I'm heavy, I'm heavy."

You make yourself look like what you are not. You become, metaphorically, something else.

Heavy and light as a study tests your skill of transcendence.

For this study you have to have a strong imagination in order to hold together the thought and the psyche and the body. This is the challenge of performing.

Design your motion to let the illusion come through. Don't think so intensely that it gets buried in the brain.

If you can get the essence of these qualities of illusion, then you have the chemicals out of which you can make everything.

Abstraction will allow greater creative freedom.

Fool around with each factor for a while—the shape values, the way the spaces fall. Find out where you have a predilection for time, space, and above all discover motional flavor, which is your real trade.

Nobody designed specifically in shape or motion. There was a lot of vague stuff. You have to be exact.

Don't be cliché. Don't repeat what we've all already seen. It's been done. You may never have done it before, but I'm here to tell you it's already been done.

That last shape was stunning. You should have started there. Don't think that how you began composing is the final order of your structure. In this case you should have begun with the last movement. It would have set a standard for the rest of the composition.

Don't be interpretive. Heavy is not necessarily sad. It could also be glad. Think of a happy elephant.

You make us see what it is you want us to see. You make us see that you are heavy, and you do not allow us to see anything that distracts from that heaviness. This is chicanery, aesthetic chicanery.

A snake does not see himself as slippery nor does a bunny think of himself as cute and cuddly, although I wouldn't put it past some of them.

CRITS ON THIN

Be thinner than thin. Design the shape that thinness takes.

The opening vision was great. Then you turned profile and lost it. You have to sense what the audience sees.

A real choreographic attempt with nice detail. Don't think of the body emotionally; transcend this. We want the form.

Good torso quality. Could be more strongly inventive.

At first I felt you were explaining yourself rather than the thing itself. Later it got more engrossing. At first it looked decorative. Later you gave it more body.

Your eye focus was too hard. This always calls attention to the person instead of to the thing being done.

Poor design on the going to the floor. Don't go to the floor just to have something else to do.

It is gratifying to see you going into choreography and structure.

Best transition we've seen so far and a very hard one to make.

See if on the next problem you can stress more motional qualities. It gets a little static. You had better think in terms of flatness. Your front fall became heavy which ended on an off-key note.

Concentrate on motion; release yourself from tight arms and tight trunk. Challenge yourself with more motional interior and delicate qualities.

Many of you do stunning things in improvisation, because your intuition is at work, but stiffen up in comp because your brain is making judgments. Try to get the skill of their cooperation with each other in structuring form.

You have to bear in mind that the onlooker sees things from a vantage point that is not necessarily yours. Place yourself in their seat.

If your beginning isn't clear, you lose your audience and it's very hard to get them back. Remember you have only a limited time to make your statement or state your case. The audience cannot go back and reread something, as they can in a book.

You are dealing with a nonliteral art form. If you want to verbalize about it, you have to find appropriate words—maybe even make them up.

Be clear. Is the gesture vertical or horizontal? Being everything at once is confusing.

Transcend the action and become it. Good actions allow you to do this. We are not looking for self-expression. Scratching yourself is not art, no matter how good it feels, it is nature. You can, however, mix nature and art for an effect. It would be interesting though for you to abstract scratching and make a dance of it. Try it.

You should experience the work of as many fine artists, in all disciplines, as you can. You can feed and perpetuate yourself in this way. Only when you see it do you know art.

The whole thing is the skill of learning dynamics. The excitement of changes and contrast, and being able to toss them around.

CRITS ON BONELESS

Now change it to boneless. It is without bones, without any kind of hard structure to hold it up. But don't lose the tensions of the space, the time, or the shape. You are merely qualifying the motional values.

Now I want you to qualify the motion as though you were incredibly brittle, so brittle that if I were to strike you with one of my drumsticks, I could shatter you. Realize how that affects the time and space, and obviously the shape. It results in a different kind of motion.

Not boneless enough. It was more sloppy than it was boneless. Jellyfish move through water, bonelessly. They can also move very quickly, though boneless!

Now you can start alternating between brittle and boneless.

How long dare we hold the tension of this shape before it has to do something else? This long, this long, or longer?

Don't be afraid to test not moving.

Let's go on and take the next step. You've done the shape of it now. You've gone from the shape and added the space in between the shapes. I want you now to become more aware of how the time illusion can be added. How can we add the time element to make it more exciting?

WEEK 17: REVIEW TECHNIQUE

This time is for recapitulation and review, for digesting the rich meal that has been served. It's a time to see what has been absorbed and what still needs clarification.

This week should be handled with simplicity. The instructor should present basic technique and creative material, simply and clearly. Students should have some ability now to combine the basic principles into the totality required for artistry.

The focused contributions of the physical body, the psyche, the intuition, and the senses should be permeating the movement. Students should now be aware of the major principles of time, space, shape, and motion. Movement, as a result of motional awareness, becomes enriched and enhanced. Dance becomes identified as an entity and objective in itself.

Murray Louis teaching carrying a shape across the floor. 18th Street class, New York City.
Photo courtesy of the Nikolais/Louis Archives.

Continue with invention and technical challenge all week.

As the theoretical challenges develop, the emphasis on technical skill in class should not lessen. If necessary, technique class can be condensed to allow more time for improvisation.

Include the brief review below before every class, or frequently. Move through all the review material at a lively tempo. Move past the brain's understanding into the body's understanding.

DIMENSIONS

During pliés review:

Height.

Width.

Depth.

BASIC SETUP

Legs

Hips

Abdomen

Chest

Neck

Head

Adjust weight placement.

Rotation of thighs. Knees over ball of foot.

As a unit, pressed forward.

Lifted to create separation between hips and chest. This middle area is pliant, flexible to create the vertical motion of up and down or arching in all directions.

Lifted and placed over hips and toes. Sternum up and through, shoulders down and grained outward into sideward.

Lengthened into head.

Reaching up.

CLASS PLAN

TECHNIQUE

Premise

Review of technique.

These periods of review are basically periods in which to clarify areas that need strengthening. These are left open to the teacher. They are periods to work on details in a detailed fashion. Add such a class whenever you need one.

Monday

Review: Space-volume, three-dimensional spatial forms, peripheral two-dimensional planar designs, linear designs.

Clarity of structure through clarity of body articulation.

Time. Shape. Motion.

Tuesday	Create phrases using these basic materials and perform them with an understanding of their motional content.
Wednesday, Thursday, and Friday	Throughout the weeks, make notes of what needs to be reviewed. Often it takes a bit of time for certain points to sink in. Some things the body needs time to absorb. Make notes of these things. Repeat them, review them, and master them.
	See where weaknesses lie technically and correct them.
	Challenge the class technically and creatively. Do not get involved in lengthy talk sessions. Move it along.
	Get the body to learn things, and the body will answer its own questions. Work toward a knowledgeable and experienced body. You are simultaneously training the body and psyche to speak for the dancer.
IMPROVISATION	All this week should be given to presenting gestalt, res, a seed, the identity of a beginning, and the nature of a movement. Extend and develop these beginnings, with awareness of transitions, in solo, duets, and small groupings.
OPEN IMPROVISATION	The lid is off. Make things happen. Instant choreography and instant performance. Relate to each other.
COMPOSITION	Choose a kinetic gestalt and develop it into a kinetic study.

WEEK 18: REALISM TO ABSTRACTION

TECHNIQUE

Premise

Technique classes deal with development of kinetic and technical phrases. Improvisation classes will deal with the "reality to abstraction" premise.

Monday

Swings—arms, legs, and torso.

Tuesday

Leg extensions and body parts. Hip and chest isolation.

Wednesday

Catch steps, quick change of weight transfer. Off balance, fast footwork.

Thursday

Moving into space: dimensions and circles. Hips and chest leading.

Friday

Turns, air work, jumps, and leaps.

IMPROVISATION

You have been working abstractly throughout this course—that is, you've been translating everything into the abstract, nonverbal language of space-time-shape-motion. Now we will deal with the other meaning of abstraction: to extract the essence or essentials from a realistic or literal object or state of being and retranslate those principles back into the abstract language of space-time-shape-motion. Through this you gain a motional vocabulary for composition.

Reading a dance. Boston dance workshop, 1959.

Monday

Abstraction of emotion.
Get the whole class on their feet.

Step 1: devise an acting or mime experience related to a character, subject, or emotion. Move under those literal and emotional motivations. Then stop at the height of the experience. Stop at one frame where the whole body is possessed by this emotion, subject, or character. Then check:

What three parts of the body were dominant?

What space was dominant? Open and out, tight or closed, or both? What volumes or peripherals were used?

What time was used: fast, slow, staccato, still, held, erratic?

What shapes were used: angular, curved, round, off balance?

What motional quality: thin, hard, light?

What energy level: tense or released?

Step 2: divorce yourself from the mime and compose with these selected elements representing the literal state of the emotion. Combine and juxtapose them interestingly. If they all spoke of the emotion singularly, they would speak of it even stronger when voiced in combination.

Step 3: perform the resulting dance with the original flavor and fervor. Perform the study with the emotion not locking the body, but released throughout the new form. This is a method of abstracting emotion. Because the elements came from the original gestalt, they will contain the nature of that gestalt or flavor, but within a different abstracted structure.

Step 4: adjust the choreography and fulfill the performance.

Time allowed for choreographing short study: thirty minutes.

Time for showing and comments: fifteen or twenty minutes.

Tuesday

Animal specific.
Choose an animal size and weight. Decide on a speed and time of its actions and its spatial concerns, perhaps its distinguishing body parts and nature. Go through the abstraction process. Put them all together compositionally and create an animal gestalt. Let the resulting study permeate you with its inherent character and perform it as such. Don't add the animal's commonplace quality to it.

Wednesday

Abstraction of a human.
Create a pantomime of a selected type of person. Go through the abstraction process. Boil it down: get the essence, the idiosyncrasies of a person, of a very rich personality. One always thinks of the literal characteristics of people, but there are many kinetic characteristics as well. Find them. Find the movement, energy, and body parts that are inherent to this person.

Thursday	A piece of furniture.
	Using the process of abstraction, work with shape, density, and period (for example, Rococo) to play the role of the furniture. Is it to be sat on, to be eaten from, to hold up a fancy vase? Do not be a person using the furniture; instead, be the furniture. Transcendence, the physical human reference, creates an illusion through decentralization and imagination.
Friday	Poeticism, for example, the word "beauty."
	Keep the studies short, but honed down and made into a simple statement.
	Create from improv ideas.

CRITS ON ABSTRACTION

It had a basic dignity, strength, and quivering alertness, which charged the air. Check out its spatial qualities. These two dancers were creating a state of animal panic, but you weren't aware of them as dancers. They were there, performing what they choreographed. This is the whole idea. We are working toward the skills of professional artistry to reveal the nature of choreography.

Think in terms of poetic imagery. Everything we see you do should have an element of beauty in it. Its totality is its statement.

Even the most unlikely subjects may turn up as a study of great beauty.

What constitutes beauty? The thing itself has as complete a gestalt as possible. The artist weeds out extraneous materials and lets coherence come through. Consonance is the essence of beauty, and a sensitive performance will reveal that essence.

It has something to do with the stimulating level of your selection. You may very well achieve a gestalt that is relatively uninteresting, but you should work toward one that challenges the mind and imagination.

Justify it in your manner of performing clarity and eloquence.

It is not always possible for us to see beauty in terms of our contemporary environment. Where does beauty lie in junk or discarded material? Nature can find beauty in the most terrifying and destructive events.

Think in terms of beauty. I'd also like to have a title from each of you. Provocative word combinations.

Communicate through motion and the passion of doing rather than emotion and the tension of obstruction.

Poeticism deals with depth. The more you get into those layers, the more details you communicate.

We have to accept the dance on her (the performer's) terms, not on yours (the viewer's). You can like it or dislike it but we should primarily see the creative aesthetic intent.

What would you say about an actor just crying? There should be some vertical depth to go past the surface display, to maintain interest.

The message here was implied on the first gesture, but you left it at that. We would hope that, like a writer with an essay, you would develop your premise beyond the title.

It wasn't without quality, but there wasn't much interest. Somehow there wasn't a facet of uniqueness.

Gesture is nicely done but clichéd, seen often in ballet. You're just walking around waiting for the prince to get his arrow out.

It's hard to say whether that premise can be done beautifully enough.

There's a certain loveliness in the control of the walk, and so on. But we're really in the same boat. What we saw was "standing, thinking, walking, thinking." What you were thinking about was never revealed to us. Let's see if I can help correct it. The hardest thing to do in the world is to stand innocently and do nothing.

Don't confuse poetry with "artistic-ness." So far everyone has tried to be delicate and polite. Poetry can also be very oafish and blunt.

Student: "That was realization of Life, Earth, Heaven." Nikolais: "My gosh, that's a little much to tackle. You aren't the first to walk around thinking noble thoughts and saying nothing. The idea is much too big. These are literary themes."

Your movements were too symbolic.

Remember that you are placing yourself in a position, as an artist, of being a brilliant conversationalist on the subject. Live up to it. At least don't make the cardinal error of being boring.

From a state of mind, you have to manifest something in motion.

It needs to build. There are two ways to do this:

a stronger motivation in the beginning that continues to motivate, or

showing different facets of the same subject.

It's as if you have a vision of something here. Now twist it and see something else. Get farther away from it. Get another perspective.

It's curious that in your attempts to go deeper, you got shallower.

It seems to me that as young people today you would want to be working in a contemporary area. I think a romantic thing can be done in a highly contemporary style. Look at Wyeth's realism, echoing time and space. A great many of Picasso's abstract paintings are basically romantic.

When you choreograph, you are on your own, alone. This can be a desperately lonely time to contend with, since you have only yourself to turn to.

When you use a title, you have the privilege of beginning to point the direction of the onlooker's viewing.

WEEK 19: DIAGONALS

TECHNIQUE

Premise

Establish diagonal control.

The four diagonals on a horizontal plane are forward right and left, and backward right and left. Dancer's diagonals exist in relationship to the body's front. Architectural diagonals exist in relation to room forward.

Establish forward orientation: (1) The body diagonals constantly change their orientation to the room's forward as the body moves. (2) The room or stage diagonals are stationary. (3) When in motion, the body's diagonals differ from the room's diagonals.

The challenge in practicing diagonals is the ability to shift the body's forward orientation to the body's diagonal alignment quickly. Moving obliquely offers a curious experience to the movement range. Maintaining the body's diagonal while dancing is the challenge here.

Body's diagonal orientation for walking diagonally forward left and right:

Head—cheekbone.

Chest—pectoral muscles.

Hip—pressed both forward and sideward. Diagonal is centered between.

Leg—thigh is turned out.

Feet—foot moves from closed third position to open fourth (modern dance positions). Passing leg crosses closely in front or back to continue diagonal line.

Body's diagonal orientation for walking diagonally backward left and right:

Head—diagonal back of head.   **Chest**—shoulder blade.

Hip—back diagonal hip.   **Leg**—turned out.

Feet—foot moves from closed third to open fourth tracing diagonal line on floor. Passing leg crosses closely behind to continue diagonal line.

The care of the legs and body in open fourth position should be carefully maintained.

Move out of the plié positions closed third into open fourth.

Graining diagonal face, chest, hips, and legs.

In forward diagonal locomotion, the crossing leg is always in front. Reverse for backward walking.

All of the leg and foot techniques of walking are applied as well as pressing the body into the diagonal direction.

Review locomotion in "Diagonals" from Week 1.

Establish the diagonals of the head, chest, and hip and the diagonal spatial direction. Here the body locomotes with the diagonals of the body parts leading. Move into body's diagonal direction as opposed to walking forward into room's diagonal. This is a marked difference, and it is important to maintain. When in motion, the diagonal of the stage almost always differs from the body's diagonal. When in motion, one has to constantly be aware of the fixed room or stage diagonals.

Monday

Determining the four body diagonals.

Forward diagonal right and left, backward diagonal right and left.

Moving forward DR—forward DL—half turn—backward DR—backward DL—half turn. Repeat across floor.

Be aware of how the body creates a cleaving diagonal path into the room's architecture. This fluidity is essential for accuracy.

Project the body direction as definitely and as strongly as possible.

Directional transitions are made by passing through the vertical.

Evolve diagonal air work. Hops, under- and overcurves.

Tuesday

Add level changes and quarter turns.

Insist on accuracy of facing and footings.

Create accurate level transitions through vertical into diagonal grain.

Build patterns and challenge diagonal accuracy.

Increase speed of diagonal change.

Wednesday

Leading with the diagonal of body parts: head, chest, and hips.

Taste the distinction of the three body parts: chest, head and hips.

Thursday

Variations: locomotion and curved or half-circle forms with level changes.

This is very challenging. Don't despair if it becomes chaotic and discouraging. Rest and try again.

Friday

Variations: add rhythmic shifts of body parts.

IMPROVISATION

Free improvisations all week stressing diagonals.

Be careful not to let the forward eye focus diminish the intensity of the diagonal movement.

Monday

Use half and quarter turns. Dancers change their diagonal going with each new architectural forward. This will demand very quick thinking and spatial orientation.

218

Tuesday	Diagonals with level changes: relevé, low, and normal.
	Sense the quality and textural changes in the torso.
Wednesday	Lead with changing body parts: head, chest, and hips. Include all four directions.
Thursday	Free: class choreographs duets.
Friday	Free: class choreographs with small groups.
COMPOSITION	Diagonals.

WEEK 20: CIRCLES

Circles are a combination of turning and locomotion action. The dancer cannot create a circle unless he creates a center or axis with the first step. The circle is the perimeter or boundary around the axis. The locomotion path prescribed is a circular one. One "walks the circle." As an introduction to circles, it is advisable to work with quarter demarcations of the circle so that one is accurate in judging step length and time allocation. The width of the circle depends on the steps allocated to it. Half, quarter, and three-quarter circles are then mathematical divisions of the step allocations. The dancer practices the process of decentralization with circles. The axis of the circles becomes the center, and the body conforming to this (centripetal) force leans inward and shapes itself accordingly. Leaning away from the center (centrifugal) is another range of action.

During a change of circular direction and locomotion, a turn in place or pivot is involved. The pivot occurs in vertical, during which the body arcs into its new direction.

In designing circles, transitions are quick and accurate. The body leans into the axis and shapes itself to the upper arc of the circle. An arc in any direction is also part of a circular form. The circle can be walked in all directions: forward, back, side, and diagonally, and on all levels. You can add half and quarter turns to change locomotor directions. You can also change time values and add more complicated body shapes.

Begin with walking a circle with centripetal leaning into the axis. The length of the perimeter of the circle conditions the length of step and time value. The feet trace the curve of the perimeter. This necessitates the outer leg taking longer steps. By shifting the arc of the upper torso leaning away from the axis circle, a centrifugal circle can also be prescribed. Here the hip leans into the axis, and the head prescribes an outer peripheral circle.

For sideward walking, the front of the body faces the central axis point. The walking pattern differs slightly from the normal sideward walking in that all the close walking steps cross in front to maintain the forward arc of the body.

The circular locomotion engages the body in rotation. For example, when one has arrived at the quarter circle in walking a circle, it should be noted that the body has also rotated one quarter. At the half-way mark it has completed a half turn, thus facing opposite the beginning point. This differs from another possibility in which the body does not rotate and still revolves about an axis. This form of circle may be described as having a stationary axis.

The stationary axis circle is executed by the feet stepping in a circular form around a stationary axis while the body maintains its facing. The body does not turn. An example is given in the following:

Step sideward right on the right foot.

Cross diagonally in front of the right with the left foot.

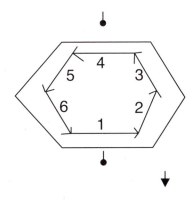

Cross diagonally in front of the left foot with the right foot.

Step sideward left with the left foot. The axis is now behind you.

Cross diagonally behind the left with the right foot.

Cross diagonally behind the right with the left foot.

Step sideward right with right foot. The circle is complete.

Walking a backward stationary axis circle simply reverses the process. Here without the body turning or changing its facing a loco-motor circle is accomplished.

As the dancer becomes more skillful in creating circles, he can change their form to ellipsoids and other elongated curved forms. One can create an acute angle one-eighth of a circle and an obtuse angle three-eighths of a circle, but in doing so be aware that the forward orientation of the body will change. These degree circles are different to perceive and offer more problems than they are worth. The half-circles as well as right-angle half-circles should be practiced first.

Above all, the dancer should remember he is dealing with a circular form and curve his body appropriately by rounding out the angles.

Look at the circles chart of possible forms. Keep devising new patterns all week with both beginner and advanced students. One can never get too much experience in circles.

CLASS PLAN

TECHNIQUE

Premise

Mixing half and whole circles.

Leaning into axis and leaning out from axis.

Stationary axis.

Forward and backward circular walking and combinations.

Sideward going: facing in or out of the axis.

Walking with quarter- and half-turns for new facings.

The body is always curved to shape the circle you are prescribing: left, right, front, or back, except for stationary axis circles.

Monday

Walking half circles

Facing the left wall, which is now a new forward, curve the body to the axis on the right. Start right leg. Go five steps to trace a half circle.

Arrive facing the opposite wall. Shift torso to the left then continue walking a smaller three-step half-circular path.

Repeat across the floor.

New pattern: walk three-step half-circular path in scallop form. Forward half circle half turn and backward half circle.

Alternate three- and five-step half circles—forward and backward.

Mix forward walks with half- and full circles.

Tuesday

Sideward and diagonal walking to prescribe front and back circles.

In a sideward walk pattern when facing the axis, the sideward cross leg is always in front. With back to the axis, the crossing leg is always behind.

Body rounded forward or back according to axis location.

Invent new floor patterns. Insist on accuracy of execution and time arrivals.

Alternate forward with side circles.

Body changes arc during transitions. These transitions can later lead to hop shift of weight. (Turns on hops.)

Judging step length and form and arrival points.

Be patient, be patient. Insist on accuracy. This is a great challenge for dancers. Applying architectural accuracy while both counting and shaping the body is a bit tricky (in the beginning).

Wednesday

Mix forward and sideward horizontal level walks with circles.

Change walking levels: low, high, and so on.

Insist on accurate body curves to indicate where axis is.

Make sure the group moves in unison.

Eventually the class will have a lyrical circular flow.

Keep rhythms in threes and fives so that the feet alternate stepping when changing circles.

Add small overcurves to patterns. Keep this for final kinetic build.

Thursday

Begin with basic half- and full-circle simple pattern.

Continue with more interesting phrase development.

Walk out new phrases carefully. Check new body facings and arrival points. Check location of the center of the new circle.

Run, run, leap. Forward runs and leap curve body to R. or L. in the air.

Friday

Front: new circle pattern with stationary axis variations.

Backward circle pattern with stationary axis variations.

IMPROVISATION

All week: circles in duets and small groups.

Choreographer for duets or trios.

You cannot start any kind of circle until you are relatively aware of home base, where it will end, and at what points you will arrive. One can think of the dancer and choreographer as a geometrist, accurately devising circles, ellipsoids, spiral, acute and obtuse portions of the circle, and so on.

COMPOSITION

Compose a study using everything involving circles. As in all compositions, you will be judged by invention, structure, and performance. The circles referred to in this lesson are those achieved by the bending of a straight path into a curve.

In the chapter on locomotion, we stated that a direction of forward locomotion implied that all body units would proceed in concerted action to that space directly forward of the frontal surfaces. Thus, in a circle, a forward walking may also be achieved by aiming the frontal surfaces at the desired line and keeping them focused on that line. Now, instead of the frontal surfaces being aimed at a straight line, however, they would, in the case of a clockwise circle, bring the right side of the body in relation to the center of the circle while the frontal areas shape and grain to the circumference.

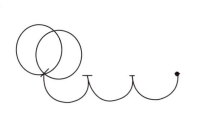 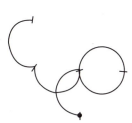 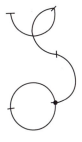

WEEK 21: FALLS[*]

INTRODUCTION

Falls can be intimidating. They can also be a little dangerous if they are not controlled. Children are closer to the ground, and so are less fearful of the distance to fall to the ground, but an adult body cannot be treated with the same abandon. It might help to begin a class of falls with careful and controlled dropping down and breaking the fall comfortably until the control of descent is transferred to the developed strength in the thighs.

Falls can be a very inventive area, and a very personally motivated activity as well. The dancer should give the same care with the descent as to the getting up. The fall is not necessarily a gravity pull, but a controlled, often designed, release to the floor.

The teacher should present the basic modern dance falls as a triple operation: the descent to the floor, the action on the floor, and the recovery from the ground. Mind that this is a basic fall. There is a world of invention to be discovered in this area.

The descent is made on one leg as the other leg folds back and behind the standing leg. (1) The body reaches its lowest level in vertical and then (2) slides out onto the floor into its intended direction. For the slide, the weight is taken on the outside of the palm of the hand, or hands. From this position (3), some transition is created to bring the dancer back up to his feet, such as a low turn or a momentum swing of the upper body or arm.

In a fall and a face-down roll-over recovery, the free arm crosses in front of the body to facilitate the rolling over and then up onto the feet.

CLASS PLAN

TECHNIQUE

Premise

Falls: front, back, and side.

Once down, develop ground patterns such as low locomotion with arms and legs creating movement details.

Make the floor a familiar space for rolling, and so on.

All of these variations can be demonstrated and explored in place before coming across the floor. Take the time to do this.

Wear kneepads.

Do not land on knees. Do not land on knees. Do not land on knees.

Monday

Mix falls with floor patterns that include various locomotions and turns and levels.

---

[*]Students should buy and wear kneepads while learning falls.

Control release to gravity. Lift body up to go down and start to shape body for slide out.

Develop lifts to hops before descent.

Do not land on knees or other bony parts.

Tuesday

High-level to low-level turning spiral down to floor. Crossed legs and resting on seat.

Reverse to come up. Centripetal outward throw helps torso to rise.

Develop speed of descents and recovery.

Do not land on knees.

Wednesday

Across-the-floor pattern including a fall and coming up out of the fall.

Develop a pattern of action on the ground to include a way to come up by careful placement of legs and feet to push up, thrusting hips through.

Do not land on knees.

Thursday

Vary descents to ground.

Locomotion patterns across-the-floor prepares the body for falls.

Do not land on knees.

Friday

If everyone isn't bruised to death, work on speed of descent and rise.

Do not land on knees. It is surprising how deaf students are, as you hear kneecaps hit the floor. Keep repeating, "Do not land on knees." Make them repeat it.

IMPROVISATION

Follow technique class development. Spend part of each class on choreography, solos for each other, and duets. Be inventive on descents and risings.

During improvisation and for composition, let the dancers, once they promise to use their best judgment, invent all sorts of falls. The dancer needs to understand the controlled use of the body for any violent action.

Upper body leans away from hips on descent.

Try not to lead with the buttocks when getting up. Vary the timing within the fall. Vary speed of getting up and recovery. Invent outcome while on the floor, but no matter how long you decide to remain on the floor, there is always the getting up to choreograph and consider. Don't forget or ignore this. Don't get comfortable once you are down.

Falls have a different connotation than using the floor and floor work. Be sure to understand the difference.

COMPOSITION

Inventive use of falls.

WEEK 22: SUSPENSION POINTS

INTRODUCTION

A single point in the body is pressed upward while the rest of the body falls away from that point, giving the body the look of hanging away or being suspended from that point. Although the body hangs from the point, it is the upwardness of the pull that is being stressed, not the downward hanging. Here, we are seeking the quality of being lifted from the ground. This requires intense graining.

Suspension points demand concentrated strength and willpower. The power of the upward pressure allows for many exciting movements. An invisible string created by the will lifts us.

Theoretically, the suspension point should be the highest part of the body. There are obviously some limitations to this in positions that do not allow for it, but with a strong performance, one can overcome limitations with illusion.

The transitions for suspension points occur within the body. When a point is released, it is as if the invisible string holding the body up has been cut. The descent to gravity begins, only to be stopped by the next suspension point lifting the body up. Graining to the transfer of these contrasting points through the body should give the up and down movement a distinctive motional feeling. For motional excitement, one should play with how far down the body can go before the next point catches and pulls it up. This creates the suspension point range of kinetics of dropping, catching, and lifting.

Varying the points of suspension from the front of the body to the back and increasing the speed make for an exciting torso participation.

The lifts have an energy, which can take the body into the air, into jumps, turns, and other kinetic variations. Explore, while on the floor, points which standing make difficult to suspend from such as the hips and parts of the legs.

Suspension points necessitate a pinpoint graining of the rest of the body to that point.

The head does not hold a vertical focus, but falls away to further reveal the suspension point, unless, of course, the head is somehow involved with the lifting point.

CLASS PLAN

TECHNIQUE

Premise

Suspension points.

The suspension points of the chest follow the eight locomotor directions of the body.

Forward is the sternum bone. Backward is directly behind the sternum; back rounds appropriately to press the back point upward. Side R. and L.—the pectorals grain to the side of the chest and the shoulder opens backward a bit. Back side R. and L.—the shoulder rounds a bit forward to allow the side point to become evident. Diagonal forward R. and L.—the shoulder rounds back for the strong pectoral point to press up. Diagonal back R. and L.—top of shoulder blade presses up. Diagonals are a combination either forward or backward with sideward. Visualizing these subtleties of sideward and diagonal are important.

In transition the body releases to gravity and the new point catches and lifts.

The dancer needs strong willpower to upward for each point.

Grain to points, but do not look at points. Let the eyes and head find their relative position sideward to the point.

Practice the eight chest suspension points before coming across the floor.

Monday

Chest has eight points of suspension: front, back, side, side, and four diagonals.

Define points.

Find sensation of body falling away from point.

Suspend from shoulders, elbows, and fingertips.

Remember physical strength of upward pull. Drop point and transition within body to new point.

Mix points inventively.

Try lifting and turning on high point.

Do not let the suspended locomotion project stronger than the suspensions. When the suspensions are carried across the floor, they are suspended, not held in place. The upward graining is kept alive.

Note the distinction between suspended movement and suspension point. Suspended is a sustained moment while suspension deals with gravity and single points of vertical.

Tuesday

With undercurves, the suspension points are pressed further up at the height of the undercurve.

Add other body points to undercurve high points: shoulders, elbows, and so on.

Pivot turns at height of suspension.

Lift from the floor with several different successive points and descend changing points.

Wednesday

Down to floor and rising with three different points lifting body to vertical. Perform the strength of upward willpower.

Quick drop and lift of points. Move into air work.

Thursday

Suspension points in air work: turning and lifting simultaneously.

Lifting to maximum height quickly will start a turning action. Use this energy for interesting turnings. Change suspension points in the body while turning.

Investigate suspension turn variations: turning with suspension from lower back as arms and legs are thrown out with centripetal force. Double turns. Half turns transfer points while turning. Sternum to lower spine. Visualize ice-skater images.

Friday

With sternum pressed up, step turn across the floor.

Change body parts during turn, pressing points upward with each turn—pulsing action.

The suspension points of the chest at upper pectoral locations are surrounded by musculature, which can grain down and away from the point to further reveal the suspension points.

In technique when the point is released to gravity, the next point in the body catches and quickly picks it up. Although these transitions occur within the body, the dancer should make them visible.

When a suspension point has been lifted to capacity, a rotary action results because the movement has nowhere else to go except around itself.

In transitions, sense the spatial flow of motion through the body and outside of it. Feel the release and pickup of suspension points.

Rise from floor through a series of suspension points.

Notes

Body rotates on highest point of suspension.

Descend to floor with suspension points pressing up.

Suspension walks are leveled as one's height level is carried evenly across the floor. The suspension is stressed, not the walk.

The suspension points throughout the body are almost similar to those points used for spatial markings in peripheral action. Their purpose, however, is decidedly different.

IMPROVISATION   Follow daily technique class premise. Evolve and lengthen phrases.

COMPOSITION   A study in suspension points using ideas presented in class.

CRITS

Single suspension points are what keep you up. Your legs are no longer primary supports for your body, your point of suspension is. Make your conceptual image strong enough to create this physical fact.

You all have articulated so politely, but none of you have given me the lusty message of up, of suspension!

Up means directly up. Not peripheral around to reach it.

Elongate yourself to such a delicate point that you rotate.

Get your fannies moving and feel the dynamics of suspension.

The word suspension suggests "hanging from," but don't think of it that way. Think of pressing up into that point.

You are going to create very fine points in the body. Press all your energy into the fine point and let all the rest hang away from it.

It is a problem of inner focus and grain. Your path of transition, from point to point, occurs within yourself.

Drop and catch. Release that point and pick up another quickly or you will drop to the ground.

These lifting points are continuous. Once there is no point of suspension, your body will collapse.

Experience suspension points from the arms, elbows, ears, and shoulders. Imagine a sky hook lifting almost any point of the body.

Your head has too much "attitude" in it. Let me see a single point of lift.

WEEK 23: PERCUSSION AND PROP EXTENSION

INTRODUCTION

Percussion basically means to strike. It can also mean to strike and produce a sound. Together with the voice, stamping and clapping were some of the earliest percussive accompaniments to dancing. Percussive in dance is not only the body part that strikes, but also the force invested in the strike. Any part of the body can strike. Some parts are obviously more fluent than others. The hands and feet offer the most mobility.

The next consideration with percussive action is the force behind the strike. This can vary from a caress to a knockout punch. The control of this force bespeaks the performing range of the

Props improvisation. UCLA, 1970.
Dancers: Raymond Clay, Sara Shelton, Michael Balard, and Frances Tabor.
Photo courtesy of the Nikolais/Louis Archives.

dancer. A tap, a sharp rap, and a leaden blow are all part of the effort range.

The brilliant range of great tap dancers, from their timing and rhythmic wit to their fascinating legwork, reflect how this singular percussive skill has become an art form in itself.

The dancer should also take into consideration the surface on which the strike occurs. The floor and the leg contact obviously are primary factors. The hardness of the contact surface will condition the sound. The dancer has his own bodily surfaces he can use as well, such as clapping the hands or other body parts. Although using imaginary spatial contact points to strike upon does not offer sound, the striking gesture is a percussive one nevertheless.

Both tangible and imagined surfaces can serve as part of the percussive act. Here the dancer's skill to suggest a spatial reference, which can be struck, comes into play. Focus and projection also help him form these invisible surfaces into realities. These invisible spatial forces can also strike the body or a specific part of the body from the outside.

Rebound is the result of a percussive strike. Its characteristic path is a trajectory away from the point of contact. These strikes can redirect the action into another direction or can repeat as in a bounce.

Rebound and bounce are variations of percussive strike. They release different energies at their points of contact.

To ricochet is to bounce off one point of contact and strike another.

CLASS PLAN

TECHNIQUE

Premise

Percussive, rebound, and bounce.

Percussive and rebound: create a momentum that will rebound from an imagined or real surface. Also create a surface in space as a surface for rebound. Make this point of contact and the degree of force visible. Create a distinct path of rebound.

Percussive action involves qualifying the contact, touch, tap, slap, and so on, with or without rebound, but usually associated with rebound.

The sound of the striking can be developed into compelling rhythms.

Percussive is to strike. Rebound is to bounce from. Bouncing is a series of repeated rebounds.

The strike requires a single energy with the contact surface.

The energy involved has a range of intensity or force from soft to hard.

Monday	Add percussive accents to locomotion pattern. Kicks, push-offs from jumps, etc.
	Various body parts—shoulders, elbows, head—strike accents against themselves to create rhythmic interest. Feet strike against the floor, palms to thighs, elbows to hips, etc.
	Arms and legs create spatial surfaces to strike or rebound from. One body part creates a surface; another part strikes. The resultant movement can be eccentric and interesting.
Tuesday	Create pattern using strike energies and time changes.
	Body parts strike and are struck by imaginary outer forces.
Wednesday	Create pattern with various body parts striking floor and space.
	Bounce from floor and spatial points.
Thursday	Create patterns using everything already introduced.
	Emphasize transition paths between strikes, for example, ricochet.
	Patterns of reverberation (continuous bounces).
Friday	Create a technically and rhythmically challenging pattern using everything introduced. A tapping dance, with feet, with hands, etc.

IMPROVISATION— EXTENSIONS (PROPS)

Think of a prop as something that will texture and extend the shape of the body. Say to yourself, "I can now only move the way these new extended shapes allows me to move." You have to give up a good deal of your centralized self when working with extensions and become the new thing, the new gestalt, however bizarre the new shape may appear.

Do not handle objects as unrelated props. They become a part of you, an extension of your body.

1+1=3. You and the new entity not only make a combination of the two but also create an entirely new third entity.

Decentralization: place your center into the newly created entity and instill it with a neuromuscular energy of its own. Project into it and through it. Bring it to life.

Do not think of fabric, for example, simply as a garment, a costume. You will now create a new entity with an extension. Give it a life of its own. Certain kinds of fabric have more animation than others. Rayon has a wonderful fluency and weight. Jersey is also great. Others are difficult, such as limp fabrics, as they have to be manipulated constantly. Choose an extension with a potential life of its own. You are going to find the life or mobility of that fabric or prop, and you are going to go with it. Work within it and its motional capacity.

Do not treat your extension simply as an adornment. Assume the mobility, fluency, hardness, resilience, or any other dominant quality of the extension. The extension will alter the condition of the whole body.

Monday	Skirts.
	Do not wear as a skirt, but as a garment that will reshape the body and become a part of this new creature's identity. You can attach this garment to any part of the body. Try three solo dancers at a time, two dancers in one skirt. Choose a fabric that has an intrinsic motional quality.
Tuesday	Sticks or hard linear objects.
	The object becomes an extension that reshapes the body, not a held adornment but almost as a new arm or leg. Three dancers show at a time, solo, then related.
Wednesday	Found objects—anything—a shoe, a garment, crumpled paper, a broom, and so on.
	Again, here the dancer's form is transformed into a new entity. Three dancers show at a time.
	Be prepared for some bizarre results. Go with whatever is brought to class. Tell dancers that they have to clean up whatever mess they make.
Thursday	Combine three different dancers and their extensions as a trio.
Friday	Group (half the class) interaction with extensions.
COMPOSITION	Use any property desired as an extension to create a new entity or illusion.

CRITS WITH EXTENSIONS

Don't play with the extension property. Use it.

Don't wear it as a skirt. That is such an ordinary relationship. We've seen it a million times.

Try not to handle props, they're part of you, like an elephant's trunk. This will considerably temper your whole movement. Find the motional facility and nature of it; it's the new entity with its new limitations and illuminations we are after. Temper your motional range, and balance yourself with it. Begin to sense what it can do and go with it.

When the person becomes more dominant than the new entity, the person is out of balance. When the property becomes more dominant, the property is equally guilty of imbalance. When it is evenly balanced, the new entity will emerge.

Before you begin, shape yourself with this new extension as part of your body. Impart your neuromuscular system into this extension.

Extend out of self, out of preconceived concepts, and achieve other images. The costume is not to cover, but to extend the shape of the body. Light and sound can also extend an image.

WEEK 24: LYRICISM

INTRODUCTION

Lyricism is the epitome of dance. Lyricism is complete release of tensions. Your performing attitude is lyrical, unimpeded. It is sheer motion. The mind travels with the movement itinerary. Psyche and body try to stay as one. Constant change, constant evolution, constant motion, but always constant. We are not interested in creating artfulness at the moment, but in discovering the uninterrupted flow of motion—that is lyricism. Lyricism has no pause and no disruption. It is a fairly stable, balanced going: not fast or slow but more or less constant. Try to remain in a constant speed that never varies. We can't rule out repetition, but it is best if we can do it without communicating repetition. You have a hunk of matter, your body, to be moved around. Move it steadily with a balanced energy. "Cool it." Don't be languid, since lyricism already has a calm, odalisque quality to it. Never let your arms out of your inner eye vision. All things happen in relation to space and time. Treat eyes and face as if they were a common center shared by arms, body, face, and so on. If one is out of key then the whole is out of sync. Lyricism is an uninterrupted going. Anything not going conflicts with the lyrical nature of the action. The body sings with a clear, open voice.

CLASS PLAN

TECHNIQUE

Premise

Lyricism: a sustained action without any interruption to the flow. Constant evolution. Constant, even change of time, space, shape, and motion.

The skill here is to be able to move over and through all the dynamics of the dance without altering the flow of the energy. Going into and coming out of climaxes without any disruption. A sort of cruise control.

Motional and movement quality blend. Achieve air and floor work without visible preparation.

Monday–Friday

Teach the whole class a different four- to eight-measure movement phrase every day using arms and torso, using any phrase already designed for other classes. The phrase should include accents and dynamic changes. The dancers should dance these with a lyric, uninterrupted, sustained quality. Acceleration without rushing. Accenting without pausing. Pausing without stopping. This is the ultimate challenge of motional flow—a constant control of energy.

These phrases should then be expanded and lengthened across the floor.

IMPROVISATION

Improvising lyrically all week. Choreograph for each other. Choreographer directs and corrects dancer to move lyrically without visible interruptions. This is also a challenge for the choreographer's verbal skills to see and make lyric corrections.

COMPOSITION

Lyric study.

CRITS ON LYRICISM

Too much hardness in eye and body. Give a sense of having no barriers. The eye seems to be staring in one spot, but motion is going in another.

It needs no impulse to change direction, particularly downward, when gravity comes into play.

Keep it even.

See if you can feel the motional flow. More songlike.

Shoulders too tight and hard.

Don't let gravity take over. Control it.

Take out the swing quality. Give it more of a "riding the undercurve" feeling.

Don't stop at the end of a straight line: put a little curve at the end for transitions. There is no stopping in lyricism.

Release the tension. Use only the necessary amount of energy required.

He first engaged the arm motion and then a trunk action, which is a nice thing to do. He did it smoothly.

Choreographically it was fine, but the performance was too submissive. Your psyche hung behind the motion.

We would like not to see the origin of the motion. No impulses.

Try to get pure essence out of it. Your psyche and physical did not come into focus with each other.

It was more like a dance of nostalgia, of past doing. It was not immediate.

The body is involved as an entire entity. Remember, you cannot use any single part without affecting the rest.

Hers almost hit it. It was a little faster and more mobile.

There are three phases to motion: (1) passivity, (2) disturbance, (3) adjustment. Blend them into a continuity.

The body is a thing of weight, and it must respond to motional laws. Internal laws: psyche, strength, and control. External laws: gravity, momentum, and friction aerodynamics. Your new "body" must do the same.

ADJUNCTS TO CHOREOGRAPHIC AND PERFORMING SKILLS

THE EXPLORATORY STAGE AND APPLICATION

Discipline usually refers to boundaries that must not be transgressed. Its purpose is to better understand the nature of that which exists within these boundaries. Our perceptions are set up like hundreds of sensory microscopes that view the motional scene, which we then store in our memory bank of feelings. These memories become the major part of the palette from which we later choose our motional vocabulary.

Even at this preliminary stage, we already face an enormously complex array of variables. Take the lifting of an arm, for example. By moving the arm, we have taken it out of stasis, the first state of motion. In effect, we have disturbed it from its still position. This disturbance is the second phase of motion. The third phase is the outcome, the arrival at the desired end position. We have completed the three phases of motion: passivity, disturbance, and outcome. However, the physical definition alone is inadequate. We must explore the necessary sensory perceptions required of this aesthetic, motional experience. We now must set up boundaries—guidelines to the intent. Choices can be arbitrary but, once chosen and stabilized, they become unalterable qualifications, which will define the gesture for the purpose of focusing the sensory perceptive memories of both dancers and viewers. Here are only some of the decisions we must make to qualify the sensory perceptions:

What speed has been allotted to the gesture?

What is the shape of the arm during the process?

Does it change speed during the act?

Nikolais choreographing, 1976.
Dancers top to bottom: Susan McDermot, Joseph Zina,
and Lizabeth Bagnold.
Photo by P. Berthelot.

Do we sense the weight of the arm?

Is the arm sensitive to the peripheral sweep?

Is the arm conscious of its tactile change in space?

Does the arm sense its kinetic progress through space?

Is there consciousness of a completed intent?

These qualifications can go on and on as we solidify the definition of the action more and more. Quality refers to the balancing of all factors involved so that a single satisfactory sensation emerges from a properly balanced combination of all sense factors involved.

It is when the sensory perception recognizes this sensation that it can put the understanding of a motion into a memory bank to be used later at will. Once this is done, we can pass on to another experience.

The experiences with the arm now pass on to other body parts and begin to redefine the kinetic qualities of those parts. Bear in mind that the more meticulously we explore each experience, the more precise each experience becomes, and the more exactly the kinetic and sensory experience is engraved on our perceptions.

Obviously, we do not dance with only one arm. There are correlations between it and other body parts, each adding its union and orchestration to the other. Each new correlation arrives at a new statement and definition—related but qualified by the new semantics introduced by each addition. Some simple explorations could be pursued as follows:

Mirrored symmetry with opposite arm.

Succession—one side followed by the other.

Broken-up succession: parts of a phrase swapped back and forth from right arm to left arm, and so on.

One arm pursuing the motional phrase against a ground base motion engaging the other arm.

In creating movement structures, you will discover that you have no concrete image to rely on. Your decisions will depend wholly on your judgment of motion. This is exactly the practice we must begin to engage in. The difficulty is that you have no concrete point of reference. You are obliged to search out the aesthetic content of the sensation you personally derive from your choreographic invention.

You have one advantage in addition to all the richness that is included in the unique gesture, which involves the unusual sensory perception of that gesture. A strong feeling for the gesture is impressed on the memory bank, then *offers* a fertile starting point for the technique of choreography and performing skills.

By *unique gesture*, we do not mean some exotic pattern never seen before; we are referring now to some texture, some discovery of the way you do the movement that gives it a feeling it would otherwise not have. The uniqueness of the dancer's nature thus reveals itself, which identifies the work as being his. It is his signature on the creation.

From this vast motional spectrum it is possible to be more specific. Your unique decision as to the nature of the movement will make it specific.

METAKINESIS—THE PROCESS OF COMMUNICATION OF MOTION

Our ability to perceive behavior sensorially is the essence of our communicative power. Our success as performing artists lies in the ability to invite the onlooker into our sentient experiences. It requires doing it in such a way that self-indulgence does not set up a murky barrier between the performer and the audience. A great performer understands that this sharing enables him to control the audience's reaction.

Empathy, an essential communicative mechanism of art, rests in our sensory and psychological functions. It enables man to feel the value of external happenings by their comparative reference to his own feelings. A pain felt by someone else can only be conceived by us through our own knowledge of pain. Empathy is, therefore, a vicarious experience. It is indirect, caused by our observation of an actual happening outside of ourselves. When we speak of a person as being particularly sensitive, we do not mean that he is more than ordinarily skilled in perceiving his own discomforts, we mean that his empathetical reaction to external conditions and happenings is particularly refined. In dance, this empathetical response is called "metakinesis."

Similes and metaphors are all empathetical in that the quality of one thing is made comprehensible by its empathetical comparison to another. When we say, "He ran like a deer," "He was strong as iron," "steady as a rock," "sharp as a tack," "big as a house," "good as gold," or "His heart is made of ice," we are relating to the feelings we have about things. Feelings derive from our empathetical reactions to our experiences of those things.

Empathetical response can be provoked in any of the senses. These responses may be circuitous, traveling through various associations, or an even more obscure subliminal path. We attempt to understand the substance of our world, its objects, people, animals, plants, by vicariously becoming them. The more completely we can do this, the more enhanced our spectrum of knowledge and feelings becomes.

Metakinesis applies to the onlooker's reaction to the motion. An audience understands motional abstraction by vicariously entering the action performed by the dancer. Metakinesis is the vicarious experience of motion. What the dancer feels about his motion should be what the viewer will feel.

If the dancer has no feeling for his motion, or if what he has in mind is not happening in his motion, the onlooker can be confused. He will be obliged to invent his own meaning, which might not be the same as what the performer or choreographer intended.

To perform effectively, the dance artist must acquire a highly sensitive metakinetic skill. He must transcend himself and become two beings inhabiting one body—himself, his physical instrument, and the thing being created. He can change his identity to a thing, creature, or abstraction; however, motions of this metaphoric figure will be guided by the feeling that he, as a real being, has acquired, which he now projects through his imagination into his created role.

One often hears a dancer say, "That movement doesn't feel right," meaning that, in tasting the action, his metakinetic evaluation finds the motion lacking in certain respects that oblige him to make adjustments. To substantiate quality values, the dancer directs the narrative line of the dance back into himself, for judgment from the metaphoric figure.

Through this tasting and evaluating judgment, the created metaphoric figure grows stronger and more identifiable. The performer can then give the action an immediate, first-time freshness with each performance. With abstraction, empathy thus used is the basis of the creative process, particularly during improvisation, where dancers make intuitive judgments quickly.

Dancer-choreographers are often called on to produce compositions consisting of many elements: colors, sounds, divisions of time, structures of space, light values, and so on. They create these by skills derived from direct empathetic experiences. Through selection and control, the artist is able to construct a comprehensive metaphoric entity in dance terms. In turn, the viewer will respond empathetically to the art structure, retranslating it back into his own area of meaning and response.

The artist must make certain that his experiences are not private. His associations or empathetical experiences must be available to everyone if he is to achieve any level of universality.

We can refer to a Pavlovian example of sorts: if a child is repeatedly given a tasty treat, and, at the same time, someone bangs a dishpan, the sound will become a pleasant association to the child. If the child now proposes to express himself musically, he may bang a dishpan because of his pleasant personal association to it. However, although the child may have expressed himself honestly, the sound lacks the common association of pleasure to his audience.

Such purely personal associations are common to everyone and are part of our own private and obscure world. They can, however, serve as spice to the "main course," but as a main course they are too private.

The metaphoric medium of dance is the all-inclusive principle of motion. The metakinetic response of the onlooker derives from his vicarious ride within the itinerary of the dancer's action. The quality of action fills him with that sensation of motion specifically designed by the creator. It is a metaphoric representation of the artist's aesthetic intent.

The dancer's technique requires an extended refinement of his feeling for motion and all the many elements related to motion. He increases his motional knowledge by direct kinetic and metakinetic experiences. These become his language, his sentient symbols of communication. His technical skill lies in the control of these elements, for this is the stuff of which his art is made.

Despite our concern for the metakinetic event in dance, there is another possible aspect of dance that cannot be overlooked. Although we speak of dance primarily as a motional art, it is simultaneously a visual art. Music, obviously, is sensed through the ear, and, consequently, the sensation of sound enters the brain via the psychodynamic paths and interpretations peculiar to that organ.

Sight is more complicated in its psychological entry into the mind. One may theorize that all sensation derives from motion—which is primarily the sense of change. Without change, sensation ceases to exist. In both the art of color and the art of sound, there are certain possible reactions that may be close to kinesthetic interpretation.

But when an artist speaks of motion in a painting, he is not speaking of a metakinetic reaction quite like the one experienced in dance. The motion in painting differs in kinetic value from the art of dance. In sound, too, we may respond by tapping our foot in response to rhythms, but this is not quite the same as our metakinetic response to dance action.

Dance, although it is an art that is seen and may sometimes be received in purely visual terms, is usually translated into a metakinetic response. In other words, it is possible for dance to enlist reactions through the eyes in a manner similar to the eyes' response to color in painting. Here, then, one may reduce or, as far as possible, eliminate kinetic sensation and appeal to the eyes directly. Through this visual reception, dance can coax the eyes into the psychological area usually engaged for painting. This is an aspect of dance that has been employed innocently and frequently from the earliest primitive ceremonies until today. Yet, in it, we find problems of definition.

Definition has the power to illuminate as well as to arrest and often obscure meaning. We commonly associate dance with kinetic experience, so

a dancer employing a large quantity of direct visual rather than kinetic appeal may leave some of his audience confused. It is somewhat like expecting ice cream and tasting cheese instead. No matter how excellent the cheese, the taste is unexpected. The word dance prepares the onlooker for a kinetic experience. The lack of kinetic appeal may so upset the onlooker in his anticipation that, no matter how great the aesthetic value of the visual experience, he will be unable to shift receptivity to that particular area of understanding.

Yet this optical event of dance is legitimate both as dance and as art, despite its strain on the confines of definition.

More important than the purism of definition is the event of art.

METAPHORIC QUALITY

There are certain tensions or forces that must be executed to emphasize a particular quality of action. In abstract dance, such extra force is often required to qualify an action. I refer to this as the dancer's skill in creating illusions, his ability to become something that, in reality, he is not. It is a practice of motional adjectives or metaphors. We can refer to classical ballet, in which the major objective is to make dancers seem to be lighter than their actual weight.

Creating illusion is a major function of the choreographer. The task here is to design motional phrases that deliver metaphors to the onlooker. Awareness of motional illusions such as hard, heavy, fast, light, thick, thin, and so on gives the choreographer and dancer additional technical and interpretive skills, which enrich technical achievements.

One assignment I usually give in a composition class is to create a study in speed. Invariably, a dancer will exhaust himself by running around the studio to convey this effect. However, the more ingenious dancer will stand in one spot and choreograph fast, jerky motions of body parts, which will create a far greater illusion of speed. Of course, choreographic invention is involved here as well as performance illusion.

Another example is a study of "heavy." Again, this is a choreographic challenge as well as one that concerns performance. Heavy, in this instance, refers to motion that makes the dancer appear heavier than he actually is.

Or with the state of "hard" and "light" to alter the condition of density in the body. To sense an increase or decrease of an imaginary amount of molecules in the body to give the illusion of compactness or looseness.

In all of these instances, we are involved in the control of abstract quality. We are not talking about a fast person or a heavy one, or hardness or lightness, but about abstract qualities that can be used in abstract expressionistic invention.

The dancer must learn to use his illusional skills to emphasize the colorations of the choreography. His artistry is judged on these terms. He must have a distinct feeling toward these illusional qualities, many of which are nonverbal but sensed. Only then will the metakinetic process work.

ART AND MEDIA

Art is not concerned with purity of media. Its sole concern is with the materialization of an aesthetic communication. Certain socio-dynamic climates may create the need to combine certain arts in order to produce an effective result. In the late Renaissance, for example, the combination of music, scenic art, drama, and the vocal range gave rise to opera.

Recently, there has been an even greater urgency to mix media in order to make contemporary aesthetic statements. The painter begins to sculpt his canvas. Sometimes the sculptor makes a work that not only moves but makes sounds. An art of theater (aside from drama) is now evident in which all the arts function toward a totality.

Art has no particular concern for the traditional specializations or limitations man imposes on himself. Art is by no means pure in this sense. It does not demand that the artist be rich or poor; nor does it require a particular religion, race, or politics. It doesn't care whether the artist is a male or female, homosexual or heterosexual. Above all, art places no limitation on the artist's media other than its suitability for the ultimate art idea. Consequently, the purist may find his purism to be a limitation to his understanding and development. More so now than ever before, the purist who pronounces that such-and-such is not dance may very well be exchanging diamonds for gravel.

For art cares only for art and has complete disregard for whether it takes the form of dance, painting, sculpture, music, or any other media. It cherishes loyalty only to itself and therein rests its strongest values. It is only in such an absolute dedication without coercion that it can stand within the framework of art.

The education of the artist deals with the refinement of his senses and perceptions and in the development of skills so that he can state his findings through the medium of his choice. When his medium is color, we call him a painter. When it is sound, we label him a musician. Shapes of things are the province of the sculptor. The dancer communicates through motion.

Dance very often has combined with the actor's domain, and this combination of dance and drama has placed a limit to the scope of dance as an art in itself.

However, the great choreographers and performers of the traditional modern dance period made considerable use of combining the arts of dancing and acting, such as Martha Graham's consummate Theater-Dance, Clytemnestra.

Ballet also uses literal and nonliteral devices. Many of its early choreographers, instead of mixing the abstract and the literal, deliberately stopped a section of abstract dance and proceeded to a wholly literal mimetic action, only to return again to purer dance. Here, each level supported the understanding of the other by sequential—rather than as in the early modern dance, simultaneous—exposition. The larger picture makes evident that we are evolving toward a new theater of abstraction.

In the arts, rules, direct or implied, are doled out daily through the tradition of critical reviews as well as pedagogical processes and learned writings, which harass the budding artist on all sides. It is indeed a wonder that a stroke on the drawing board or a gesture in space can be free from a judgmentally restrictive tug on the arm caused by some critical conclusion that preys on the primary impulses that make the synapse between the art source and the medium.

QUALIFICATION

Definition is concerned mainly with boundaries of understanding. It sets limitations on meanings and streamlines comprehension. Often it jumps these boundaries and admits confusions by adding embellishments, which obscure and reduce values essential to the arts.

Germinal definition is essential to the creation of an artistic thing. That is, the raison d'être springs from a basic source that is unique to the vision of the creator.

How does one find, create, or come upon a unique art experience? I recall an experience I had with a painter friend: a wise old gentleman. I had received a packet of drawings made by school children. They depicted their reactions after seeing one of my concerts. I showed them to my painter friend. He went through one after another making two piles. As he did so he said, "This one is; this one isn't." When he finished. I asked him, "Is or isn't what?" He said, "You can easily see that those in this pile are personal reactions. With the others the children were taught what to see." Seen that way, the differences were immediately apparent.

In exploring motion, we are also searching for definitions. But we must eventually make our own definitions. It is true other artists' findings often give us clues to these decisions. The profession abounds with methods. Students imitate artists' performances with hope that with their proximity to the artists' genius, some of it will rub off onto them.

The most rewarding process is the richness of worldly exposure: exposure not to one thing but to many. One has to eventually make choices, but choice is more likely to be fruitful when one has quantity to choose from.

At this point we are involved in a complex kinetic experience, the process of selection: the recognition of unique qualities when they happen. There are two basic possible processes: one is when the artist specifies a kind of motion, the other is when the artist allows a motion to occur under its own dictates.

In either case there is the necessity of passing aesthetic judgment on the experience. In both instances there should be an associative experience or feeling, not necessarily literal but nevertheless intuitively recognizable, which will allow one to judge their applicability and make further choices. Obviously, this process is not going to occur with every gesture.

There is a third possible process. That is where a dancer has an image of a feeling of what he or she wants to occur. Then begins the process of searching out which motions coincide with this feeling or image. One danger to be avoided is falsely implanting a feeling on a motion when that feeling has no affinity for that gesture.

Many of these qualifications relate back to metakinesis. Metakinesis differs in that it does not refer to the empathetic feeling caused by someone else, but rather on the feeling the artist causes on himself. In the case of motion, it is a reflection back into the self: one that opens up memory sensations, either abstract or literal.

The dancer and the choreographer both evolve from a basic understanding and experience of the dance art. One pursues the performance of the art; the other, the making aesthetic continuity of its design.

In the search for distinction, one must pursue one's own motional definitions out of which can arise the unique gesture, which distinguishes the truly creative and performing artist.

WEEK 25: THE SHOWING: PERFORMANCE

PREPARATION

Present a good, persistent warm-up. After the warm-up, there should be a last showing of the studies and dances. These events are very important in that they mark the progress of the students as technicians, choreographers, and performers.

To Instructor

Give last crits that will keep clarifying and improving material. Try to bring out the best possible performance.

Arrange dances for a balanced program.

Prepare staging with simple lighting if possible, also prepare stage area.

Technical preparation of music and cueing will require extra time.

A bit of personal grooming: leotards and tights—hair—simple makeup.

If there is no stage and auditorium available, employ the largest studio space. Place the dancing area at the end of the room length. Place the audience seats at the opposite side facing the "stage." Then leave as open a space as possible between the dancing and the viewing area. If the audience increases, allow it to sit on provided mats in this open space so that there is still a sense of distance between audience and dancers. Make sure that the audience entrance and exit areas preferably behind the audience seating, do not cross the dance space.

With various levels of choreographic efforts being shown, it is important to devise a program that will show all the participants to their best advantage. Nikolais designed a staging that allowed all students to show their studies regardless of study length. The shorter studies that merited showing were put together in the first part of the performance. Everyone served as a chorus, which marked the stage and introduced each dancer. The chorus moved in groups and formed architectural patterns throughout this section, which revealed and absorbed the shorter studies. This gave the forty-second studies, for example, the chance to participate in a five- to ten-minute experience on stage. One piece of suitable music or sound ran continuously and accompanied the whole staging.

We presented the studies that could hold up as dances separately as solos, employing whatever sound they were created to. On occasion, a short group work from the repertory of either Nikolais or myself would serve as a finale.

PERFORMANCE

Performance is the enactment of the finished product. It is the point where all the elements of production pull together. The curtain is up and the last ingredient necessary is present: the audience, the viewer.

The ball is rolling and there is no turning back. Of course, once the curtain falls the entire event can be changed for the next performance. But befores and afters have nothing to do with performance. Performance is the now, the cauldron where everything fuses together.

For the dancer it is a time of advancement on every level. Whether the performance is good or bad, the performer has gone forward. There is a greater realization of self, of choreography, of the fulfillment of movement; a newfound control and ability. The body has dealt with adrenaline, and the mind with clarity and fear. The dancer has had his first experience with the nameless black hole that is the fourth wall, the audience, from which encouragement and silence emanate. This new arena makes the studio classes seem like a child's playpen.

Transformation seems a suitable word to describe the change that transpires. The stage lights blind you—your breath unexpectedly faltering, the muscle cramping, and the choreographic blackouts all challenge and force you to new internal strengths. You discover a new level of your abilities that carries you through degrees of challenge you've never experienced in studio work. Performance will eventually lead to professionalism, and with professionalism come new challenges that must be risen to and achieved. But first performance is a first step.

There are two areas to be dealt with in the performance of choreography. One is the quality or intent of the movement and the other is the technical structure of the movement itself. They should be mastered separately and then put together and performed as a total experience where the quality and structure mingle and serve each other. To perform one without the other leads to either an indulgent or arid performance.

The less theatrical environment of a studio showing will allow the structure and quality of the dance and dancing to be more visible. Form, content, and performance define choreography.

Projection and Aura

In a sense, performing is a motional conversation between the dancer and the audience. When one dances for his own pleasure the conversation is contained and doesn't have to cross the footlights, it is in a sense performing to an interior viewer; however, our purpose here is to project out to an audience and to bring it in.

When an audience doesn't exist, the dancer has to create one in his imagination and project out to reach it. For example, in the plié series, the wall (not mirror) the dancer faces becomes the back of the theater and the dancer reaches out and extends his movement to not only touch that wall but to go through it. The dance studio no longer has walls or ceilings. The dancer in all of his extended movements reaches through these confines and expands himself to heroic proportions, using the spatial currents to carry his actions to fill the imagined auditorium. Surprisingly, this takes a great deal of physical strength.

When a dancer walks out on a new stage, he sizes up the demands the space is going to make upon his performing energies, and he knows how hard he is going to have to work that night. Projection is expanding the personal aura to fill a house. But first, of course, comes creating an aura, that marvelous enlivening of the space around the body.

244

GENERAL CRITS

I want you to concentrate but I don't want to see concentration.

For the dance artist, the muscle must be connected to the imagination.

If you're going to make a mistake, make it a big one! Very often, it is your intuition telling you, this is what you should have done, but it's your propriety that thinks it's a mistake.

Every artist has to be terrified by his art. That art is the same dragon of doubts that eats you alive at 4 o'clock in the morning.

Immediacy is the act of presence.

Einstein's theory stated that all matter contains energy. When a mass is disturbed, energy is released. So disturb yourself and release some energy. Make Albert E. proud of you.

Performance is the presentation of the finished product to the audience.

Don't be obvious. Be subtle, penetrating, and perceptive. Don't show me all the things we already know.

Don't overset the studies. But practice them, know them. They should breathe a little bit differently with each showing. That will keep them alive. Make sure the dance still contains its initial excitements, however.

When you are consonant with the inner detail of that motion, you are in a state of dance.

Manners, idiosyncrasies, and style: these are not in the domain of the student, yet. Practice the clarity of your art. Later, you can do anything you want because I know you will have chosen to do so.

I would rather you be outrageous than timid, because the outrageousness we can tone down.

I didn't see you. It wasn't pungent enough to reach across to me. If it's so without character that I can't see it, I can't criticize it, let alone respond to it.

Traditional movement is not pungent. Nor is tradition. You have to analyze and instill tradition with fresh motivation.

A dance is never completed until it is performed. The cycle is not completed.

Don't think emotionally, but passionately. Passion is not restricted to emotion. It is the strength of fulfillment of the intent. Emotion is a particular condition, a specific state of response. Passion is an energy that embodies intent.

You taste the experience of shape so deeply, so convincingly for yourself that you begin to understand shape as one of the important principles of dance. Therefore, when you execute movement either as a performer or as a choreographer, you can count on the knowledge and conviction that these highly experienced "tastebuds" give you.

Remember, the process of the viewer understanding what a dancer does is the process of metakinesis. Another word would be *empathy*. I understand what you do by virtue of the fact that, as I look at you, I vicariously occupy your body. Therefore, what you feel I feel. If you don't feel strongly about the shape, don't expect me to feel strongly about it.

You sometimes can insist that we understand what you are doing. Your performing conviction can make up for the strength of your choreography.

Also, the persistence with which you show the thing is important. I can't just stick my arm out; my body must say, "Look at that arm." While you are doing it, it must have an importance that hits the onlooker right in the gut, or at least in the eye.

It isn't that it's never been done before, but somehow you must bring to it a force that makes it important for the first time.

[Criticism to a professional-level dancer] Divorce yourself a little bit from all your skills and abilities—from all your hard-earned performance values. They are limiting you now by creating a self-conscious veneer.

The torso has to get lush. You have to have a sound in your own ear. Not enough resonance inside you. It has to be a certain kind of delight, a delight of you in the movement shape, in the senses. Like a nude dip in the pool at midnight. You are bathed all over in that tactile sense. Little crystals glitter all over you as if with reflected starlight. There has to be more suppleness in the coming and going of the arm's roundness. Cushion more into the downward of it. Never stopping . . . soft breath . . . arms lush—Harvest moon! Suspension of the whole body immersing itself in the space around you.

Intimate is when the gesture or dance is shared with audience. Personal is when the dance is reserved for the dancer alone. The audience is kept at arm's distance, made to feel a prying viewer and unwelcome. Crit: Don't be personal with your movement. Share it. Reflect it out.

When one sees a successful study for the first time, especially when it came out of left field, it has a certain nervousness and brilliance it will never have again. Because as a viewer, you'll be prepared for it. That's why every performance must have a first-time look.

Once the dancer loses his concentration on what he is performing, he slips from the art of motion to the "marking" of movement. Skipping over that fine line is the difference between motion and movement. One practices and learns the mechanics of a movement and, once learned, performs it with its motional quality, which identifies and fulfills it. "Marking" is movement; "performing" is motion.

Bodies go wrong; it's nothing to get hysterical about. Eat regularly. Pop blisters. A & D ointment for split feet. Don't take class on an empty stomach. Have breakfast—you need fuel. Release into a fall . . . melt . . . collapse. Don't push when you know you're exhausted.

I saw you wind up for the next phrase. You gave me time to anticipate where it was going.

You did the gestures. You did them on time. But I wasn't at all convinced that there was a performance interest in it. I did not see you permeating yourself with an idea, to such a point of conviction, to the point that it becomes inescapable to the onlooker what the gesture intends. And even if the gesture isn't great, the dancer should at least have faith enough to perform it with zest.

Don't spell out and deliver what the public expects or knows.

A real artist has to be disturbing . . . in a quiet way, in a poignant way—or in a shattering way.

You "see" dance in a manner unique among the arts. It enters you not so much through your eyes. It gets to you here [taps heart] as well as all up and down your backbone! As a performer, you project to the audience a kinetic sense, through their spinal cord. They also see the dance through their spine.

You have a responsibility as a performer once you've hit on something that starts an audience's imagination going. You can't pull the rug out from under them. When you start off with a powerful opening, your job is to live up to it. If you can't go with it—drop it rather than destroy it. Come back to it later when you can deal with it properly.

The audience is embarrassed watching a performer who is ill at ease with his materials.

The audience does not only see what the dancer is doing . . . . it feels what the reaction is on themselves. Don't ever lose sight of what you're doing. The only way the audience gets a reaction to what you're doing is by how you're doing it.

[Student] I had a feeling, while I was working on this study, that muscle tone—muscle tension—had a lot to do with time. When I did it here, I was so nervous I forgot to breathe. I felt a tension that didn't allow the "slow" to be slow enough or the "fast" to be fast enough or the time separating them. Suddenly, when I was performing here, there was a muscle tension that prevented the ease necessary to perform time properly.

[Comment] That's always the case when you get nervous, that's for sure. The emotions are like a cup—they can only hold so much. Whenever it runs over, then it goes into tension. But if you fill your motivation so strongly with that which you are doing, there's no room for tension to evolve. And I know with performers, no matter how nervous they are before a performance, they can be absolutely shaking, but if they know absolutely the quality they are seeking when they go onstage, they can zero in on that and the tension seems to go.

In a choreography where you're dealing with tensions, you have to be careful not to interpret them dramatically.

The moment that you create a dramatic story line about the tension, then it goes into centralization and we see you in conflict with it.

I remember there was a girl from the Midwest, and her behaviorisms seemed distinctive. Her sense of space was different, her sense of volume was different. Different from a New Yorker's, for example. Whatever part of the country you come from, there is a possibility of a different flavor in your work.

All she would have to do is perform it better. What you could do sometime after you've done it is to give the dance to somebody else to perform and then watch and see who tastes the movement better, you or they. It is interesting to see the difference in impact of the same dance structure performed by two different people.

Being extraordinarily absorbed in what you are doing is not the only chore of the performer. The performer must also be aware of what is being communicated. I don't care how great a performer is, and how deeply they are involved, they must keep in mind what is being communicated. You must put yourself into the eye of the audience, to make sure that what they see is what you intend them to see.

You ask yourself the question when choreographing: "How do all the sensitive parts of me relate to what I'm doing?" These sensitive areas communicate in the nuance range. Delicate, subtle nuances occur when you begin to work with usually unexposed areas. You are exposing the vulnerable, the unprotected, tender parts. When you want bigger, broader tones, you work with the more callused parts . . . with the bones, perhaps. See how, in the development of the sensitive instrument, the body, how each of these areas effect a different timbre. You can orchestrate with your body, depending on which parts you expose. You're also dealing with the space around you, which carries and resonates what you're showing to the onlooker.

A professional performer is someone who can deliver the "goods" with every performance.

Or you can do "ME" dances: "This is ME dance #1 . . . then change costume," "This is ME dance #2. Change costume"—and so on. [Students laughed in self-recognition.]

The thing about this is she doesn't know yet how deeply she's gone into it. As she matures as an artist, her depth will reveal itself to her. Maturity has answers as well as unexpected rewards.

The worst moment in the theater is lighting the dance. You stand and stand. You just have to suspend yourself while your body gets cold and your mind drifts off, and once again, you ask yourself, "Why am I doing this?"

Choreographers have multiple responsibilities. They have to account to their audience, to the choreography itself, to their dancers and to themselves.

Practice going into the state of dance all the time. Especially when your body is in a pedestrian state. Walk with the lift of a special person, of a dancer.

The body has developed certain relaxing techniques to prevent injury from falls.

There is music-musicality and dance-musicality. Musicality does not belong solely to the musician's realm. In dance, the flow, the lyricism of phrase, textural quality, and clarity of time all deal with musicality. Musicality is one of the dancer's graces.

Conflict is the art of drama. Dance is basically an abstract art. The moment you assume the actor's role, then your training would have to be differently oriented.

[Student] But music itself has tension and conflict. [Nikolais] Let's say it has dynamics. You do use tension and conflict, but you use them differently. You don't use them as in a dramatic situation. You use them to create energy changes or dynamics.

In your art, you have to learn what not to do, or what not to show, as well as what to show.

You have to know when you're repeating something for the sake of emphasis. Know your purpose of repetition.

Basically, you're working on a classical principle. I don't mean ballet classical, I mean classical in the Greek aesthetic sense. Every gesture you make is an ongoing thing. It is never a retreat from somewhere. It is going to the next place. It is balanced in all its aspects. There is no emotional content as in the sense of being mad, sad, or glad. There is emotion, but it is a different kind that psychiatry and psychology hasn't as yet identified. The interest of the motion is the motion itself, not the dramatic content. It's a different kind of excitement. The sensation of that particular motion becomes a part of your storage house of imagery and experience. When you move your head, feel it as a sensation rather than as an emotional or situational activity, or empty physical gesture.

Like a Steinway concert grand piano, when you press one note, the sounding board of the whole piano reflects the resonance of that particular note. So should your body resonate. You can send vibes through your whole body. It denies kinesiology and physiology to a certain extent, but it does happen. Sense if you can do that. Send sympathetic vibes through your whole body.

Transitions are the subtle joining of movements. This responsibility usually rests in the performer's domain. It is a performance skill.

TRANSITIONS

How the dancer shapes himself to link movements and phrases bespeaks his performing artistry. The subtlety of the dancer's performing sense, and how he handles choreography, gives each dancer his own distinction. Choreographers cannot always control these individual physical distinctions and depend on the dancer's contribution to enliven the movement. Through transitions the dancer claims choreography. Through his linking of time and space and shape and motion, the dancer presents his artistry.

Transitions can be linked to finely tailoring a dance to a dancer. When he makes an arm gesture, the dancer is aware of how the rest of the body responds to the movement, how his bodily fabric adjusts.

The dancer, for the most part, knows his body's capabilities best and therefore must be responsible for performing transitions seamlessly. Transitional routes differ in each body, because the proportions and temperaments of each body differ. When dancers are changed in roles, it is this adaptability, this subtlety of transitional ability, that marks their skills. These transitional skills illuminate the professional dancer.

EMOTION

Emotion is far too complex a subject to deal with in any depth here, but generally, this is how it is dealt with in this technique. First, we must consider the age of the students, who usually range from children to young adults, and their general limitations of maturity. Young people often substitute frustration or psychological disturbance for emotion.

As it is most commonly understood, emotion is a very personal function. It is not taught but is innate, and its motivation often comes from murky sources.

Emotions are a stronghold of the ego, bastion of the self. They tend to dominate the movement and thereby flavor the movement with a personality overlay. The idea here is not to remove the inherent emotional flavor of a movement but to replace it with the passion of the doing. Not to be limited to emotional motivation, but to seek out the broader motional palette of dancing inherent in the movement.

Every physical movement contains a degree of emotion within it. In performance, when the movement is presented in its fullest, it is automatically colored with its inherent emotion. Emotion is feedback from the movement, which is generally of an abstract nature.

Mixing the role of the actor with dancer is a common practice. To perform them properly, however, they involve two markedly different trainings. Certainly, should the role call for a strong character or dramatic situation, then those dancers involved should have some coaching to perform the additional demands. An untrained dancer performing emotionally charged material can put a viewer in the uncomfortable position of watching clumsily performed acting.

With the clear and strong technique of mime, for centuries the ballet solved the problem of narrative exposition. With abstract movement, there was no reason to train the dancer in the verbal skills to achieve an emotional dramatic range. When the dancer achieved the totality of motion, the emotional quality was part of that totality and lent the movement its appropriate dramatic color.

Passion is a better word than *emotion* to use for the abstract arts, of which dance is one. Passion is the intensity that possesses the body to vividly carve space, evolve the subtlety of time and duration, style the intricacy of the body's shape, and release the motional flavor of movement. There is some analogy here to Jackson Pollock and his impassioned involvement with casting paint as an abstract expressionist technique.

Actors use their verbal eloquence to express a character's emotion. In the same sense, dancers learn to use their motional eloquence to release the emotion within motion.

Usually, the "boy meets girl" relationships are taken for emotion. Sexy attitudes and come-ons are often substituted for emotion. If dancers can evoke passion, motional passion, without tension or strain, they will have opened the door to a rich performing range for themselves.

The skills of characterization and emotion are not the skills that one learns and develops in dance training. The abilities of emotional temperaments must already exist in the performing artist. Imbuing motion with emotional overlay requires a specifically choreographed structure.

In the process of abstracting emotion, one can take the literal emotion, translate it into its abstract components, and choreograph with these elements.

If there is a strong emotional intent in the choreography, the choreographer selects his movement vocabulary accordingly to reflect that intent. But pasting an emotional overlay on movement that doesn't necessarily contain that emotion is like "pinning a rose on a tomato plant."

* * *

In introducing the idea of the human body as a potential abstract shape, I was able to conceive of the action of that shape as abstract motion. In the earlier period, the dancer assumed a role—just as an actor does. The motions then, although not mimetic, and consequently abstract or closely bordering the abstract, illuminated the emotional substance of the character the dancer assumed. In my instance, because in theory (and often in practice) the dancer assumed no role, he became, instead, the vehicle of the motion. Motion in my concept is the medium, and the total communication (or message) is contained therein. Such a concept is wholly congenial to the idea of decentralization.

Definition of dance in such a concept is clear. Basically dance is motion that has no purpose beyond itself. It is not necessarily an explanation of the figure performing it, and consequently does not include mime or sports activities. As such it defines itself as clearly as does music (the art of sound), painting (the art of color), and sculpting (the art of three-dimensional form). None of these arts needs necessarily rely upon the representational image for its definition. The definition (in basis) is in the medium itself.

Bear in mind that I am not championing such purism as the requirement of the art. We must be aware that the arts do not court purism. Definition is for identification, training, dictionaries, encyclopedias, professors, and artists who need to reaffirm a basis from which they may depart into new ventures and understandings. I should add here that although we do not have scientific, psychological affirmation, I believe it is the condition of motion that causes emotion. However, because the word emotion is semantically so broad—embracing everything from our reaction to a Bach fugue to the complexities of a love affair—I would need to write a thousand pages to state my experiences in this area of thought. For example, my piece _Scenario_, with its screams, laughter, and hysterical outbursts, expresses man's need for emotion as a relief from boredom with life and as a necessary primal appetite.

CONSONANCE AND SUMMATION

Nature, man, and motion, together form a triumvirate. They are integrally bound together and the value of dance occurs in the summation of all three.

Along with other creatures, man has been endowed with a sense of consonance. This sense of accord is also our sense of beauty. The beauty that "rests within the eye of the beholder" is a rightness or balance as the early Greeks knew it. This process of finding consonance is not only a sense but a fundamental drive as well. Out of this drive man endeavors to correct himself to gain accord with nature and with his own living processes.

We find nature is tolerant of many things that are not altogether fitting to its order and growth. Man, too, is not always fitting in his behavior. But, being endowed with this sense of consonance, man possesses the wherewithal to repair deficiencies, and even to correct organic structures. This suggests that the sense of consonance or beauty is actually more than a sense but a force as well. Even beyond this we may find that consonance may be an aspect or characteristic component of the nature of energy itself. We find that consonance is not a passive affair even when it is (if ever) achieved. In the time-space aspect there is constant change and even consonance cannot remain static without destroying its nature.

It is also out of man's deficiencies and derelictions in relation to nature that his compulsion to create art arises. His desire for consonance compels him to create it, artificially, often by ignoring nature's rules and materials and creating his own.

Returning to primal dance, perhaps it is now possible to see it in better perspective. We might find that it is the result of an instinctual drive compelled by a necessity to experience the extent of one's consonance with nature. It is certainly nonpathological. We may find that in the primal act of dancing, man is in his most totally sane moment, that he is then as fully human as he ever will be.

In the preceding chapters, we have rushed into space, juggled with time, molded our bodies into different shapes, and experienced the distinction of motion. Hopefully, there have been discoveries. And, just as pertinent, we have begun to establish a language of motion, of dance. Through this, we now need to train ourselves to pull our visions of dance into more disciplined focus via our mental binoculars. This brings us right back to the beginning, to a consciousness of space, time, and shape out of which disciplined aesthetic motion can take place. So, back to standing presence in stillness we go.

A multitude of germinal points of technical practice rest within the concept of the dimensional balance—standing in stasis. It is impossible to achieve this performed, standing presence by practicing it alone. All areas of dynamic weakness must be strengthened and enlivened beyond the point of balance so that the midstate of stasis is truly a middle or still point. The dynamics of consonance cannot be achieved by pressing toward consonance. One must have the power to reach that midpoint so that the muscular tone is at ease in the balanced state.

Until the dancer has developed a secure general technical ability, achieving the idea of stasis will remain a theoretic ideal. Although the principles of stasis have been outlined in terms of the upright standing position, they are applicable to all shapes in stasis.

Passion, soul, spirit, emotion, and feeling are all terms used to describe the life-energy of art. Yet, for the most part, they are amorphous terms that offer no real definition to the act of the performing art; they merely make reference to a power or drive. They can be as wrong as they are right, and as over-abundant as they are lacking. In reality, when they are lacking in force, it is usually due to the dancer's lack of will to be sentiently present, which translates into weakness in action. When the teacher or choreographer demands more passion, spirit, or emotion to enliven an action, he is apt to be misunderstood by the dancer and the results misinterpreted by the audience. He is not saying, "Be passionate," in the emotional sense; he is saying, "Put fuel in the car and turn on the engine."

One can readily see that extraneous passion or emotion will more than likely throw the quality of immediacy out of balance. Instead of creating a resonant and consonant figure, one is apt to end up with a disturbed-looking creature, one in the throes of unexplained psychical distress rather than an ideal, alive presence.

Stasis requires motivation. The motivation is the stimulation a performer gives himself to willfully, without bias, stand within the upright presence of himself in space and time with the sense of willingly being there and nowhere else.

The psyche must now match its energies to the energy of the movement. A tardy psyche will jar any action out of stasis as it rushes to become present with the action.

The moment we act beyond the state of stasis, we create another structure in time and space. Be it fast or slow, large or small, here or there, where and how, or any other qualification, the new identity sets up different orbits of time-space happenings that the self then sets out to activate and bring into balance with the laws of energy that govern all life.

The dancer's action in time-space is different from the actor's. An actor dealing with drama to create a dramatic situation needs an element of conflict. To the contrary, a dancer's goal is unrestricted achievement_motion that is devoid of conflict to his interest, both externally and within himself.

When his desire for action is within the possible range of his physical and psychical accomplishment, there will be no drama of conflict between him and external forces. There will be no comedy or tragedy in terms of failure or inadequacy or fulfillment. Comedy and drama are created through choreographic juxtapositions, which are then performed with consonant fulfillment. The laws of nature become protagonists—not barriers. The dancer longs for nothing he cannot achieve. He looks not in anger but in consonance with his environment. His motivations are not secondhand. They stem from his immediate self-determination to act and to complete the immediate action.

The dancer does not practice failure. The dancer's challenge is to effectively act within the confines of his specifically allotted space and time. His fundamental practice is that of achieving consonance. The impulse, the motivation to move, the follow-through and the ending are an absolute fulfillment of his desire.

The basic dance—action is one in which there is no visible time-space lag or aggression between the impulse or motivation and the action. Just as one may have immediacy or presence in stasis, one may also have immediacy or presence in action. Being present within the doing requires a vivid perception of the dance in progress. This, in turn, illuminates the itinerary of the choreography, and thus the nature of the motion as a thing in itself is communicated. This is the fundamental difference between motion and movement. In movement, the end purpose of the movement is primary; in motion, the sentient awareness of the ongoing action itself is the objective.

Basic dance requires consonance within action, not desire beyond it. When a dancer runs, the excitement is not in his wanting to get somewhere before it is too late; the excitement exists in the run itself. When energies, either physical or psychical, are exaggerated beyond the requirements of the intended action, the result is dramatically emotional rather than motional, or emotional in addition to motional. The resulting implication is that of desire beyond attainment. On the other end of the motivation scale, insufficient energy also reflects emotional implications.

The dancer's art is motion and, consequently, physical change. The presence of the psyche makes the performance visible. The thought must permeate the flesh; otherwise, the buried thought and the external action will lack the look of self-determination.

The look of the eyes is the most vivid manifestation of intent—not necessarily in their focus, but in their alertness. When the eyes do not dance, it is often because they are detached from the actual event they look back into the brain toward the mental image of the action instead of furnishing vitality to the action itself. Their inward vision is usually a fair clue that other body parts are similarly enrapt with the internal rather than external.

The dancer's process is, of course, far more complex. It is not his body that directs his mind; it is his mind that now shapes his body, shapes the action, and shapes the time and space in which the action occurs. Because the dancer is a performer, his motivation takes hold of his instrument and directs its itinerary in time and space, giving fulfillment to the action. If he does not do this, then he will lose a great portion of his motional aliveness, his kinetic vitality. The body in such tenantless action can then only be a symbol of motion. Metakinetically, to the onlooker, the moving figure will not carry with it the sensations of its action. Worse yet, the dancer will miss out on experiencing a great percentage of the sensation of motional feedback to himself. In consequence, his wide range of association with time and space—the very crux of his power—will be lost.

In training, we need only to define a simple pattern to observe the process as the dancer imbues his instrument with the ability to accomplish it. The careful eye of the teacher will see the overzealous ones, the misinformed ones, the unaccustomed and weak ones, and try to correct the dead spots that occur.

The order or exposition of this book does not imply any order of procedure in technical practice. It is unlikely that anyone will achieve a fine quality of stasis within a short time. It is unlikely that stasis can be achieved by practicing it alone. Stasis is part of the sum total of dance.

In the second phase of motion, disturbances, we might substitute the word change because, even in the smallest act, everything must change. The dancer is essentially dedicated to his facility of causing change. He must change his physical orientation, his physical shape, his whole molecular grain, his aura. Everything changes his advent into space and time.

Although we must arrive at a single comprehensible event, the contents of that event are beyond total conception, because so many operable factors within it are still beyond human comprehension. Yet, as explained in the chapter on sensory perception, we have the power of isolating and separately exploring a great many of these factors. What's gratifying is that the more we comprehend these factors individually, the better we begin to understand the whole picture.

Our basic practice is to feed motivational energies, to the extent of their absorption, into the act. One moves without reticence, fear, wishfulness, arrogance, vacuity, anger, confusion, cuteness, or any undue passion, spirit, or emotion, no matter how fetching or self-satisfying such a qualification may be. The dancer's satisfaction comes from the balance of the action—for this is the very essence of art dance. Its reason is self-contained. The dancer reveals his molecular, living grain: his unhampered flow of action. His result is an innate, innocent dignity, rich in clarity of presence, transparent to the depths of the individual. It shows his state of life right to the very bone, unobscured by the veneer of excess passion or the fog of reticence. He is a live thing, one with an innocent bravado, beautifully and consonantly balanced within himself, his world, and his universe.

A BRIEF REVIEW

Imagination is bringing your inner vision to both the act of creating and performing.

Art improves one's sensitivity to life itself—don't treat art as a separate thing.

Don't be predictable.

On jumps: hold muscles in a state of elasticity for the landing.

Sustained movement ignores gravity and other conflicting forces.

Use passion in the doing, not as an emotional message.

Feed from each other, not on each other.

A rule of improvisation—if you can't think of anything, look, see and relate to what is going on around you. As an artist, you take the ordinary into the extraordinary.

Be deliberate and secure with footing. Wavering makes the audience feel insecure.

Four dedications:

> In technique class, you do whatever the teacher tells you. The teacher is boss.

> In improvisation, the creative realm, you are the boss. Your body tells you what to do.

> In choreography, the art or what you are creating tells you what to do.

> Performance puts all three together and delivers it to your audience's level of receptivity.

Don't knock anyone off balance.

Don't show worry about difficult movements.

Follow where the movement takes you.

Don't go so fast that your partner loses contact with you and your intention.

Give the motion enough time to register visibly. Make time to let the movement visibly sink into the viewer's eye.

Create interesting relative details.

Don't get too comfortable with the energy.

When you collide, use that intrusion to develop your movement in an unexpected way. Don't break your concentration and apologize to each other—just don't let it happen again.

Sense each other without looking at each other. Use the eyes in the back and sides of your head.

Try to investigate something new in warm-up exercises each day.

When change occurs, feel the dynamic that results.

Precarious balance lends kinetics to movement.

Kinetics keeps an audience alive rather than comfortable.

Try to make time visible as it passes through your body.

Now you're dancing because you're investing quality in the movement.

Stillness is not locked—the internal juices are still flowing.

Allow the upper thighs a pliancy as they support the torso.

It is not necessary to stop after moving fast, even though it is convenient.

Quick change of focus is an easy way to look as if you are going fast.

A constant reminder about "turnout": don't force the ankle out but persist with the rotation of the thighs.

The torso extends itself outward through and into the extremities.

Your projection of where you are going is often stronger than the point of where you are. Sense where you are a little more, and reduce a little bit where you are going. It has that faraway look to it.

The sternum articulates the chest and makes it eloquent.

Allow your reactions to take you into space and into locomotion.

Get traditional forms out of your system—invent new forms of locomoting.

Movement must be allowed to create its own quality to arrive at a motional definition.

Learn how to see and feel what works and what doesn't.

There are no formulas for successful work. You must individually find out what works for you, for your premise.

The longer you can develop a phrase, the more skillful you will become as a choreographer.

Don't handicap each other by holding or restraining each other.

Don't swallow the movement without sensing the flavor—taste it, chew it, digest it.

The art of dance is about revealing quality.

In technique class, don't stop because you give out. Continue till the end of the movement phrase. That's the only way to develop endurance.

In duets think of yourself as a four-legged animal—each leg knows what the other leg is doing.

Vague soft edge movement gives a partner nothing to bounce off of.

Disassociate yourself from the stylistic dominance of your ego.

Know where a movement is going and go with it.

Go organic—the way it wants to grow.

Recognize what your mannerisms are so you don't repeat them all the time.

Put your stops at unexpected places—don't let the viewer predict your phrasing.

There is a difference between stopping and stillness. Moments of stillness should be inserted in unpredictable places.

Don't pass through a dozen wonderful things without tasting them.

Influence what your partners are doing, and in turn be influenced by them.

The overcurve has an upbeat preparation: a buoyancy, a bubble.

Don't possess the art so much that it can't breathe—release it.

Be sure to be in the act, not outside looking at it.

A fixed focus makes your gestures appear to be explaining the focus.

[Nikolais quotes Wigman] "Isn't it funny how when you put a pair of tights on them, they forget they're human."

Non-image dancing is devotion to the intelligence of motion itself. Intelligence is knowing why a movement occurs, its non-literal purpose.

Abstraction—to be the essence of the thing, not the thing.

Never let any action occur without some participating image in your mind. Keep everything alive.

Sense the length of time for an improvisation. Sense when to end them.

In stasis one grains to the direction of stillness.

Direct the audience to what you want them to see.

Dancing is a compulsion, not a choice.

It is important to take the time to study each element on a specific level, limiting yourself to that element. By this process you will increase your palette of colors.

Show me the whole pie, not the ingredients.

Nature has all the time it needs to make beauty and it is called nature. We have a limited lifetime to make beauty, which we call art. However, in time, through familiarity, art takes on a natural appearance.

You don't have to be able to name a quality, just reveal it.

Improvisation is not a mindless display. Something in you is in control of every movement.

When dealing with shape do not break away from the opening shape too quickly. Develop it!

If your intuition says, 'it works,' it works.

Describe the space around you, and make it tangible.

[Claudia G. quotes Hanya] "It is getting harder to teach because people know too much."

POSTSCRIPT

The idea of decentralization, which is the opposite of egocentricity (where the whole body is filled with the center of itself), is important to this study of dance. When you decentralize, you don't emphasize yourself over the thing you're doing. One difficulty is that because the eyes, nose, ears, and mouth—our main means of connection with the world—all relate in one direction, we have a natural tendency to give spatial emphasis to what is ahead of us. The back of our body becomes far less sensitive, though it is just as important and can easily be overlooked. The past is like that too.

Writing a book on dance technique may sound like a fairly mundane job, but writing one on creative dance presents a challenge all its own. The danger in dealing with pedagogy is falling into the trap of pedantry. Even more daunting is the challenge of capturing the creative impulse. Creativity deals with the psyches of both the artist and the viewer. Penetrating both is a rich basis for the field of psychology. But can it fit into a book?

There is no single progression in teaching creativity. The logic of a class jumps from one point to another until, very often, a class ends successfully, but with an entirely different premise having been accomplished than the one that was intended. The richness of the teacher's own experience and character will constantly assert itself through the anecdotes, stories, and professional background that he uses to flesh out a class. Generosity is a requisite.

All this ambiguity leads to the fear of mistranslation when corralling a subject like teaching into the confines of a book page. Finding a format was the key to this book, a book dealing primarily with creative dance and technique. Since the classes, which both Nikolais and I taught, were shared with active and creatively volatile dance and choreographic personalities, the classes' freewheeling temperament and direction stimulated the imagination. Similarly, all of us learned a great deal from both the successful and the not so successful studies and performances in class.

How, then, does one make order out of all this? Aside from the class lessons, there is a purposeful jumping of order and continuity. Ideas are reiterated, since 50 percent of all teaching is reiteration. Similarly, I have tried to express something about finding the right tone for the classroom. I have included the crits to suggest that, not to provide explicit directions.

The memories of our fifty years of teaching are remarkable, the results were often inspiring, and the experience was certainly unforgettable. I only hope that in some way I have made that spirit cohere and come alive, and that the insights brought together here will pass some of that fervor on to other classrooms.

What Is Dance?

Nikolais would sometimes ask a beginning creative class, "What is dance? Anyone got a definition? Any ideas?" The more you probe, the more complex the answer appears.

Dance seemed to be defined in musical terms. Rhythm seemed more important than pulse. Very few mentioned "the message" in their definition. The session always ended in a general sense of embarrassment, because, however simple the question was, there seemed to be no consensus on this subject.

This opened up the students' eyes to the wide range that dance contains. It led to an understanding of the art's complexity: from the identification of the body parts as the instrument, to space and time, to creative invention, to grasping the scope of the art of dance. It was obvious that dance has a deep, inclusive definition.

ABOUT THE DVD

The five films that comprise the series "Dance As an Art Form" began filming in 1970. They were edited over a two- or three-year period, released completely in 1973, and proved to be very successful.

During the 1960s I toured the United States frequently. At that time, the major sponsors for modern dance were the schools and universities that contained dance departments and dance programs.

On one occasion, in 1969, I was appearing at UCLA, which had an excellent modern dance program. The arts and humanities program divided the year into four quarters. In these quarters the school offered music, dance, art, and theater. Every freshman was required to take this course.

I arrived on campus during the dance quarter. The large auditorium was filled with what seemed like hundreds of freshly scrubbed young people, and the sides of the room were lined with latecomers. The lecture began. The lecturer read and commented on the work of two notable modern dance performers, and in about ten minutes had lost her audience. Dance was not to be listened to. Dance was to be seen, especially for beginners. What a pity, I thought, to miss this great opportunity because, in all honesty, there was no material to describe or present the scope of modern dance, its principles, its philosophy, and its analysis. What was available was limited to films and photographs of dancers and dances; there was nothing about the art itself.

As I sat listening to the lecture, I made a promise to myself that I would do something about it.

These five films resulted from that episode in Los Angeles. I filmed in various parts of the country and with various dance departments. Included were the University of Utah, UCLA, the University of Arizona, Duke University, the University of Florida, and in New York City at our studio in "the Space."

The sections are:

The Dancer's Instrument—the Body

Motion

Space

Time

Shape

In addition to the material they contained, they also gave a picture of how young people dressed and looked then. I tell my students today, "This is what your parents looked like." The films presented the dance ideology and pedagogy as it was forming, and the then-hip look of the dancers' hair and clothes just confirmed the transiency of style.

For this DVD, the five films were reduced from their total length of two and a half hours to eighty-five minutes to adapt to the structure of this manual.

The films are still available separately from the Nikolais/Louis Foundation for Dance (Nik-Murry@mindspring.com).